METHODS AND METHODOLOGIES FOR RESEARCH IN DIGITAL WRITING AND RHETORIC
CENTERING POSITIONALITY IN COMPUTERS AND WRITING SCHOLARSHIP, VOLUME 2

Practices & Possibilities
Series Editors: Aimee McClure, Mike Palmquist, and Aleashia Walton
Series Associate Editor: Jagadish Paudel

The Practices & Possibilities Series addresses the full range of practices within the field of Writing Studies, including teaching, learning, research, and theory. From Richard E. Young's taxonomy of "small genres" to Patricia Freitag Ericsson's edited collection on sexual harassment in the academy to Jessie Borgman and Casey McArdle's considerations of teaching online, the books in this series explore issues and ideas of interest to writers, teachers, researchers, and theorists who share an interest in improving existing practices and exploring new possibilities. The series includes both original and republished books. Works in the series are organized topically.

The WAC Clearinghouse and University Press of Colorado are collaborating so that these books will be widely available through free digital distribution and low-cost print editions. The publishers and the series editors are committed to the principle that knowledge should freely circulate and have embraced the use of technology to support open access to scholarly work.

Other Books in the Series

Heather M. Falconer, *Masking Inequality with Good Intentions: Systemic Bias, Counterspaces, and Discourse Acquisition in STEM Education* (2022)

Jessica Nastal, Mya Poe, and Christie Toth (Eds.), *Writing Placement in Two-Year Colleges: The Pursuit of Equity in Postsecondary Education* (2022)

Natalie M. Dorfeld (Ed.), *The Invisible Professor: The Precarious Lives of the New Faculty Majority* (2022)

Aimée Knight, *Community is the Way: Engaged Writing and Designing for Transformative Change* (2022)

Jennifer Clary-Lemon, Derek Mueller, and Kate Pantelides, *Try This: Research Methods for Writers* (2022)

Jessie Borgman and Casey McArdle (Eds.), *PARS in Practice: More Resources and Strategies for Online Writing Instructors* (2021)

Mary Ann Dellinger and D. Alexis Hart (Eds.), *ePortfolios@edu: What We Know, What We Don't Know, And Everything In-Between* (2020)

Jo-Anne Kerr and Ann N. Amicucci (Eds.), *Stories from First-Year Composition: Pedagogies that Foster Student Agency and Writing Identity* (2020)

Patricia Freitag Ericsson, *Sexual Harassment and Cultural Change in Writing Studies* (2020)

Ryan J. Dippre, *Talk, Tools, and Texts: A Logic-in-Use for Studying Lifespan Literate Action Development* (2019)

METHODS AND METHODOLOGIES FOR RESEARCH IN DIGITAL WRITING AND RHETORIC

CENTERING POSITIONALITY IN COMPUTERS AND WRITING SCHOLARSHIP, VOLUME 2

Edited by Victor Del Hierro and Crystal VanKooten

The WAC Clearinghouse
wac.colostate.edu
Fort Collins, Colorado

University Press of Colorado
upcolorado.com
Denver, Colorado

The WAC Clearinghouse, Fort Collins, Colorado 80523

University Press of Colorado, Denver, Colorado 80202

© 2022 by Victor Del Hierro and Crystal VanKooten. This work is released under a Creative Commons Attribution-NonCommercial-NoDerivatives 4.0 International license.

ISBN 978-1-64215-166-4 (PDF) | 978-1-64215-167-1 (ePub) | 978-1-64642-388-0 (pbk.)

DOI 10.37514/PRA-B.2022.1664

Library of Congress Cataloging-in-Publication Data

Names: Del Hierro, Victor, 1988– editor. | VanKooten, Crystal, 1980– editor.
Title: Methods and methodologies for research in digital writing and rhetoric : centering positionality in computers and writing scholarship / edited by Victor Del Hierro and Crystal VanKooten.
Description: Fort Collins, Colorado : The WAC Clearinghouse ; Denver, Colorado : University Press of Colorado, [2022] | Series: Practices & possibilities | Contains 18 chapters by Ann Shivers-McNair and others. | Includes bibliographical references. | Contents: volume 1. Section 1, The journey and the destination : accessing stories of digital writing researchers ; Section 2, Memory and documentation : digital archives and multimodal methods of preservation — volume 2. Section 3, Ethics and intangibles : unique challenges of digital research ; Section 4, Digital tools for understanding discourse, process, and writing : languaging across modalities.
Identifiers: LCCN 2022050587 (print) | LCCN 2022050588 (ebook) | ISBN 9781646423828 (v. 1 ; pbk.) | ISBN 9781646423880 (v. 2 ; pbk.) | ISBN 9781642151664 (v. 2 ; PDF) | ISBN 9781642151671 (v. 2 ; ePub) | ISBN 9781642151541 (v. 1 ; PDF) | ISBN 9781642151558 (v. 1 ; ePub)
Subjects: LCSH: Online authorship—Research. | Discourse analysis, Narrative—Research. | Storytelling in mass media—Research. | Internet research.
Classification: LCC PN171.O55 M48 2022 (print) | LCC PN171.O55 (ebook) | DDC 808.0072—dc23/eng/20230111
LC record available at https://lccn.loc.gov/2022050587
LC ebook record available at https://lccn.loc.gov/2022050588

Copyeditor: Tony Magialetti
Designer: Mike Palmquist
Cover Art: "Digital Rhetoric Collage," by Valentina Sierra Niño. Used with permission.
Series Editors: Aimee McClure, Mike Palmquist, and Aleashia Walton
Series Associate Editor: Jagadish Paudel

The WAC Clearinghouse supports teachers of writing across the disciplines. Hosted by Colorado State University, it brings together scholarly journals and book series as well as resources for teachers who use writing in their courses. This book is available in digital formats for free download at wac.colostate.edu.

Founded in 1965, the University Press of Colorado is a nonprofit cooperative publishing enterprise supported, in part, by Adams State University, Colorado State University, Fort Lewis College, Metropolitan State University of Denver, University of Alaska Fairbanks, University of Colorado, University of Denver, University of Northern Colorado, University of Wyoming, Utah State University, and Western Colorado University. For more information, visit upcolorado.com.

Land Acknowledgment. The Colorado State University Land Acknowledgment can be found at https://landacknowledgment.colostate.edu.

Contents

Acknowledgments vii

Introduction 3
    Crystal VanKooten and Victor Del Hierro

SECTION 3. ETHICS AND INTANGIBLES: UNIQUE CHALLENGES OF DIGITAL RESEARCH

Chapter 10. Developing a Black Feminist Research Ethic: A Methodological Approach to Research in Digital Spaces 29
    Constance Haywood

Chapter 11. Toward a Feminist Ethic of Self-Care and Protection When Researching Digital Aggression 45
    Erika M. Sparby

Chapter 12. Reflections on a Hip-Hop DJ Methodology. 65
    Eric A. House

Chapter 13. Trauma-Informed Scholarship in Digital Research and Design 81
    Shannon Kelly, Eric Rodriguez, Stuart Blythe, and Ben Lauren

Chapter 14. Considerations for Internet Participant Selection: Algorithms, Power Users, Overload, Conventionalization, and Participant Protection 105
    John R. Gallagher

SECTION 4. DIGITAL TOOLS FOR UNDERSTANDING DISCOURSE, PROCESS, AND WRITING: LANGUAGING ACROSS MODALITIES

Chapter 15. Studying Unknown Unknowns: Lessons from Critical Making on Twitter 117
    Whitney Lew James

Chapter 16. Language Policing to Language Curiosity: Using Corpus Analysis to Foreground Linguistic Diversity 133
    Laura Aull

Chapter 17. The Pleasurable Difficulty of Programming. 159
    Benjamin Miller

Chapter 18. Multimodal Methods for Mapping Multimodal Composing Processes 185
    Christina Rowell

Contributors 209

Acknowledgments

Working on this book has a been a labor of love. I want to thank my co-editor, Crystal for inviting me to join her on this project. We both got a chance to learn a lot on this project and I am grateful for her willingness to be completely collaborative and at the same time pragmatic when necessary. We were thoughtful when we needed to be and moved quickly when we could to move this project along. As soon as we decided on our authors, the only thing we wanted to do was get their work to the field as fast as we could.

Big shout out and love to all of our authors. Without them this collection would not be what it is and I appreciate their patience and energy throughout this project. Thank you for trusting us with your work. Thank you to Kat Stevenson for your editorial work on our project.

Finally, thank you to my partner Laura. Your endless support and love is appreciated and recognized.

– Victor Del Hierro

Thank you to Victor for taking on this project with me and seeing it through, and for teaching me to learn from ways of being and researching that I've paid too little attention to in the past. Thank you to all the authors in the collection for your thoughtful work and willingness to share not only your methods and methodologies, but your identities and experiences. Thank you always to my family and my partner Ben: I couldn't do this without you.

– Crystal VanKooten

METHODS AND METHODOLOGIES FOR RESEARCH IN DIGITAL WRITING AND RHETORIC

CENTERING POSITIONALITY IN COMPUTERS AND WRITING SCHOLARSHIP, VOLUME 2

Introduction

Crystal VanKooten
OAKLAND UNIVERSITY

Victor Del Hierro
UNIVERSITY OF FLORIDA

Coming Together across Computers and Writing: A Playlist as Introduction—Track 1

Over the course of creating this edited collection, we did not imagine that our CFP would attract so many responses, nor that our manuscript would grow into 18 chapters. We received so much excellent work and so many important methodological stories that we now present two volumes of *Methods and Methodologies for Research in Digital Writing and Rhetoric: Centering Positionality in Computers and Writing Scholarship*. The introduction that follows is the same introduction that we wrote for Volume 1—it tells the story of one future for digital writing and rhetoric research that moves toward being conscious of who we are, how we can come together, and telling the stories of our work. We appreciate you reading and engaging with both volumes.

We find ourselves living and working at such an exciting time in the field of rhetoric and composition and its sub-field of computers and writing. College students are writing and reading in a wide variety of formats and spaces, and they use computers, phones, and other digital devices to connect to audiences online through words, images, and sounds. Researchers continue to study these and other forms of 21st-century communication, and we too have laptops, cell phones, software programs, digital cameras and microphones, and more to assist us. With the use of digital technologies, though, comes researcher responsibility and new questions. How does the prevalence of the digital in rhetoric and writing affect the questions we ask, the methods we use to answer these questions, the knowledge we make, and the teaching practices we employ?

We developed this edited collection in response to these questions, perceiving a need to revisit where computers and writing today stands in its use of digital methodologies and methods. Drawing on Gesa Kirsch and Patricia A. Sullivan, we define *methodology* as the overarching theoretical approach and design of research, and *methods* as the tangible research practices that are enacted within a study. In this collection, we explore methodologies and methods that are shaped with and through *digital* tools and texts: electronic and computerized tools that allow what Doug Eyman calls "a new form of production enabled by information and communication technologies" (20), and multimodal texts composed with both "fingers and codes" as Angela Haas has described (84). As scholars of digital writing and digital rhetoric, we study communicative products and practices at the intersection of textual production and rhetoric, where a text is defined as any object that can be read or interpreted (Eyman 21), and rhetoric involves practices related to oratory, language, persuasion, style, human action and motivation, ideology, and meaning (Eyman 13–17). Jonathan Alexander and Jacqueline Rhodes further describe digital texts and related practices as having been affected by technological change, as developing over time, and as "enriched by the experiences and traditions of many diverse people and communities" (4). Because of this variety, some difficulty arises, as Eyman notes, when "applying traditional rhetorical theories and methods to new media compositions and networked spaces," and thus "new methods and theories may need to be developed" (18). Specific attention to *how* the digital informs and shapes theories that ground research and the specific methods used is crucial. The authors in this collection provide windows into the process of theory-building and method development for research related to various digital sites, tools, and approaches.

Our conversations about digital methodologies and methods have ultimately been steered by where in the field we stand and what our disciplinary landscape represents. At the outset of this project, both of us wanted to fill the need for a resource for scholars of digital writing and rhetoric: for much of our own research and that of our colleagues, we felt like we were constantly figuring out digital methods and methodologies on our own as we proceeded with our work. We wanted to emphasize that there is a broad landscape of scholars doing important work in digital rhetoric and writing that we knew could provide starting points for others, and we sought to bring some of this work together in one place. As editors, we searched for a balance of chapters that would help us get at granular questions about methods and how they related back to the development of digital methodologies, while seeing how far we could push the possibilities of what could be understood as part of methods and methodologies for digital writing and rhetoric.

One place we often found ourselves coming back to in our discussions was one of our disciplinary homes: computers and writing (C&W). The field and the conference represent the audience we want to speak directly to with this book. For both of us, our work "fits" at C&W. We have presented many times at the computers and writing conference, we have networked there, and we have attended C&W presentations by many authors in this collection. Thus, one of our goals is to highlight voices from C&W. But we also want to expand our methodological discussions and discourses, to shift our attention to diverse scholars and to other parts of the field that might not be our own. C&W, like all conferences in our field, is still overwhelmingly white, but there are many researchers who identify as Black, Indigenous, and people of color (BIPOC) who are designing and implementing digital research related to and aligned with work in C&W.[1] Another goal of this collection, then, is to highlight the voices of BIPOC scholars doing digital work. Finally, we want this collection to speak across and beyond C&W and encourage researchers to look at and listen to a variety of digital research. We both are members of the C&W community, for example, but in the past, we did not interact with each other at the C&W conference: we come from distinct positionalities and different pathways. Perhaps in part because of our differences—our research interests, the technologies we use, the communities we inhabit and study, our race, age, and gender—we existed in the same academic community for several years without meaningful interaction, inhabiting different corners of the field.

As co-editors of this collection, we now take a different approach: we speak together from a new place, a shared corner, where we highlight our similarities and our differences and use our varying strengths and points-of-view. One of our similarities, for example, is that we both love music. Crystal is a singer; Victor is a DJ. So we frame this introduction as a playlist, juxtaposing and mixing our voices, histories, and positionalities with scholarship to lead you into the chapters to come. We also intentionally use our differences, demonstrating one way that this collection might enter the disciplinary discourse within and adjacent to C&W, and drawing on the collective vision that comes from distinct positions. Crystal approaches this work with strong grounding in composition studies and a desire to seek out digital method/ologies due to the multimodal nature of composition. Victor approaches the collection drawn to the work of BIPOC scholars who have used and developed digital methods and methodologies to trace long histories of technology work in their respective communities. Together, we forge and widen pathways for authors in the collection to share research insights grounded in multimodality, positionality, and community. In volume 2 of the collection, we focus on researchers' stories, exploring how positionality impacts research and vision for the field, as well as how new tools are changing what is possible for digital writing and rhetoric.

Our Histories: How Crystal Learned that Research Inquiry is Always Multimodal—Track 2

The field needs more scholars to share digital writing and research experiences so that others can learn from and build on their mistakes and successes. Thus we begin by each telling our research stories and sharing some context about where we come from personally and professionally. Through conversations with scholars in the field and with each other, we have come to know that thinking critically about identity and positionality in relation to digital methods and methodologies is a crucial part of any discussion on research. We understand that there is no way

---

1. A note from the publisher: The WAC Clearinghouse practice is to capitalize names of racial and ethnic groups. The editors and contributors to this collection have chosen to capitalize *Black*, *Brown*, and *Indigenous* but not *white*.

to fully consider what future technologies await us, yet one constant is the impact of the researcher and their unique and multiple points of experience.

In 2009 as a first-year graduate student, I (Crystal) composed a video to go along with my seminar paper for a course entitled *Introduction to Composition Studies*. My paper explored the use of sound and music in composition studies, providing an overview of work in rhet/comp that demonstrated how sound might be used and emphasized in writing classrooms and in research. I wasn't required to make a video as part of the project, but I felt that writing about the importance of composing with sounds, but including no sounds or music in my paper, wasn't a very appropriate approach. Thus I chose to make a companion video to hand in with my more traditional paper, and in the video, I put songs together with images of musical notes, people singing and playing instruments, and people dancing and moving their bodies. I concluded the video with singing, my voice ringing out a bit awkwardly that "composition needs music." Of course, others in our field had been making such a call already (Halbritter; Selfe; Shankar), but in that moment—my first year of graduate study, my first Ph.D. level seminar paper in rhet/comp, my first attempt at joining the conversation—it seemed amazing and freeing and *fun* to me that I could sing my thesis to my professor, that I could illustrate my argument by lining up photos to the driving beat of a song that I loved and literally got me moving, and that all of this was part of my *writing*.

This story of my first academic video composition demonstrates that research inquiry, critical thinking, and making knowledge are always entwined with multimodal expression, and thus with new (or at least newly accessible) digital technologies for composition. In rhet/comp, we do not always fully acknowledge or explore the multimodal nature of inquiry because of print-centric research traditions, time or technology constraints, lack of training and mentorship for new researchers, or publication venues that favor alphabetic-only composition. But digital technologies that facilitate multimodal inquiry—a laptop, free video editing software, a laptop microphone—were immediately available to me as a grad student and easy to learn how to use, and as I began to use them, I found that the multimodal processes they facilitated stimulated different kinds of thinking and engagement, not to mention a lot of joy. I sat on the bed in my small graduate-student bedroom, hunched over a laptop, lining up images with song beats for *hours*, bobbing my head to the music while I considered the rhetorical qualities of notes, sounds, melodies, and beats. I was sucked into the editing, to the flow, to the hearing and composing and the inquiry.

Thus when it came time to decide what to study for my dissertation project, I knew that multimodal expression of ideas was going to be at the core of my research. My dissertation was a qualitative classroom study in which I observed and interviewed first-year composition students and instructors, looking for evidence of if and how students developed meta-awareness through video composition. To conduct the study, I collected various kinds of digital data: I observed and recorded class sessions, I conducted and recorded one-on-one interviews with students and instructors, and I collected videos that students composed. (To read more about the methods and findings from my dissertation, please reference VanKooten "Identifying . . ."; "Messy Problem-Exploring"; and "'The video was what did it' . . .").

The training I received in how I might approach designing and conducting such a study came from several sources. I took one course in *Qualitative Methods in Educational Research*, where we read about and discussed fundamentals of qualitative inquiry within education: epistemology, validity, reliability, interviews, observations, data analysis, politics, ethics, and the presentation of data. I also took one course in *Multimedia Writing*, in which I composed several videos: a remix video, an interview-based informational video, and a final project video where I interviewed several undergraduate students who had taken my writing courses and then used this interview footage to make a video argument about their learning and the rhetoric of music. This final video project within *Multimedia Writing* served as a pilot study for the kind of work I would do on a larger scale in the dissertation: observing and talking to students, recording their narratives and interactions, and using the digital recordings for analysis and presentation of conclusions, and it also led to my first academic publication, where I used both prose and video to present arguments (VanKooten "A New Composition").

In addition to coursework, I was mentored through the process of composing my dissertation using video and other digital tools and methods by several professors, most notably by my dissertation co-directors, Anne Ruggles Gere and Bump Halbritter. Much of my learning, though, about specific digital methods and the possibilities of the digital for inquiry came because of me jumping in, asking for advice, and figuring it out as I went along. After the dissertation, as an Assistant Professor, I continued using video to pursue similar research questions, and my work expanded to include more classrooms, more student participants, and more video cameras. As I collected new video data and analyzed it using a combination of multimodal and traditional print-based methods, I found myself constantly reflecting on how humans and technologies interacted, and I worked toward written and multimodal expressions of findings. I've written elsewhere about the process of coming to articulate and employ what I now call a methodology of interdependence through video as method (VanKooten "A Research Methodology . . . "), and I describe there how much of my methodological wayfinding (to borrow an apt word for learning from Jonathan Alexander, Karen Lunsford, and Carl Whithaus) occurred as I experimented with cameras and editing software and learned as I went about the affordances and limitations of video for qualitative writing research.

My wayfinding went a little like this: I made some bad recordings and videos, and some that weren't so bad. In the process, I wrestled with ethics—again and again as the study progressed—and I still came up against ethical and procedural questions that I didn't know how to answer. What I thought would be simple was not ever simple, and I often received conflicting advice: use pseudonyms for student participants/use real names; record with one camera/record with multiple cameras. I made choices, tried something, reflected on the choice, and moved forward. I edited footage together in a way that was confusing, or that wasn't as respectful of my participants as it could have been, or that didn't acknowledge my own role in the research interaction. I reflected, got feedback, and revised. I made some videos that were overly simplistic, hard to understand, and weren't very useful. And then I made something that I thought was kind of good, maybe—a video sequence that sparked a new insight. And the combinations of images, interview clips, sounds, and words began to speak to me, to reveal new pathways for moving forward.

I am so fortunate that with support from others in the field and in my personal life, I was able to publish my digital book, *Transfer across Media: Using Digital Video in the Teaching of Writing*, through Computers and Composition Digital Press in 2020. In the book, readers can see and hear my process of seeking out digital-methodological pathways that were new to me, and they can also explore digital data and video analyses and findings. For me, though, these pathways were not always easily discovered, and I needed and wanted more guidance along the way.

With this edited collection, we want to shed light on and widen similar hard-to-find or seemingly narrow methodological pathways for research in digital writing and rhetoric. Through these chapters, we offer seasoned and emerging scholars in computers and writing and rhet/comp some help and advice as they work to develop their own digital methods and methodologies for research. While it might seem like you are the only researcher who wants to use digital and online tools to collect, analyze, and present data about writing and rhetoric, and who is grappling with the many complexities of doing so, there are, in fact, many researchers in our field who have gone and are going through a similar confusing, messy, and exciting digital research process. We seek to present and amplify their voices in the chapters to come.

Our Histories: How Victor Learned to Problem-Solve with Digital Tools—Track 3

I (Victor) like to joke with my friends in academia that I hate reading. I always tell a version of this joke to my students and tell them that is why I decided to study Hip-Hop. The truth of that statement is actually more about the relationship I have to education. Growing up in the late 1990s and early 2000s, it was the digital music turn which meant that digital tools have been at the center of my life, and, by association, a part of my learning.

Maybe my favorite memory of the interaction between digital tools and my education history was the year I received an MPIO FL300 mp3 player for Christmas. It was tiny, the size of a fun size snickers, but it was a full gigabyte of memory and featured a tiny microphone on the end. Later that year, I sat in my junior year high school English class—an AP class that we were told was the hardest class we would ever take and would prepare us for college. At the start of the year, students in this class were advised that if we were not willing to work hard, we should tell our counselors to switch us out of the course. As the youngest of three siblings, during a time when my older siblings were away for college, I was eager for a taste of what college life would be like.

I was excited for this class where we would read literature and talk about the world. We would challenge ourselves to think hard about the complicated texts. We might read some Shakespeare and others in the canon that my college-aged siblings were reading. However, over the course of that class, I grew increasingly disappointed in my educational experience and increasingly agitated at schooling in general. The culmination of this moment was when our English teacher went on some tangent and decided we needed to go back to the basics. Instead of engaging with difficult literature, we would be having vocabulary spelling tests. The whole class groaned at this announcement, and I could not have been more pissed off about having to do a spelling test. After all, we had all already transitioned to writing our papers on computers! Spellcheck would have our backs.

That night, I sat in my room begrudgingly studying for this spelling test while listening to my mp3 player. At some point, I looked at my MPIO FL300, remembered the tiny microphone on the end of the display screen, and suddenly had an idea. Fueled by all my indignation about the spelling test, I held in my hand my tool for rebellion. That night, I schemed to cheat on my test by recording the spelling of each word on the test using this microphone, and then playing back the recording in my ear during the test. Frankly, this instance of rebellion really kickstarted my first experience with a digital tool, helping me begin to understand how to best use these tools for any situation. I recorded drafts, quickly learning that I would need to speak softly but clearly so I could hear the spellings using only one earbud on the side opposite of the teacher's desk. I spelled the words slowly so I could write them while preserving a natural spelling speed. Finally, I had to remember to leave the playback setting on "repeat one track" mode so I could listen back the second time and make sure I spelled everything correctly.

Reflecting on this experience, I could make several connections to scholarly inquiry, including arguments about education, innovation, and lived experiences with digital composing. I could also say this was my first experience with post-humanism, as this mp3 player was just an extension of my own memory as I listened to the sound of my own voice spelling out the words no different than what was happening in the head of any other student in the room. I knew I was cheating, but I felt justified because I felt like I was getting cheated out of an education. Two wrongs may not make a right, but I know this experience set off a continuing relationship I have had with schooling that I continue to grapple with as an educator. This relationship is one of skepticism that is perpetually directed at institutions of learning that are not transparent about their methods and methodologies or about the motivations for the pedagogical decisions that inform schooling. In my experiences of public education, there was hardly any discussion by school officials about the decisions they made. Or at the very least an inkling that my teachers also recognized that there were some cracks in the system. In the example of my AP English class, we were simultaneously supposed to believe that we were gaining a college credit worthy experience while being disciplined with lackluster pedagogy. At all phases of my schooling, I have strived to hack, resist, rebel, and survive by finding solutions to problems that a Chicano studying Hip-Hop might encounter. I have learned which educators are truly invested in helping their students, and which ones are just interested in gatekeeping. I have also learned that there is risk in finding innovative solutions, and that these solutions sometimes don't work, but you can still learn from the experience.

I share this story to locate my experience in digital rhetoric as one that comes from problem solving. Often the problems that I find myself solving are linked directly to not accepting the status quo while simultaneously making sense of the methods and methodologies we gravitate to for our solutions. In this collection, we are excited to highlight work that draws on digital methods and methodologies as tools to solve problems while doing so from lived experiences. We bring knowledges and approaches to our digital methods and methodologies that draw from all our experiences of digital tools and all the ways we have learned to leverage them. Many of the authors in this collection echo the same kind of innovation that draws on lived experience, problem solving, and a rejection of average or getting by. And so, I and my co-authors ask, what problems are you interested in solving? What versions of the status quo are you rejecting? What digital tools are you playing with to go higher?

Who We Are: Crystal's Positionality Statement—Track 4

Many of the authors in this collection powerfully highlight how positionalities and identities intersect with and shape methodology in meaningful—and at times subversive and emancipatory—ways. Scholars of color in the collection, queer scholars, and differently abled scholars, these strong and persuasive voices demonstrate the importance of acknowledging oppression, privilege, and positionality when a researcher speaks and writes. Across the collection, then, you will notice that we have asked all authors to include a positionality statement or a positionality story that links identities and digital methodologies, and Victor and I offer editorial positionality statements here in the introduction. Through writing explicitly about positionality, the authors and editors entered a process of what Jacqueline Royster and Gesa Kirsch label "strategic contemplation" at the intersection of identities and research methodologies and methods. *Strategic contemplation*, a feminist orientation, asks us to "pay attention to how lived experiences shape our perspectives as researchers and those of our research subjects" (Royster and Kirsch 22). Royster and Kirsch remind us that explicit attention to positionality can bring "rich, new dimensions in scholarly work when we deliberately seek to attend to the places where past and present meet, where our embodied experience, intuition, and quiet minds can begin to notice the unnoticed" (22). In the pages that follow, it is our hope that researchers in computers and writing and beyond can learn from these new dimensions together.

I start my positionality statement by introducing myself and the place where I work and live. My name is Crystal VanKooten, and I am a white, cisgender, able-bodied woman. I work as an Associate Professor of Writing and Rhetoric at Oakland University, and I live in Rochester Hills with my family: my partner Ben and my two young kids, Sabrina and Paul. The land on which Oakland University stands is the ancestral, traditional, and contemporary lands of the Anishinaabe, known as the Three Fires Confederacy, comprised of the Ojibwe, Odawa, and Potawatomi. The land was ceded in the 1807 Treaty of Detroit and makes up southeast Michigan. I recognize these roots to acknowledge that the arts and humanities have been practiced where I live and work long before the arrival of Europeans such as myself.[2] I am half Dutch and half German; I am a Christian; I am a musician (I play piano and love to sing in choir); I am a teacher, a writer, and a video-maker.

I recognize and acknowledge that many aspects of who I am shape the work that I do and the ways that I can do it. Because I am white, straight, cisgender, able-bodied, and Christian, I am privileged in a society and a schooling system that often unfairly recognizes and rewards these qualities as natural or normal. I have benefitted from my white skin, for example, in that I almost always had teachers and professors that looked like me and shared many aspects of my home culture. I fit in at school, and I always loved it, partially because my schooling experiences were dominated by a familiar and comfortable white culture. Now, as a professor in a predominantly white university culture, I am only recently learning to see and prioritize the importance and impact of race in my work—and the dire need to address racial inequities and white supremacy head on—in part through working with and reading the writing of scholars of color such as Victor and other authors in this collection. In 1995, Gesa Kirsch and Joy Ritchie urged feminist researchers to "acknowledge the way race (and for most composition scholars this means examining their whiteness), social class, and other circumstances have structured their own thinking and how that, in turn, has shaped their own questions and interpretations" (10). Today, I see that my white privilege allows me to remain unaware of or even ignore such urging, which can negatively influence the experiences of research participants, my research findings, and the audiences I am able to speak to within the field.

I have benefitted, too, from an able body in my research. I often carry heavy camera and microphone equipment with me, and I freely walk about a classroom

---

2. I am grateful to Oakland University and the Center for Public Humanities for sharing this land acknowledgment.

research site with a camera in hand. When I compose video products, I see and hear the material I'm working with, and standard video-editing tools generally work well for my body and my abilities. While I am a woman who lives within a patriarchal society, I have experienced few extremely damaging or limiting instances of overt misogyny in my professional and personal life, at least that I am aware of. Because I am married and am a mother, I split my time between family and work, but I receive heavy familial support from my partner and my parents when it comes to childcare, allowing me to focus a great deal of time on my work and scholarship.

These reflections on my identity, positionality, and privileges make clear some of the pathways I've traveled and assistance I've received that have led to and facilitated my research and the use of digital methods and methodologies in that research. I share these parts of me while acknowledging, as Kirsch and Ritchie point out, that my experiences are reflections of ideology and culture and that we all inhabit "split selves" where "multiple and often unknowable identities" exist (8). I recognize that these pathways might be open, closed, or partially blocked to other scholars and researchers reading this book, and I commit to working toward opening as many entry points as possible and providing adequate assistance to all who want to engage in similar work.

Who We Are: Victor's Positionality Statement—Track 5

What up doe! What it do? I (Victor) always open my presentations with these greetings because I always want to honor and show love to two Hip-Hop communities that have sustained and nourished me as an academic: Detroit and Houston. Specifically, I want to honor my Southwest Detroit homie Sacramento Knoxx, who inspires and reminds me that Hip-Hop is still about community and resistance. In addition, DJ Screw and Houston Hip-Hop taught me that you can show love to those who came before you while making your own lane and still staying grounded in your community.

I enter this discussion of digital methods and methodologies through Hip-Hop. DJs in Hip-Hop have used records to travel across time and space, listening, learning, and keeping alive records they grew up with as well as records from different eras across all continents. These DJ practices are acts of knowledge making and a practice that I treat as the foundation to my work in Hip-Hop. Furthermore, I credit Hip-Hop for giving me the opportunity to learn how to enact migratory practices as a productive and relational activity. I have learned to find comfort in being a migrant and understanding that migration is my grounding for my relationship to people, culture, and land.

I grew up in the borderlands of El Paso, Texas and Ciudad Juarez, Chihuahua. Growing up, I really did not know the impact crossing back and forth between nation-states had on me. And while reading Chicanx studies scholarship helped it make more sense, it was not until I spent time in Michigan in graduate school making an intentional effort to understand my relationship to land and to Indigenous communities that I started to understand my identity as migratory.

The borderlands taught me about the value of border crossing, Hip-Hop taught me how to respect the spaces you cross into, and migration taught me to be purposeful in my engagements and movements. I draw on this orientation of borders, Hip-Hop, and migration to understand my own positionality and my approach to research. For example, knowing that Hip-Hop is a Black space, I always want to ensure that my movement within Hip-Hop is pro-Black. And while Hip-Hop has embraced me in some spaces, I know that Hip-Hop, like Black people, is not a monolith. So, in every space I engage within Hip-Hop, I do my best to enact a purposeful movement into different spaces. What is purposeful movement and why does it matter? For me, purposeful movement is the foundation to my positionality because it asks me to identify why I am deciding to move into a space and as part of that decision I have to identify whether or not that space is for me. This process is iterative and an important part of my practice of relationship-building.

This brings me back to Hip-Hop, DJs, and the connection to purposeful movement, aka migration. As I have started to play with my own turntables, one of the first revelations made to me was how much data was needed to play records. In addition to what I will call the raw data, the information pressed onto the records, was the information needed to perform as a DJ: how the needle works; the role of the platter; the way to use your hands; the feel of different records. All of these are tools for examining and understanding the raw data on the record. And then there is the part where you commit what is on the record into your own memory: sounds, words, artists, track locations, and so much more. As the hands and the needle physically make their way across the record, you develop a relationship. Hip-Hop taught me how to move over records with purpose by paying attention to language, place, and stories. DJs emphasize this purposeful movement as they develop relationships to records by connecting the physical movements to the content as they apply their analytical frameworks as they listen and compose. A Hip-Hop DJ listens with purpose because their movements require it; this is their digital method.

The ways that Hip-Hop has taught me to listen have been a grounding practice for understanding my own identity and positionality and how it exists in relation to other people, communities, and identities. As a cis-man Chicano, I do my best to be conscious of who and what I embody as I move between spaces and engage with people. I listen for stories because they ground humanization. I pay attention to language, specifically how people describe themselves, their communities, and the places they occupy. When they feel familiar, I make connections, and when there are no connections, I keep listening. When stories sound personal, I respect boundaries. If I did not catch it the first time, I wait for the next time or ask for a rewind. Hip-Hop grounds all my relationships with any kind of knowledge-making experience. I will always make sense of my understanding of scholarship in writing and rhetoric through what Hip-Hop has taught me.

Digital Methods and Methodologies in Computers and Writing—Track 6

In the next several paragraphs, we review prior scholarship within C&W and rhet/comp that has led us to our current moment of collaboration and this collection. Published in 2007, *Digital Writing Research: Technologies, Methodologies, and Ethical Issues* provides a look into several kinds of digital writing research occurring at the start of the 21st century. In their introduction, editors Heidi McKee and Dànielle DeVoss note that there was "little extended and published examination by compositionists of the methodologies used and ethical issues faced when studying writing with/in digital technologies" (12), and they also call attention to an assumption in writing studies that non-digital methods could be applied across digital spaces with little or no changes (13). McKee and DeVoss survey the limited amount of work on digital methods for writing research that had been conducted at the time, mentioning research in the 1980s on writing processes with word processors and computer software, and a few published studies and discussions of methodological approaches in the 1990s (McKee and DeVoss 12–17). The 90s also included calls for new attention to context; to critical, feminist approaches; and to ethnography and empirical work within digital writing research, as well as web-based research in other fields such as technical communication, information architecture, and computer programming (McKee and DeVoss 15–18).

The chapters within the McKee and DeVoss collection offer views into several kinds of digital research that was occurring at the start of the 2000s: research on digital communities (Banks and Eble; De Pew; Sidler), research on global citizens and transnational institutions (Sapienza; Pandey; Smith); research on the activity of writing through digital technologies (Hart-Davidson; Addison; Geisler and Slattery); research on digital texts and multimodal spaces (Blythe; Hilligoss and Williams; Romberger; Kimme Hea; McIntire-Strasburg); and research on the research process and research reports (Blair and Tulley; Burnett, Chandler, and Lopez; Hawkes; Reilly and Eyman; Rickly). Overall, McKee and DeVoss's collection presents wide coverage on a range of research angles and topics within computers and writing, illustrating that the sites and questions for digital writing were changing and that methodologies should be reshaped for these new contexts, technologies, and tools.

At the same time in the mid-2000s, scholars like Adam J. Banks and Angela Haas were developing groundbreaking work bringing together digital and cultural rhetorics. Angela Haas' 2007 "Wampum as Hypertext" brought to the forefront what digital methods and methodologies looked like from an Indigenous perspective, rewriting the history of hypertext while tying it back to embodied practice. Adam J. Banks' 2006 *Race, Rhetoric, and Technology: Searching for Higher Ground* (winner of the 2007 Computers and Writing Distinguished Book Award) and 2011 *Digital Griots: African American Rhetoric in a Multimedia Age* brought African American rhetorics to the center of digital writing. Haas and Banks are representative of the work being done by BIPOC scholars that expands our understanding of digital methods and methodologies. Additionally, Dora Ramirez-Dhoore's 2005 article "The Cyberborderlands: Surfing the Web for Xicanidad" traces early conversations of identity and race on the internet, and Samantha Blackmon's 2004 article "Violent Networks: Historical Access in the Composition Classroom" reminds us that even though computers entered the classroom more frequently, there was still a major digital divide to account for in terms of access and the historical lineage of institutional racism. The genius in all this work is not about identifying new tools for digital writing, but instead connecting longer lineages and discourses to conversations on technology and writing. Banks, Haas, Ramirez-Dhoore, and Blackmon insist on bringing methodologies to digital rhetoric that identify and keep communities at the center.

Since this mid-2000s moment, other scholars have continued to build on these publications in digital writing and rhetoric. We list them briefly here to honor their contributions and to point to how a variety of work related to digital tools has shaped research inquiry in the field. To be blunt, if you haven't read these works and you do digital research, get to reading! First, we have been heavily influenced by the work of scholars in C&W who study writing and rhetoric through video and other related technologies (many of whom are women), listed here in alphabetical order by author name: Megan Adams' use of digital storytelling connected to place; Sarah Arroyo and Bahareh Alaei's visually stunning video remixes; Laura Gonzales's use of video coding software to examine rhetorics of translation; Bump Halbritter and Julie Lindquist's use of video to examine scenes of literacy sponsorship; Alexandra Hidalgo's feminist filmmaking methodology; bonnie lenore kyburz's video experimentation and theorization of film-composition; Lehua Ledbetter's work on YouTube bloggers; Casey Miles' Queer video filmmaking; Andrea Olinger's analysis of visual embodied actions within interviews; Laquana Cooke, Lisa Dusenberry, and Joy Robinson's work on gaming; Ann Shivers-McNair's use of point-of-view (POV) researcher video; and Josie Walwema's studies on intercultural and transnational digital communication.

Overall, these authors demonstrate how digital research tools like a video camera or video editing software function as much more than a "note-taking device," but instead as an integral part of the research ecology that then "demands a retooling of the methodology" (Halbritter and Lindquist 185). We have learned much from technofeminists, as well, who have discussed multimodal methods within a technofeminist research identity (Almjeld and Blair), shown their work through authoring digital dissertations (Adams and Blair), and have extended "conversations in technofeminism, digital rhetorics, and computers and writing, with an increased attention to intersectionality" of race, gender, class, and sex (Haas, Rhodes, and DeVoss).

We also draw from and build on the work from those using digital research and technologies as what Regina Duthely calls a "disruptive political force" (357) to address injustice. Duthely argues that Hip-Hop provides a foundation for digital and multimodal composition in our field, and that we can learn much from online Hip-Hop communities that use digital tools to build community, resist dominance, reaffirm Black experiences, and generate hopeful narratives (355). A.D. Carson's *i used to love to dream* is an apt example, and as the first peer-reviewed rap album, it paves new ground for digital methods related to the presentation of scholarship and simultaneously disrupts dominant forms of discourse within academia and foregrounds Black expression. We are listening, as well, to colleagues from the Sound Studies, Rhetoric, and Writing community and conference who record and mix sound to connect to communities and fight against oppression and injustice (Aguilar, Bravo, Craig, Milburn, Petchauer, Rodriguez, Valenzuela, and Landa-Posas). For these authors, composing and performing with digital tools such as turntables or audio and video editing software is a way to share stories and to disrupt harmful narratives and practices in society.

Extending Work on Digital Methods and Methodologies: Positionalities and Technologies—Track 7

From the history of work on digital methods and methodologies that we present in Track 6, we learn that the digital affects all aspects of research, including methodology and methods. The use of digital technologies for writing research is thus always experiential, contextual, and rhetorical. The authors in this collection are navigating complex experiences, and one way that they build on prior work is that they purposefully—and at length—share methodological stories, experiences, and knowledge gained. They do so with an explicit attention to researcher positionality and how that positionality affects the work. The results are methodological narratives that are personal and professional, individual yet foundational. Our authors, much like Victor with his MPIO FL300, use the digital to solve problems, to challenge the status quo, and to address inequalities. Sometimes they do so by using familiar digital technologies in novel ways, exploring the use of social media, online repositories, a handheld sound recorder, online corpora, or a camera, for example. Other times, they explain the use of relatively new or less familiar technologies such as digital mapping apps, Twitter bots, audio-visual captions, or computer programming code. Overall, the collection usefully combines attention to human positionality and digital technology to dig into important social issues and questions related to writing and rhetoric today. And because our authors have so many important experiences to share and diverse methodological narratives to tell, we have divided the collection into two volumes. In Track 7, we provide an overview of the sections and chapters in each volume.

Telling Research Stories for Activist Ends

In Volume 1, *Section 1—The Journey and the Destination: Accessing Stories of Digital Writing Researchers* focuses on the stories of researchers arriving at their current digital-methodological practices, with attention to how digital methodologies open opportunities for reflective scholarship that is at times activist minded and at others an opportunity to check our privilege. In chapter 1, "Lessons Learned from an Early Career, Five-Year Project with Digital Methods: Accounting for Positionality and Redressing Injustice," Ann Shivers-McNair traces the relationships between bodies, things, contexts, and practices in her experiences as an early-career digital researcher. With careful attention to her own positionality and to networks of relationships with BIPOC women scholars in rhetoric and composition, she describes work on an ethnographic case study of a makerspace where she used video recording and still photography. Specifically, Shivers-McNair reflects on how digital fabrication technologies like 3D printing and the use of video and photographs for storytelling are intertwined in her work, and how both aspects are often influenced by her own multiple identities and white privilege.

In chapter 2, "Flipping the Table and Redefining the Dissertation Genre with a Digital Chapter," Temptaous Mckoy discusses the methods behind the digital chapter in her award-winning dissertation. Connecting digital publishing with digital methods as fundamental to doing digital scholarship, Mckoy argues that leveraging a wide range of experiences in and out of academia helped her realize the potential of her skill set based in her own lived experience. These skills and practices, including networking, social media strategy, fund-raising, and relationship building, allowed her to utilize a wide range of digital methods to complete her project through an iterative process that eventually led to the digital chapter. By wanting to create a digital publication that would better tell the story of her research, Mckoy was led to the acknowledgment, development, and deployment of her digital methods to complete her research.

In chapter 3, Janine Butler brings together theories of sound, access, interdependency, articulation, and voice to reflect on her methodology and methods, which include the use of audio and video technologies. The chapter, "Strategies for Accessing and Articulating Voices through Digital Writing Research Projects," details processes for accessing a professional voice through signed, captioned, and voiced-over videos; as well as processes for accessing research participants' voices through transcribing and video recording. Butler urges digital writing researchers to join her in further exploring ways to make sounds visible and visuals sonic so that more people might fully access and articulate their writerly voices.

Chapter 4, "'Tell Virgil Write BRICK on my brick': Doctoral Bashments, (Re)Visiting Hiphopography and the Digital Discursivity of the DJ: A Mixed Down Methods Movement," is a reflection from Todd Craig on hiphopography, a term originally coined by James G. Spady, as a research methodology that intermingles with classroom praxis. Hiphopography, for Craig, embraces inclusion through digital resources, always inviting, invoking, and involving participants of Hip-Hop culture into the processes and products of research and teaching. Craig organizes his reflections as a set of tracks, mixing in samples from an online meme, a track from the Buffalo, NY based Hip-Hop collective Griselda, his own theory of Hip-Hop DJ Rhetoric, Nelson Flores and Jonathan Rosa's raciolinguistic theories, and James G. Spady's work on Hip-Hop.

As editors, we wanted to open the collection with these chapters because they emphasized the journey of research. Methods and methodologies are learned, expanded, and understood best through experience. As the authors retrace their research steps, we are grateful to them for sharing their stories. Through their narratives, Shivers-McNair, Mckoy, Butler, and Craig give us access to their identities and digital research stories in ways that inspire us to build on their work and learning. Sharing stories is a vulnerable and engaging act that motivated us to further shape this collection by asking all the authors in the book to acknowledge their positionalities as they describe their scholarship. We hope you share in our gratitude to these authors for the stories they provide in their chapters.

New Perspectives, New Tools

Section 2 in Volume 1 contains methodological perspectives that utilize evolving 21st-century digital technologies to document histories, experiences, and phenomena. In the section, entitled *Memory and Documentation: Digital Archives and Multimodal Methods of Preservation,* the authors explore various applications and tools for archiving, recording, and mapping that extend current approaches to looking and listening across time and experiences. In chapter 5, "Digital Story-Mapping," Eda Özyeşilpınar and Diane Quaglia Beltran employ digital story-mapping (DSM) as a methodology and method to explore space and place, embodied storytelling, and multimodal writing in two projects: Özyeşilpınar's reading of the cartographic narrative within the *Israel in Pictorial Maps* atlas, and Beltran's writing classroom where students interrogate historical memory on a university campus. Through these projects, Özyeşilpınar and Beltran demonstrate how DSM offers possibilities for uncovering counterstories and silenced experiences of under-represented groups.

In chapter 6, "Social Network Analysis and Feminist Methodology," Patricia Fancher and Michael J. Faris explore the question of "who appears?" in two research projects through social network analysis (SNA). Fancher examines solidarity, inclusion, and exclusion in a community of early 20th-century women physicians, and Faris presents a citation network analysis of queer rhetoric studies, exploring citation patterns relating to scholars of color. Fancher and Faris conclude with three feminist methodological principles for the use of SNA, and they call for more attention to questions of power, embodiment and emotions, and the complexities of defining and visualizing networks.

Next, Kati Fargo Ahern asks us to consider ethics, ownership, IRB-related issues, and the consequences of the practice of field recording sounds. In chapter 7, "Recording Nonverbal Sounds: Cultivating Rhetorical Ambivalence in Digital Methods," Ahern describes field recording as a method, gives details on two sonic methods projects, and encourages researchers to actively cultivate ambivalence as they choose whether or not to field record. To assist us in this cultivation, Ahern offers a heuristic based on Indigenous digital composing and Indigenous sound studies that includes consideration of sound's purpose, land and space protocols, relationships, and potential benefit.

In chapter 8, "Digitally Preserving the Home through the Collective: A Communal Methodology for Filipinx-American Digital Archiving," Stephanie Mahnke and James Beni Wilson describe the digital archiving of artifacts from the Philippine American Cultural Center of Michigan. Mahnke and Wilson detail communal methods that challenge traditional notions of the archive through seeking balance between the creation of a digital infrastructure for a large set of collections and a community-engaged praxis that attends to narratives and place/space. They discuss grounding their archive in shared identity, communal decision making, local Filipinx history, the cultural center as a physical collective place, intergenerational succession, outreach, access, and financial sustainability.

Bibhushana Poudyal then discusses what minimal computing and community praxis offer digital archival research in chapter 9, "Counter, Contradictory, and Contingent Digital-Storytelling through Minimal Computing and Community-Praxis." Drawing from her experience creating an online archive of images depicting life in Kathmandu, Nepal, Poudyal describes how digital archives can be a dialectical space for deconstructing representations of the Other. She also reflects on openings for working with community members through digital archiving, even as a researcher with few resources, and argues that digital storytellers must learn to pay attention to and reflect the heterogeneities within diverse communities.

Taken together, the researchers in section 2 ask us to consider how mapping and archiving, how recording and networking create a space for preserving and sharing knowledge and for challenging racism and inequalities within the past and the present. The maps, graphs, sounds, and archives they describe help us to visualize and hear digital representations of cultures, events, and locations, and to consider our own roles in the ways we look back and remember in our research and our lives. They help us think about the potential for the digital to preserve— and to alter—the ways the world around us is constructed.

Negotiating Challenges in Digital Research

Digital writing research presents challenges that are contextual, rhetorical, and at times uncharted. While we might imagine that digital writing research presents *new* challenges, and it does, we are reminded that there will always be *people* navigating the technology. In Volume 2, *Section 3—Ethics and Intangibles: Unique Challenges of Digital Research* focuses on complex methodological situations that arose for authors: working with marginalized groups on the web, dealing with online digital aggression, centering Black rhetorics and Hip-Hop DJ practices, negotiating trauma in community engagement projects, and selecting participants within the vastness of the internet. Overall, the authors point to the necessity of continually considering digital ethics when encountering unfamiliar, challenging, or potentially harmful situations. In chapter 10, for example, Constance Haywood draws on her experiences researching online to suggest that Black feminist theory has much to teach digital writing and rhetoric researchers. In "Developing a Black Feminist Research Ethic: A Methodological Approach to Research in Digital Spaces," Haywood calls rhet/comp researchers to give prioritized attention to the lived experiences of Black women and to the ethics of working with research participants and communities online, especially with those who are multiply marginalized. Black feminism guides and specifies how we might do this, Haywood argues, through critical self-reflection, radical reciprocity, consideration of multiple identities and histories, and a commitment to liberation through protection and privacy.

In chapter 11, "Toward a Feminist Ethic of Self-Care and Protection When Researching Digital Aggression," Erika M. Sparby recounts their experience studying and navigating digital aggression on the popular message board site 4chan. Connecting their work to the growing body of research in writing studies on digital aggression, Sparby highlights the importance of researching digital aggression while acknowledging the inherent potential for harm in doing so. Specifically, Sparby advocates for a feminist ethic of self-care because of the emotional and intellectual toll of working in these at-times dangerous spaces. Sparby offers advice on how to be proactive within this feminist ethic of self-care, including an example of how to contact administrators to help secure support.

In chapter 12, "Reflections on a Hip-Hop DJ Methodology" Eric A. House argues for the centering of Black digital writing and rhetoric practices in our field through Hip-Hop, teasing out what the DJ has to offer pedagogy and research ethics. House illustrates that the Hip-Hop DJ represents a model for digital writing that is situated in a long-standing tradition of multimodal and digital writing practices. By emphasizing DJ practices like the mix, the remix, and the sample, House pushes back on the idea of digital methods and methodologies as new or fresh, but rather sees them as part of a larger rhetorical lineage if we center Black digital writing epistemologies. Ultimately, House argues that foregrounding Hip-Hop DJs in the theorizing of digital writing methods and methodologies goes beyond simply bringing in Hip-Hop, but instead invites a dynamic understanding of the relationship between culture, embodiment, and digital composition.

Shannon Kelly, Eric Rodriguez, Benjamin Lauren, and Stuart Blythe discuss the importance of Trauma Informed (TI) scholarship and its relationship to two community engagement digital writing projects in chapter 13, "Trauma-Informed Scholarship as a Rhetorical Methodology in Digital Research and Design." The authors provide an extensive literature review on TI scholarship and offer a heuristic for conceptualizing a TI approach within digital work. Drawing on two projects as examples, the authors explain how TI scholarship shaped their research designs to prioritize participants and ensure their safety and well-being.

Finally, in chapter 14, "Considerations for Internet Participant Selection: Algorithms, Power Users, Overload, Conventionalization, and Participant Protection"

John R. Gallagher discusses the selection of participants in internet research, outlining five challenges: algorithms, power users, overload of possible participants, conventionalization of experiences, and participant protection from online toxic communities. He describes the importance of understanding these challenges while designing a study because while research on the internet can feel unwieldy, careful participant selection aids in understanding internet spaces at a granular level. Ultimately, this granular view helps researchers understand the narratives that users build in their relationships to digital spaces.

Section 3 speaks to the intangible, layered questions that arise as the digital intertwines with human participants and researchers. The people involved in digital writing research have human needs: of representation, protection, safety, and security, and the technologies we use can help to facilitate how we remain aware of and meet these needs, or they might present barriers that can compromise an ethical response. The authors in this section remind us to consider the people *and* the technologies, the original and the remix, as we design and conduct research.

Engaging with Bots, Corpora, Code, and Cameras

In Volume 2's *Section 4—Digital Tools for Understanding Discourse, Process, and Writing: Languaging Across Modalities*, the authors take us back to one of our most powerful technologies: language. In the final section of our collection, we found comfort in our roots in writing studies. At the same time, the authors in this section demonstrate the possibilities of composition when your writing and research tools involve Twitter bots, chunks of code, linguistic patterns, and even fashion. These researchers, with (digital) tools such as bots, corpora, code, and cameras, deeply engage with activism, accessibility, linguistic diversity, and multimodal compositional processes. In chapter 15, "Studying Unknown Unknowns: Lessons from Critical Making on Twitter," Whitney Lew James takes on the work of trying to better understand the relationship between social media, algorithms, and echo chambers. James brilliantly undertakes this project by engaging in the creation of Twitter bots as a method of digital making and data collection. As tools for collecting research, James argues that making bots helps us better understand how they function and how we might utilize them to better understand social media spaces. Finally, James grapples with the complex relationship and associations that bots have as social media menaces as well as with their possibilities for social media activism.

In chapter 16, "Language Policing to Language Curiosity: Using Corpus Analysis to Foreground Linguistic Diversity" Laura Aull argues for a shift in how students engage with language in writing classrooms: from prescribed rules and evaluation to language curiosity and analysis. By centering linguistic diversity as well as linguistic patterns, Aull explains that this shift asks scholars to reimagine how we engage with diverse language practices, not only in terms of language ideologies but also in terms of how we analyze and assess language itself.

Furthermore, Aull shows how a corpus approach drawing on linguistic diversity is a method that allows us to put stated beliefs about diversity into action while resisting an urge to return to homogeneity in practice.

In chapter 17, "The Pleasurable Difficulty of Programming," Benjamin Miller calls for a renewed understanding of programming through his experience building digital tools as an enriching collaborative writing process. This chapter hopes to change perceptions of programming code by encouraging non-coders to consider working in both direct collaboration with programmers and indirect collaboration with others as you develop coding literacies. Miller reminds us that all code comes from somewhere, and while you may not directly work side by side with someone, there are collaborators everywhere in online communities or in the code itself. Ultimately, Miller provides a view of composition with a digital tool that aims to both embrace the difficulty of coding while providing an invitation to programming by demystifying the process.

Finally, Christina Rowell dives deep into studying the composing processes of students within a fashion design program. In chapter 18, "Multimodal Methods for Mapping Multimodal Composing Processes," Rowell describes how multimodal process interviews evolved within her study and were born out of collaboration with participants and grounded in feminist theory and research on think-aloud protocols. Rowell details her methods for these interviews, which involve interacting with participants in the composing space, collecting and capturing various kinds of data on video, taking field notes, streamlining and combining data sources in a video editor, and supplementing interview data with various reflections and artifacts. Overall, Rowell calls researchers in writing studies to more carefully attend to the complex ecologies of humans, nonhumans, objects, materials, tools, and environments involved in composing.

Section 4 prompts researchers to make something new—and digital—that helps us better understand different ways of writing and composition. The authors describe their own experiences making and researching, reminding us that writing is ideological, activist, pleasurable, difficult, and always multimodal.

Outro

The chapters in this collection offer insight into designing and approaching research using a wide variety of digital tools and technologies. It is our hope that the chapters in both volumes provide a broad but inclusive cross section of the dynamic work occurring in digital writing and rhetoric studies. What makes digital scholarship digital? What does adding the word "digital" in front of "methods and methodologies" represent for scholars and the discipline? The tools themselves are one aspect of the answers to these questions, albeit an important one. Yet our identities and positionalities, and those of our research participants and collaborators, affect and influence the technologies that mediate our relationships and research. These relationships between humans, technologies, methods, and methodologies determine the results of our efforts towards knowledge-building, problem-solving, and ideally, as many authors in this collection demonstrate, our efforts towards redressing oppression.

As this project developed, we strived as editors to make an impact on digital writing and rhetoric by offering readers a variety of projects with an emphasis on positionalities. We acknowledge that attention to positionality is a common approach within the research designs of multiply marginalized scholars, and we honor this approach as we take it up. We hope that the stories and experiences described in this book offer starting points for those interested in digital writing research, as well as continual access points for those already engaged. We believe that the work represented here is defining what it means to do research in digital writing and rhetoric. Drawing on our own stories and those of our authors, we recognize that a multiplicity of paths can lead you to digital writing research, and so we share these narratives as an invitation to new scholars and an affirmation of those already in the field. We aim to inspire you to go for it, and to give you a little bit of help along the way, as you think about how and why you might learn to use an unfamiliar digital tool, or to reimagine your use of familiar tools for new possibilities.

Works Cited

Adams, Megan. "Affective Connections to Place: Digital Storytelling in the Classroom." *Kairos: A Journal of Rhetoric, Technology, and Pedagogy*, vol. 22, no. 1, 2017, http://kairos.technorhetoric.net/22.1/praxis/adams/index.html.

Adams, Megan, and Kristine Blair. "Digital Dissertations: A Research Story." *Kairos: A Journal of Rhetoric, Technology, and Pedagogy*, vol. 21, no. 1, fall 2016, http://praxis.technorhetoric.net/tiki-index.php?page=PraxisWiki%3A_%3ADigital+Dissertations.

Addison, Joanne. "Mobile Technologies and a Phenomenology of Literacy." McKee and DeVoss, pp. 171–83.

Aguilar, Vanessa J., Stephany Bravo, Todd Craig, Jared D. Milburn, Emery Petchauer, Eric Rodriguez, Cecilia Valenzuela, and Magnolia Landa-Posas. "Testimonios and Turntables: Claiming Our Narratives through Sound and Space." *Kairos: A Journal of Rhetoric, Technology, and Pedagogy*, vol. 26, no. 1, 2021, https://kairos.technorhetoric.net/26.1/topoi/aguilar-et-al/index.html.

Alexander, Jonathan, and Jacqueline Rhodes. "Introduction: What Do We Talk about When We Talk about Digital Writing and Rhetoric?" *The Routledge Handbook of Digital Writing and Rhetoric*, edited by Jonathan Alexander and Jacqueline Rhodes, Routledge, 2018, pp. 1–6.

Alexander, Jonathan, Karen Lunsford, and Carl Whithaus. "Toward Wayfinding: A Metaphor for Understanding Writing Experiences." *Written Communication*, vol. 37, no. 1, Jan. 2020, pp. 104–31.

Almjeld, Jen, and Kristine Blair. "Multimodal Methods for Multimodal Literacies: Establishing a Technofeminist Research Identity." *Composing(Media) = Composing(Embodiment)*, edited by Kristin L. Arola and Anne Frances Wysocki, Utah State UP, 2012, pp. 97–109.

Arroyo, Sarah J., and Bahareh Alaei. "The Dancing Floor." *Kairos: A Journal of Rhetoric, Technology, and Pedagogy*, vol. 17, no. 2, 2013, http://kairos.technorhetoric.net/17.2/topoi/vitanza-kuhn/arroyo_alaei.html.

Banks, Adam J. *Digital Griots: African American Rhetoric in a Multimedia Age*. Southern Illinois UP, 2011.

———. *Race, Rhetoric, and Technology: Searching for Higher Ground*. Routledge, 2006.

Banks, Will, and Michelle Eble. "Digital Spaces, Online Environments, and Human Participant Research: Interfacing with Institutional Review Boards." McKee and DeVoss, pp. 27–47.

Blackmon, Samantha. "Violent Networks: Historical Access in the Compositional Classroom." *Journal of Advanced Composition (JAC)*, vol. 24, no. 4, 2004, pp. 967–72.

Blair, Kris, and Christine Tulley. "Whose Research Is It, Anyway?: The Challenge of Deploying Feminist Methodology in Technological Spaces." McKee and DeVoss, pp. 303–17.

Blythe, Stuart. "Coding Digital Texts and Multimedia." McKee and DeVoss, pp. 203–27.

Burnett, Josh, Sally Chandler, and Jackie Lopez. "A Report from the Digital Contact Zone: Collaborative Research and the Hybridizing of Cultural Mindsets." McKee and DeVoss, pp. 319–36.

Carson, A.D. *i used to love to dream*. University of Michigan Press, 2020, https://doi.org/10.3998/mpub.11738372.

Cooke, Laquana, Lisa Dusenberry, and Joy Robinson. "Gaming Design Thinking: Wicked Problems, Sufficient Solutions, and the Possibility Space of Games." *Technical Communication Quarterly*, vol. 29, no. 4, 2020, pp. 327–40.

De Pew, Kevin. "Through the Eyes of Researchers, Rhetors, and Audiences: Triangulating Data from the Digital Writing Situation." McKee and DeVoss, pp. 49–69.

Duthely, Regina. "Hip-Hop Rhetoric and Multimodal Digital Writing." *The Routledge Handbook of Digital Writing and Rhetoric*, edited by Jonathan Alexander and Jacqueline Rhodes, Routledge, 2018, pp. 352–60.

Eyman, Doug. *Digital Rhetoric: Theory, Method, Practice*. U of Michigan P, 2015, http://hdl.handle.net/2027/spo.13030181.0001.001.

Geisler, Cheryl, and Shaun Slattery. "Capturing the Activity of Digital Writing: Using, Analyzing, and Supplementing Video Screen Capture." McKee and DeVoss, pp. 185–200.

Gonzales, Laura. "Multimodality, Translingualism, and Rhetorical Genre Studies." *Composition Forum*, vol. 31, 2015, http://compositionforum.com/issue/31/multimodality.php.

Haas, Angela M. "Wampum as Hypertext: An American Indian Intellectual Tradition of Multimedia Theory and Practice." *Studies in American Indian Literatures*, vol. 19, no. 4, 2007, pp. 77–100.

Haas, Angela, Jackie Rhodes, and Dànielle Nicole DeVoss. "Introduction by the Guest Editors." *Computers and Composition*, vol. 51, 2019, pp. 1–3.

Halbritter, Bump. "Musical Rhetoric in Integrated-Media Composition." *Computers and Composition*, vol. 23, no. 3, 2006, pp. 317–34.

Halbritter, Bump, and Julie Lindquist. "Time, Lives, and Videotape: Operationalizing Discovery in Scenes of Literacy Sponsorship." *College English*, vol. 75, no. 2, Nov. 2012, pp. 171–98.

Hart-Davidson, William. "Studying the Mediated Action of Composing with Time-Use Diaries." McKee and DeVoss, pp. 153–70.

Hawkes, Lory. "Impact of Invasive Web Technologies on Digital Research." McKee and DeVoss, pp. 337–51.

Hidalgo, Alexandra. *Cámara Retórica: A Feminist Filmmaking Methodology for Rhetoric and Composition*. Computers and Composition Digital Press; Utah State UP, 2017, http://ccdigitalpress.org/camara/.

Hilligoss, Susan, and Sean Williams. "Composition Meets Visual Communication: New Research Questions." McKee and DeVoss, pp. 229–47.

Kimme Hea, Amy. "Riding the Wave: Articulating a Critical Methodology for Web Research Practices." McKee and DeVoss, pp. 269–86.

Kirsch, Gesa E., and Joy S. Ritchie. "Beyond the Personal: Theorizing a Politics of Location in Composition Research." *College Composition and Communication*, vol. 46, no. 1, Feb. 1995, pp. 7–29.

Kirsch, Gesa, and Patricia A. Sullivan, editors. *Methods and Methodology in Composition Research*. Southern Illinois UP, 1992.

kyburz, bonnie lenore. *Cruel Auteurism: Affective Digital Mediations toward Film-Composition*. The WAC Clearinghouse/UP of Colorado, 2019. https://doi.org/10.37514/WRI-B.2019.0025.

Ledbetter, Lehua. "The Rhetorical Work of YouTube's Beauty Community: Relationship-and Identity-Building in User-created Procedural Discourse." *Technical Communication Quarterly*, 2018, vol. 27, no. 4, pp. 287–99.

McIntire-Strasburg, Janice. "Multimedia Research: Difficult Questions with Indefinite Answers." McKee and DeVoss, pp. 287–300.

McKee, Heidi A., and Dànielle Nicole DeVoss, editors. *Digital Writing Research: Technologies, Methodologies, and Ethical Issues*. Hampton Press, 2007.

Miles, Casey. "Butch Rhetoric: Queer Masculinity in Rhetoric and Composition." *Kairos: A Journal of Rhetoric, Technology, and Pedagogy*, vol. 20, no.1, 2015, http://kairos.technorhetoric.net/20.1/disputatio/miles/index.html.

Olinger, Andrea R. "Visual Embodied Actions in Interview-Based Writing Research: A Methodological Argument for Video." *Written Communication*, vol. 37, no. 2, Apr. 2020, pp. 167–207.

Pandey, Iswari. "Researching (with) the Postnational 'Other': Ethics, Methodologies, and Qualitative Studies of Digital Literacy." McKee and DeVoss, pp. 107–25.

Ramirez-Dhoore, Dora. "The Cyberborderland: Surfing the Web for Xicanidad." *Chicana/Latina Studies*, vol. 5, no. 1, 2005, pp. 10–47.

Reilly, Colleen, and Doug Eyman. "Multifaceted Methods for Multimodal Texts: Alternate Approaches to Citation Analysis for Electronic Sources." McKee and DeVoss, pp. 353–75.

Rickly, Rebecca. "Messy Contexts: Research as a Rhetorical Situation." McKee and DeVoss, pp. 377–97.

Robinson, Joy. "Look Before You Lead: Seeing Virtual Teams Through the Lens of Games." *Technical Communication Quarterly*, vol. 25, no. 3, 2016, pp. 178–90.

Romberger, Julia. "An Ecofeminist Methodology: Studying the Ecological Dimensions of the Digital Environment." McKee and DeVoss, pp. 249–67.

Royster, Jacqueline Jones, and Gesa E. Kirsch. *Feminist Rhetorical Practices: New Horizons for Rhetoric, Composition, and Literacy Studies*, Southern Illinois UP, 2012.

Sapienza, Fil. "Ethos and Research Positionality in Studies of Virtual Communities." McKee and DeVoss, pp. 89–106.

Selfe, Cynthia L. "The Movement of Air, the Breath of Meaning: Aurality and Multimodal Composing." *College Composition and Communication*, vol. 60, no. 4, 2009, pp. 616–63.

Shankar, Tara Rosenberger. "Speaking on the Record: A Theory of Composition." *Computers and Composition*, vol. 23, no. 3, 2006, pp. 374–93.

Shivers-McNair, Ann. "3D Interviewing with Researcher POV Video: Bodies and Knowledge in the Making." *Kairos: A Journal of Rhetoric, Technology, and Pedagogy*, vol. 21, no. 2, spring 2017, http://praxis.technorhetoric.net/tiki-index.php?page=PraxisWiki:_:3D%20Interviewing.

Sidler, Michelle. "Playing Scavenger and Gazer with Scientific Discourse: Opportunities and Ethics for Online Research." McKee and DeVoss, pp. 71–86.

Smith, Beatrice. "Researching Hybrid Literacies: Methodological Explorations of 'Ethnography' and the Practices of the Cybertariat." McKee and DeVoss, pp. 127–49.

VanKooten, Crystal, and Angela Berkley. "Messy Problem-Exploring through Video in First-Year Writing: Assessing What Counts." *Computers and Composition*, vol. 40, June 2016, pp. 151–63.

VanKooten, Crystal. "A New Composition, A 21st Century Pedagogy, and the Rhetoric of Music." *Currents in Electronic Literacy*, 2011, http://currents.dwrl.utexas.edu/2011/anewcomposition.html.

———. "A Research Methodology of Interdependence through Video as Method." *Computers and Composition*, vol. 54, Dec. 2019, pp. 1–17.

———. "Identifying Components of Meta-Awareness about Composition: Toward a Theory and Methodology for Writing Studies." *Composition Forum*, vol. 33, spring 2016, http://compositionforum.com/issue/33/meta-awareness.php.

———. "'The Video Was What Did It for Me': Developing Meta-Awareness about Composition across Media." *College English*, vol. 79, no. 1, Sept. 2016, pp. 57–80.

———. *Transfer across Media: Using Digital Video in the Teaching of Writing*. Computers and Composition Digital Press; Utah State UP, 2020, https://ccdigitalpress.org/book/transfer-across-media/index.html.

Walwema, Josephine. "The WHO Health Alert: Communicating a Global Pandemic with WhatsApp." *Journal of Business and Technical Communication*, vol. 35, no. 1, 2020, pp. 35–40.

Section 3. Ethics and Intangibles: Unique Challenges of Digital Research

Chapter 10. Developing a Black Feminist Research Ethic: A Methodological Approach to Research in Digital Spaces

Constance Haywood
EAST CAROLINA UNIVERSITY

> ". . . Black women's knowing is acquired through our various experiences living, surviving, and thriving within multiple forms of oppression. It is a self-defined, embodied way of knowing."
> – Patterson et al. ("Black Feminist Thought as Methodology")

In a world of civil unrest and unending racial violence, digital platforms allow marginalized groups the space and opportunity to connect, build community, and safely network amongst each other. They also largely make room for these groups to organize and amplify the experiences, needs, and concerns of inner communities to larger publics. For example, Black women are a group that often turn to digital platforms for several personal, political, social, and community-focused reasons; for many, their very presence in these spaces aids in their efforts to push back against the overlapping heteronormative, racist, sexist, and classist systems that harm them, kill them, and, ultimately, were not created for them.

From blogging to the use of #BlackLivesMatter hashtags, digital and Internet spaces grant Black women the ability to exist, write, and work in ways that significantly add to the varied and extensive writing and rhetorical histories that they carry. As Black women have historically used language and literacy as a means of advocacy and survival, this new and forming digital history—and the literacies and practices developing within it—has influenced digital researchers to investigate the kinds of platforms that Black women communities—and Black online communities, more generally—take up. This includes (but is not limited to) research inquiries around how Black digital platforms and spaces function, how they are managed, and how they aid in communicative processes. Given the popularity and the possibilities that these technologies afford, these spaces also yield ample opportunities for writing researchers to identify and inquire into new(er) areas of research, particularly around digital and social media writing practices (Walls and Vie), online community-building (Sawyer), and digital resistance (Duthely).

While these areas rightfully deserve more attention, it is to be noted that with the work of digital research often arises ethical dilemmas. Thankfully, as a field, rhetoric and composition has always been concerned with issues of research ethics (Banks and Eble; DePew; Sidler). In the 2004 summer issue of *College*

Composition and Communication (CCCC), the "Guidelines for the Ethical Conduct of Research in Composition Studies" was published. Briefly outlining the general values, commitments, and procedures of writing research in the overall field, this document asserts that those identifying as composition specialists should "share a commitment to [protect] the rights, privacy, dignity, and well-being of the persons . . . involved in their studies" (779). Though these guidelines did not at the time explicitly address research endeavors that take place in and around digital spaces, the shift of writing research from physical to digital does not by any means alter the grounding research principles of our field; as composition specialists, it is still among the values of digital writing researchers to ensure that those included in our research studies are protected—even if that means that we can no longer rely on prescriptive ethical frameworks to get the job done.

When it comes to digital spaces that serve marginalized populations (e.g., Black women), we find that these communities are often targeted, scrutinized, harassed, and met with an overload of digital aggressions (Canella; Reyman and Sparby; Haywood). This alone should signal to researchers that how we engage these communities in our research must be as careful and deliberate as it is contingent on our relationships to them. What happens, though, when we find that the risks associated with research and the relationships that we have with these communities directly conflict with our abilities to do the research itself? In rhetoric and composition, how do we begin to cultivate methodologies that assist us in sifting through the initial muck of emotions, processes, and ethical dilemmas that tend to come along with researching both in and around multiple-marginalized communities?

As Annette Markham puts it, "ethic is method and method is ethic." In forming research methodologies, we must reconsider our research practices to better attend to our ethical obligations to research participants and communities. For the purposes of this chapter, I forward a Black feminist methodology, as Black feminist epistemologies view and approach ethics by emphasizing the need to reflect inwardly paying less attention to outsider knowledge(s) and giving more attention to knowledge that comes directly out of embodied experience, personal accountability, acts of care, and community connectedness (Collins "Toward an Afrocentric"). In minding this understanding of ethics, the researcher is required to remain in a reflective space where their proximity to the communities that they work with determines the methods they choose to go about their work. Thus, this chapter will combine my personal experiences with digital writing research and Black feminist thought to begin theorizing a research ethic that deprioritizes research itself and places the needs and safety of community members at forefront. By centering Black feminist theory and highlighting Black feminist (AND Black feminist adjacent) research methods across fields, this chapter calls for researchers in rhetoric and composition to place more of a priority on our ethical responsibilities to research participants and communities—especially those who identify as multiple-marginalized.

A Story on Experience and Ethics

Following the Black feminist tradition, I find it both necessary and critical to theorize around these ideas through my own personal experiences. Before continuing with this chapter, I will recount a recent research experience, as it has both inspired my writing and driven most of my thought process(es)/work around digital research ethics over the past year.

In spring 2019, I began a project combining discourse analysis and rhetorical analysis to look at Black language and its role in both the formation and continuation of digital and communal discourses. At core, I wanted more insights into 1) how Black communities use Black Language (more commonly known as African American Vernacular English AAVE) and rhetorical practices within digital space(s) and 2) how Black community members use digital spaces in ways that allow them to build community and intentionally engage in larger public discourses. To do this, my plan was to examine a series of conversation topics/threads in a public Facebook group that I was part of. To gather the information that I needed, I planned to code and analyze exchanges between group members largely based on conversation topic(s), means of communication, common linguistic features of Black language (e.g., rhythmic language, call and response, etc.), and the invocation of Black rhetorical traditions (e.g., signifyin', use of cultural references, etc.). I had finally gotten to a point in the project where I felt that I had a good grasp of what I wanted to do, and I knew (for the most part) of how I might go about it. Still, something inside of me was not at ease.

The group that I wanted to conduct my work in is a public Black liberation group.[1] Anyone with access to Facebook can go search the group, join it, and access its content. Based on current digital research guidelines, there was nothing "technically" withholding me from conducting research on this space. If I wanted to, I could easily go into the space, go through with my study, and move forward with my original plan. However, as a loyal member of this group, I found myself immediately cautious when it came time to gather my data. Being privy to the kind of space that it was, the conversations that regularly took place within it, and all the important activist and liberatory work that the group regularly engaged in, I found that my own work felt almost traitorous in a sense that it would be placing an outside gaze on a space that was clearly and unapologetically FUBU.[2] It was in these moments that I felt the urge to reflect on my positionality to the group—as a member, as an academic, as a Black cisgendered woman, and as a Black feminist.

I also began to reflect on the space itself and the positions of the folks located within it. This space was public, but it was still intimate. It was rich with data,

---

1. For the purposes of this chapter (and out of respect for the community itself), I will keep the Black liberation group mentioned anonymous.

2. FUBU, a term coined and popularized by a Black-owned clothing company in the 1990s, stands for 'for us, by us'. The term is often used to represent Black collectivity.

but it was also full of brilliant-minded people with varied identities, histories, and beings. Even if I did end up doing research on this space, how exactly would I encapture all of this? From this moment, I continued to ask myself a series of questions: "Would this group want this work done?"; "Who benefits most from this work?"; "Who might this work harm?"; "Are my methods invasive?"; "What power dynamics may be at play here?"; "How might I communicate my research interests to the group?"; "Is it even my place to do this work?" Riddled with multiple unanswered questions, I decided that I would contact the community administrators and respectfully inquire into conducting a pilot study on the space.

This action came after days of wrestling with the questions that ate away at my conscience. More importantly, this decision came after I spent time refreshing myself on the tenets and values of Black feminism. Remembering that knowledge-making is communal and "requires collaborative leadership among [all] those who participate in the diverse forms that . . . communities [take]" (Collins *Black Feminist Thought* 19), I felt that the most ethical action would be to first engage in a conversation with community members, as this would ultimately determine the next steps in my research process. In the first few weeks after contacting the admins, I received no response. However, after following-up on my first email, one of the group's administrators publicly (yet implicitly) rejected my research inquiries by reiterating what the purpose and values of the group were. Respectfully, the administrators reminded the group that emails and messages inquiring into anything other than assistance with urgent, material needs would be both denied and ignored. While my name, per se, was not included in the post, I realized upon reading it that this was not the place to do research; I valued the space and the people more than I did my project. So, I started to make changes to the project altogether, with the first major revisions resulting in a change of location and purpose.

At the time, I aligned myself with this group because I carried similar values. As I write the words of this chapter, I still do. Having to abandon and reconstruct my original ideas around this project allowed me room to think more about what it actually means to work with (and protect) the people and communities that are at the center of my work. In doing this, I found that at the heart of my ideas around research ethics lies an alignment of values and self to marginalized digital communities and spaces—one that ultimately prioritizes their wellbeing and longevity over any amount of research that might be conducted (Haywood). This space of reflection has led me to begin designing a research study that bypasses me looking into the processes and inner workings of digital communities to instead examine the digital research practices and ethics carried out in rhetoric and composition. How do digital researchers in the field generally understand ethics and ethical responsibility? How exactly do our ethical responsibilities inform the methods we use in our studies? How do our methods speak to issues such as participant protection and privacy?

When it comes to digital research ethics, writing researchers tend to emphasize digital environments as places where ethical decision-making becomes reliant on several technological and rhetorical contexts. Often faced with the dilemma of how to approach ethical ambiguities in digital research, digital writing researchers often are unsure as to whether permissions should be garnered for the use of certain data and digital material. For example, how to decipher content in digital spaces as either private or public has proven to be an ongoing challenge. For Tabitha Adkins, in figuring out whether it is appropriate to use data from and/or conduct research around a particular space, it is first necessary to determine if members of the digital community maintain *consistent associations* or *remote associations*, both speaking directly to how community members participate within a given space (55–56). Because definitions of ethics vary by institution, field, and department, concerns around participant protection, privacy, and human harm are both consistent and reoccurring. It is for this very reason that digital writing researchers—and digital researchers, in general—are regularly encouraged to work from a range of ethical frameworks (AOIR).

While it is clear that there are digital scholars in the field who address ethical issues of protection and privacy by directly centering the people and communities located in their work (e.g., Adkins), I, too, am finding that articulations of digital ethics in the field[3] still largely ignore Black feminist theory as a means of methodological grounding. Perhaps this is because Black feminist theory has a history of being treated as just an "anti-racist intervention within feminism . . . [rendering] it as a disruptive and temporary event, to be addressed, responded to, and moved on from" over time (Cooper 16). Still, I can only speak from my own experiences when I say that meditating on the tenets, values, and epistemological foundations of Black feminism (Combahee River Collective; Collins "Towards an Afrocentric"; Collins *Black Feminist Thought*) is what I have found most useful in moving throughout both my life and my communities. For me, it helps to rethink and address those emotions, processes, and ethical moments I mentioned earlier that continue to emerge with this kind—my kind—of work.

Black Feminism and Black Feminist Ethics

From its inception, Black feminism has worked to interrogate the ways that Black women experience multiple jeopardy[4] as well as how they come to understand the world and move throughout it. Black feminist theory sees Black women's multilayered and complex identities (race, gender, class, sexuality, etc.) as a way to think more about how major systems of oppression very rarely exist outside of each other; instead, these systems interlock and overlap (Combahee River

---

3. The term 'field' in this instance refers to rhetoric and composition as a discipline. This includes all areas within the field that engage in digital research and study (i.e., composition studies, rhetorical studies, technical communication, etc.).

4. For a full definition of multiple jeopardy, see Deborah King's 1988 essay "Multiple Jeopardy, Multiple Consciousness: The Context of a Black Feminist Ideology."

Collective). This area of thought is not a new way to understand the complex relationships between identity and community by any means; as a critical social lens, Black feminist theory takes into consideration people's identities and social positionings to understand how oppressive systems work and locate how they might be dismantled. Because Black women have theorized around their own bodies, identities, communities, and positions in the world since the early 1800's (Sheftall loc. 342), they have used their experiences and knowledges to make room for change in various capacities (Collins *Black Feminist Thought* 31). Developed out of the notion that the Black women at center deserve autonomy and a means to negotiate AND be liberated from oppressive systems (Combahee River Collective loc. 4553), Black feminist values can be summarized into the following statements: 1) the sharing of experience makes room for consciousness in ways that build politics and spark change (loc. 4552), 2) radical politics tend to come directly out of attunements to identity (loc. 4568), and 3) Black feminist work must naturally and collectively benefit and liberate Black women by working to critique and dismantle interlocking political-economic systems (i.e. capitalism, imperialism, white supremacy, and patriarchy) (loc. 4568).

Ultimately, the work of Black feminism is about positioning oneself to do work for and with multiple-marginalized folks that immediately places their well-being and needs at center. Responsibly, Black feminism does not find priority in the promotion of self, especially if that means that the self benefits from others in capitalist and imperialist ways (which, in terms of academia, may speak directly to the things that research is often and inherently tied to—e.g., publications, job hires, tenure, etc.). In the formation of a digital research ethic, values of Black feminism can directly respond to the recurrent issues of self-reflection and positionality (and how those things might inform reciprocity) as well as measures of privacy and protection. To further frame Black feminist theory as a potential methodology and ethical grounding to digital writing and rhetorical research, I pull from the work of Patricia Collins just as much as I do the work of the Combahee River Collective, as the act of centering voices and thoughts of community members across non-academic and academic spaces is, too, a value and work ethic that Black feminism maintains.

For the Combahee River Collective,[5] a Black feminist and lesbian group founded in the early 1970s, Black feminist thought cannot exist without the understanding that oppression is influenced by issues of race, gender, and class just as much as it is influenced by issues of sexuality and capitalism. Being one of the first feminist groups to use Black feminist theory to push back against capitalist efforts, the Combahee River Collective is responsible for some of the more central, modern developments in Black feminist values and thought. As for Patricia Hill Collins, Black feminist thought is believed to "[foster] a fundamental pragmatic shift

---

5. The Combahee River Collective is named after the river in South Carolina where Harriet Tubman led a raid that freed over 750 slaves during the Civil War.

in how we think about unjust power relations" (*Black Feminist Thought* 273). This alone implies that Black feminist theory might serve as valuable to conversations around research ethics, as work around research-community relationships often speak of power through concepts such as positionality and reciprocity—concepts that are also largely found in modern feminist writing research.

Feminist researchers in rhetoric and composition have spent a rather ample amount of time thinking about how things like identity, emotion, and positionality impact research methodology and decision-making processes (Royster; Bizzell; Deutsch; Gruwell). Highlighting reflexivity, reciprocity, and transparency as issues of feminist ethics, feminist research often concerns itself with the understanding that researchers are tasked with the responsibility of handling and disseminating information that can "better the lives of women and other oppressed groups" (Gruwell 89). For example, Ellen Cushman speaks of power while presenting reciprocity as beneficial to the writing researcher just as much as it is to the community. Defined as an "open and conscious negotiation of . . . power structures [that are] reproduced during the give-and-take interactions of [people] involved in both sides of [a] relationship" (16), acts of reciprocity are the result of a recognition that the writing researcher is often in a position of power that needs to be leveled to some degree. While there is very clearly a history of reflexive practices in the field, it is to be noted that feminist research methodologies, particularly those that accentuate an ethics of care, place a rather special focus on issues of power and labor in the research process. While a Black feminist research methodology must, too, address issues of power and labor in the research process, Black feminist research methodologies address the complexities of research by 1) examining Black women's unique, lived experience(s) and 2) using that embodied knowledge to resist, radicalize, and do work that aims to set people free.

It is without doubt that parallels can be drawn between feminist and Black feminist methodologies; however, it is to be continuously pointed out that Black feminist methodologies are developed through and by Black lived experience. In a research culture where digital spaces feel disembodied, Black feminist research practices encourage the researcher to see data as always embodied—sitting/growing/evolving beyond the screen and implicated as part of participants and their everyday lives. Bottom line, to study Black women on the web (or honestly, any multiple-marginalized group), we cannot ignore the historical, social, political, personal, and rhetorical contexts to which Black women and Black internet/tech users occupy digital space. As a Black woman researcher, it does myself, my work, and my community a disservice to ignore those contexts. In bringing my knowledge(s), my emotions, my body, and all the experiences that have been inscribed onto it into the research process, I have more room to be able to make decisions in various research situations, redistribute power, and begin shifting away from research histories that have both knowingly and unknowingly subjectivized Black people. Under a Black feminist framework, considering power and position means not only assisting researchers in thinking more critically about power itself, but also making it so that conversations around power are repurposed to "[rearticulate and develop] knowledges that empower oppressed groups and stimulate resistance" (Collins *Black Feminist Thought* 32). As a digital research ethic, Black feminist theory makes room for researchers to reconsider, repurpose, and reapproach acts of self-reflection and reciprocity from embodied, critical standpoints.

Because Black feminism aims to do good in the world and good by others, it well-informs digital research ethics. Applying research methods that restore power and autonomy to the research subject works to address and correct histories of academic work that relied heavily on the Western gaze. The subjectivized positionings assigned to research participants and spaces have historically made room for those within academia to conduct studies on/around/with people and communities without feeling the need to consider their experiences, desires, and perspectives critically and responsibly in the process. This is especially so regarding digital research, as research in digital spaces can often seem disembodied and/or disconnected from humanity.

Tracing a Black Feminist Research Ethic Across Fields

Ethical frameworks are often difficult to develop, mainly because ideas around ethics are varied. In those same respects, there are several ways to understand how a Black feminist ethic might operate as well as understand what the implications of that work might be in digital writing research. Because Black feminism examines multiple identities simultaneously, an ethic of this tradition must remain open to change and interpretation. Even though Black feminist thought has specific tenets and values, it is heterogeneous in how it is conceptualized and taken up both across and within Black women communities. Thus, a research ethic pulling from this tradition must shy away from likeness and stability; since it is based mainly on drawing knowledge out of embodied experience and practice, it always has room for rhetorical deliberation and development.

With digital writing research, a Black feminist ethic inherently sees digital data as tethered to humans and human experience. In terms of the rhetorical language project that I detailed earlier, my own sense of Black feminist ethics helped me (i.e., the researcher) to do the rhetorical work of choosing early methods and working in ways that carefully examined what my next steps would be. Because a Black feminist ethic needs to consistently use Black women's knowledge and embodied experiences to determine how digital community spaces should be interacted with, it requires engaging with Black feminist texts and collaborating with Black women. In other words, at center should be Black women's thought and scholarship, regardless of whether those at center are the researchers themselves, the research participant/community, or a combination of both. In working out of the experiences and realities of multiple-marginalized identities both on and off the web, a Black feminist ethic can help make decisions around issues of boundaries (where on the web people/communities should exist without gaze) and assist with issues of embodied resistance (i.e., how to use one's experiences to intentionally preserve/provide space for said communities to exist in digital realms). An ethic of sorts can also help call for acts of critical self-reflection, radical acts of reciprocity, and commitments to the dismantling of oppressive systems. By emphasizing the protections and privacies of those most at risk of harm through all these things, a Black feminist research ethic intentionally makes space for those who have historically had their autonomy stripped in ways that they might have that autonomy restored.

There are a few scholars in rhetoric and composition who work out of Black digital spaces and Black women's online communities (Kynard; Sawyer; Duthely); however, it appears that digital rhetoric and writing research that directly names Black feminism and Black feminist theory as a place of methodological departure does not exist. This is not to say, though, that there aren't Black feminists in our field or that there aren't researchers who understand their research and work commitments through a Black feminist lens. While articulations of digital research ethics in rhetoric and composition tend to not explicitly use Black feminist theory as a methodology, traces[6] of Black feminist thought and ethics are still likely to be found. As Collins writes, "To look for Black feminism by searching for . . . Black women who self-identify as 'Black feminists' misses the complexity of how Black feminist practice actually operates" (*Black Feminist Thought* 30). This is especially so for Black feminist works outside of our field, as there are several studies that engage digital work, methods, and ethics by first considering the participants and communities at center. This is precisely why it is important to look at what is happening both inside and outside of rhetoric and composition; doing so provides a fuller view of the work Black feminist ethics can do for digital writing research in the future. Multiple scholars across fields of study pull from Black feminist theory to situate themselves to their work, understand ethical responsibility, and inform the research methods they use. Here, I turn to examples of what I would call a Black feminist and Black feminist-adjacent ethos that details methods and ethical practices driven by the identities/experiences, needs, and protections of the marginalized communities engaged.

Critical Self Reflection and Radical Reciprocity

As previously mentioned, having and/or maintaining a Black feminist orientation to the world innately keeps one reflecting on their self, their experiences, and

---

6. Natasha Jones' 2020 technical communication article titled "Coalitional Learning in the Contact Zones" is a prime example of a work within the rhetoric and composition field that can be situated within BFT. In making the argument that technical communication, composition studies, and other related fields can learn from each other, Jones uses decolonial theory and BFT to develop a narrative inquiry method. More specifically, in developing her method(s), Jones explicitly reflects on/centers the work of Black women writers and thinkers such as Patricia Hill Collins, bell hooks, and Audre Lorde.

their ways of moving about various spaces, places, and situations. When applied to research, a Black feminist approach to digital research would likely operate in a number of ways—but mostly in ways that deliberately work towards the benefit of people and communities who are misrepresented or put at the most risk. In thinking more around this, I turn to the Combahee River Collective as well as to works of digital research scholars whose practices seemingly align with what a Black feminist ethics calls for.

> As feminists we do not want to mess over people in politics. We believe in collective process and a nonhierarchical distribution of power within our own group and in our vision of a revolutionary society. We are committed to a continual examination of our politics as they develop through criticism and self-criticism as an essential aspect of our practice. (Combahee River Collective, loc. 4669–4686)

As demonstrated here, Black feminism places a high priority in thinking more around how people should situate and understand themselves, their values, and their responsibilities in collaborating with others. For example, Keila Taylor addresses the role, benefits, and responsibilities that critical self-reflection holds in Women and Gender Studies research. By reflecting on "ethical critical practices," Taylor posits that "in-depth interviews can be as radical as a political protest" because it makes room for storytelling practices and raises awareness of the kind of empathy needed in collecting data from Black women participants. With this, Taylor recalls moments in the interview processes where sensitive materials were shared (721). By reflecting on the moments in her interviewing and data collection processes where she had to make decisions around what to publish and what to keep confidential, Taylor locates a need for researchers to spend time not only developing trust with participants but paying close attention to the ways that participant histories and experiences impact the care in their research practices., In applying this to a Black feminist digital research ethic, reflexivity must be taken into consideration in digital research, particularly around how researcher's relationships with the participants and communities they engage online should be an influencing factor in how they go about their work. More specifically, this Black feminist ethic keens digital researchers specifically to how one's values 1) shape their research relationships and 2) work to locate and leverage their power/positions located within those relationships.

In social movement studies, Kevin Gillan and Jenny Pickerill help researchers to think through both the necessity and complexity of reciprocity in one's work. By highlighting that activists themselves often face tremendous risks in their work, Gillan and Pickerill suggest that researchers enact an "ethics of immediate reciprocation" which consists of the researcher aiding the activist and/or the social movement they are studying (136). In doing this, though, they take the time to address the identity of the "activist-scholar" as well as the more common issue of activist agendas being taken on in academia as a way to "further one's academic career" (136). Because this move that some activist-scholars make is the complete antithesis of what a reciprocal act should be, Gillan and Pickerill stress that when it comes to research ethics, the researcher should be honest in how they come to their reciprocations as well as how those reciprocations are maintained.

I further the work of Gillan and Pickerill to emphasize the need for what a Black feminist digital research ethic would label as radical reciprocity. Radical reciprocity maintains that "researchers . . . see their work not necessarily as the 'exchange' that more traditional definitions of reciprocity seem to nudge at, but more-so as a collective and gradual move with the communities we engage in a forward and socially-just direction" (Haywood). For the most part, this entails that researchers' reciprocal acts be formed within commitments to not do harm just as much as they are formed in full support of the communities they are aimed towards. Radical reciprocity also acknowledges that not all participants and communities seek reciprocity —especially if they are already resistant to engage with the researcher from the start. Additionally, in circumstances where research participants and communities deny a reciprocal relationship with the researcher, radical reciprocity means being willing to support research participants and communities outside of research and outside of personal gain.

In terms of a Black feminist ethic, the understandings and practices within this framework should strive to simultaneously engage researchers' positions, the overlapping identities, histories, and experiences of research participants, and the overall well-being of the at-risk participants engaged in research. Emphasizing practices like critical self-reflection and radical reciprocity, this component of Black feminist research ethics works to prevent a "messing over [of] people."

Positionality

Another important component of a Black feminist research ethic is the enacted commitment to considering multiple identities and histories located in one's work. The following excerpt digs into why paying close attention to overlaps in multiple identities and histories matter:

> We believe that sexual politics under patriarchy is as pervasive in Black women's lives as are the politics of class and race. We also find it difficult to separate race from class from sex oppression because in our lives they are most often experienced simultaneously. We know that there is such a thing as racial-sexual oppression that is neither solely racial or sexual, e.g. the history of rape of Black women by white men as a weapon of political repression. (Combahee River Collective, loc. 4563–4577)

In the excerpt, members of the Combahee River Collective contend that overlapping identities can never really be seen as separate as these identities build upon each other and create/give meaning to specific embodied experiences. When it comes to digital writing and rhetoric research, this kind of commitment works as a way to understand data as never being separate from humans nor human experience. Coming out of cultural studies, Nicole Brown discusses the use of mixed methods—specifically the use of computational tools and autoethnography—to add depth to the ways digital data around Black American women are collected and processed. Naming this process as a *methodological cyborg*, Brown's meshing of the two tools speaks directly to the method's ability to simultaneously address computation's "racialized and gendered biases within its algorithmic assemblages" and Black feminist knowledge-making practices (65). Likewise, bioethics scholars Amal Cheema et al. highlight Black feminist theory (which they use interchangeably as intersectional theory) as a methodological approach to research based on the idea that it provides health care with ways to be more "inclusive and empowering" (1). Cheema et al. posits that by 1) developing research questions around the lived and embodied experiences of research participants, 2) choosing research methods that capture social inequities and push back against the consolidations of participants' experiences, and 3) dedicating time to analyze and revisit empirical data, researchers have the ability to develop research processes that are more encompassing of people's complex identities.

With both works, Brown and Cheema et al. enact a Black feminist ethic to research because they acknowledge that data is shaped by and through people. For digital research, this means we should not only view our data-collecting practices as highly complex, interpretive, and contextual, but we should also interact with that data in ways that highlight this importance. For digital methods, this, too, means that approaches to data collection and data dissemination should reflect the digital communities we work with in the various forms they take.

Protection and Privacy

Lastly, one of the most important components of a Black feminist research ethic is a commitment to liberation. The following quote captures the kind of sentiment that current articulations of research ethics across fields and spaces seem to lack: "We realize that the liberation of all oppressed peoples necessitates the destruction of the political-economic systems of capitalism and imperialism as well as patriarchy" (Combahee River Collective, loc. 4578). In translating this through a digital research lens, I turn to works that discuss digital research sites as places where subaltern politics have caused researchers and scholars alike to "reconsider the role of digital epistemologies in everyday discourse and public pedagogy" (Hill 291). As a study out of urban education, Marc Hill submits that places and spaces like Twitter are not abstract; Black people regularly use these platforms to engage in various discourse(s), protest, and resist in very real, very tangible ways. Thus, there is a need to develop methods that approach users, communities, and data in ways that not only work to benefit research but also work to "spotlight, protect, humanize, and, perhaps, save Black lives" (297).

When it comes to a Black feminist digital research ethic, understandings of liberation within this context submit that in whatever work we researchers do, we should in some way be aiming to 1) address and undo the many hegemonic systems that exist in digital space(s) and 2) do this work with goals (no matter how impossible they may sometimes seem) to do very little harm or no harm altogether. Within this, the commitment to liberation should recognize that many online spaces occupied by marginalized communities are already active, busy, and engaged in culturally relevant, rhetorical (and often, private) work. This work, no matter how much it may provide the researcher insights to community relationships with technology, does not exist as mere spectacle. Thus, a commitment to liberation on part of the digital researcher not only keeps this in consideration but also calls for more explicitly addressed concerns around protection(s) and privacy that simultaneously validates participants' labor and existence while pushing back against oppressive and invasive digital practices. This, I believe, is especially relevant in working with Black women, marginalized communities, and several activist communities who experience harm and exploitation at accelerated rates in both physical and digital spaces. In reconsidering the roles that digital spaces provide, a need to reassess the harms that may come with researching these spaces is always necessary.

Black Feminist Ethics: A Look Ahead

Since Black feminist theory prioritizes the lived experiences of Black women and Black people, a Black feminist research ethic should absolutely do the same. Black feminist epistemologies see great value in utilizing knowledge(s) developed out of Black lived experiences, and researchers who take on a Black feminist research ethic have a responsibility in carefully positioning themselves (and their methodological practices) in ways that 1) go beyond any benefit of the self and 2) demonstrate great concern and care for all parties involved. Because Black feminist theory requires digital writing researchers to examine and consider the historical, social, political, personal, and rhetorical contexts by which Black women and Black digital citizens occupy space, it also forwards a research process that assists researchers in wading through varied decision-making processes in ways that closely examine the research situations, redistribute power (if need be), and work towards the benefit of those who might possibly be at risk/harm. Because there is little-to-no digital ethics work in rhetoric and composition-related fields that draws explicitly from Black feminist theory, it is pertinent that Black feminist theory be sought after and applied in research more intentionally in coming years. By examining Black feminist and Black feminist-adjacent research ethics both inside and across fields of study, researchers can begin to trace, develop, and use Black feminist theory to construct and employ self-reflection, reciprocity, and various other methodological practices from embodied and critical standpoints.

Because developments around Black feminism should be "tied to the contemporary economic and political position of Black people" (Combahee River Collective, loc. 4557), I can see a Black feminist ethic being utilized to do a large range of work in digital spaces. While most of this chapter has focused on the work that a Black feminist ethic can do when engaging the work and spaces of multiple-marginalized people, it is not unreasonable to imagine a Black feminist ethic being developed to address bad actors in digital spaces or being used to deliberately push back against white supremacist narratives on the Internet. Black feminist ethics must remain anti-racist, anti-misogynist, and anti-capitalist in practices, and because online spaces continue to develop and engage new publics regularly, we need new methods and ways of researching that reflect these changes.

Moving forward, I envision a Black feminist research ethic reframing the ways digital researchers within rhetoric and composition understand their work. We need more ethical frameworks that reestablish our commitments in digital research towards the prioritization of the people, communities, and spaces located within it. To do this, there needs to be explicit acknowledgment of the roles that lived experience and positionality play in digital research. There also needs to be more of a consideration of overlapping identities/histories held by digital citizens and communities and an unmoving dedication of ourselves and our work to the well-being, needs, and desires of the folks that we engage in it. It is my belief that all these things can be demonstrated through ongoing considerations of ethics as well as the simultaneous implementations of Black feminist/Black feminist adjacent research practices. Defining an ethical framework through Black feminist theory as well as through interdisciplinary works not only gives digital researchers a broader means to support and enact Black feminist ways of thinking, but it also helps to conceptualize the place and role that Black feminism might have in research ethic conversations down the line.

Works Cited

Adkins, Tabitha. "Social Spill: A Case-Based Analysis of Social Media Research." *Social Writing/Social Media: Publics, Presentations, and Pedagogies*, edited by Douglas M. Walls and Stephanie Vie, The WAC Clearinghouse/UP of Colorado, 2018, pp. 53–68, https://doi.org/10.37514/PER-B.2017.0063.2.03.

Association of Internet Researchers (AOIR). *Internet Research: Ethical Guidelines 3.0. AOIR*, 2019, https://aoir.org/reports/ethics3.pdf.

Banks, William P., and Michelle Eble. "Digital Spaces, Online Environments, and Human Participant Research: Interfacing with Institutional Review Boards." *Digital Writing Research: Technologies, Methodologies, and Ethical Issues*, edited by Heidi McKee and Dànielle Nicole DeVoss, Hampton Press, 2007, pp. 27–47.

Bizzell, Patricia. "Feminist Methods of Research in the History of Rhetoric: What Difference Do They Make?" *Rhetoric Society Quarterly*, vol. 30, no. 4, 2000, pp. 5–17.

Brown, Nicole M. "Methodological Cyborg as Black Feminist Technology: Constructing the Social Self Using Computational Digital Autoethnography and Social Media." *Cultural Studies, Critical Methodologies*, vol. 19, no. 1, 2019, pp. 55–67.

Canella, Gino. "Racialized Surveillance: Activist Media and the Policing of Black Bodies." *Communication, Culture and Critique*, vol. 11, no. 3, 2018, pp. 378–98.

Cheema, Amal W., Karen M. Meagher, and Richard R. Sharp. "Multiple Marginalizations: What Bioethics can Learn from Black Feminism." *American Journal of Bioethics*, vol. 19, no. 2, 2019, pp. 1–3.

Collins, Patricia H. *Black Feminist Thought: Knowledge, Consciousness, and the Politics of Empowerment*. 2nd ed., e-book ed., Routledge Classics, 2014.

———. "Toward an Afrocentric Feminist Epistemology." *Turning Points in Qualitative Research: Tying Knots in a Handkerchief*, edited by Yvonna S. Lincoln and Norman K. Denzin, AltaMira Press, 2003, pp. 47–72.

Combahee River Collective. "Combahee River Collective Statement." *Words of Fire: An Anthology of African-American Feminist Thought*, e-book ed., edited by Beverly Guy-Sheftall, The New Press, 1977, pp. 4506–4665.

Cooper, Brittney C. "Love no Limit: Towards a Black Feminist Future (in Theory)." *The Black Scholar*, vol. 45, no. 4, 2015, pp. 7–21.

Cushman, Ellen. "The Rhetorician as an Agent of Social Change." *College Composition and Communication*, vol. 47, no. 1, 1996, pp. 7–28.

DePew, Kevin E. "Through the Eyes of Researchers, Rhetors and Audiences: Triangulating Data from the Digital Writing Situation." *Digital Writing Research: Technologies, Methodologies, and Ethical Issues*, edited by Heidi McKee and Dànielle Nicole DeVoss, Hampton Press, 2007, pp. 49–69.

Deutsch, Nancy L. "Positionality and the Pen: Reflections on the Process of Becoming a Feminist Researcher and Writer." *Qualitative Inquiry*, vol. 10, no. 6, 2004, pp. 885–902.

Duthely, Regina. "Black Feminist Hip-Hop Rhetorics and the Digital Public Sphere." *Changing English*, vol. 24, no. 2, 2017, pp. 202–12.

Gillan, Kevin, and Jenny Pickerill. "The Difficult and Hopeful Ethics of Research On, and With, Social Movements." *Social Movement Studies*, vol. 11, no. 2, 2012, pp. 133–43.

Gruwell, Leigh. "Feminist Research on the Toxic Web: The Ethics of Access, Affective Labor, and Harassment." *Digital Ethics: Rhetoric and Responsibility in Online Aggression*, edited by Jessica Reyman and Erika M. Sparby, Routledge, 2019, pp. 87–103.

Conference on College Composition and Communication. "Guidelines for the Ethical Conduct of Research in Composition Studies." *College Composition and Communication*, vol. 55, no. 4, 2004, pp. 779–84.

Haywood, Constance M. "'I Do This For Us': Thinking through Reciprocity and Researcher-Community Relationships." *Sweetland Digital Rhetoric Collaborative*, 10 Dec. 2019, https://www.digitalrhetoriccollaborative.org/2019/12/10/i-do-this-for-us-thinking-through-reciprocity-researcher-community-relationships/.

Hill, Marc L. "'Thank You, Black Twitter': State Violence, Digital Counterpublics, and Pedagogies of Resistance." *Urban Education*, vol. 53, no. 2, 2018, pp. 286–302.

Jones, Natasha N. "Coalitional Learning in the Contact Zones: Inclusion and Narrative Inquiry in Technical Communication and Composition Studies." *College English*, vol. 82, no. 5, 2020, pp. 515–26.

King, Deborah K. "Multiple Jeopardy, Multiple Consciousness: The Context of a Black Feminist Ideology." *Signs: Journal of Women in Culture and Society*, vol. 14, no. 1, 1988, pp. 42–72.

Kynard, Carmen. "From Candy Girls to Cyber Sista-Cipher: Narrating Black Females' Color-Consciousness and Counterstories In and Out of School." *Harvard Educational Review*, vol. 80, no. 1, 2010, pp. 30–53.

Markham, Annette. "Ethic as Method, Method as Ethic: A Case for Reflexivity in Qualitative ICT Research." *Journal of Information Ethics*, vol. 15, no. 2, 2006, pp. 37–54.

Patterson, Ashley, et al. "Black Feminist Thought as Methodology: Examining Intergenerational Lived Experiences of Black Women." *Departures in Critical Qualitative Research*, vol. 5, no. 3, 2016, pp. 55–76.

Reyman, Jessica, and Erika Sparby, editors. *Digital Ethics: Rhetoric and Responsibility in Online Aggression*. Routledge, 2019.

Royster, Jacqueline J. *Traces of a Stream: Literacy and Social Change Among African American Women*, Kindle ed., U of Pittsburgh P, 2000.

Sawyer, Latoya L. "Don't Try and Play Me Out!: The Performances and Possibilities of Digital Black Womanhood." 2017. Syracuse University, dissertation.

Sheftall, Beverly. *Words of Fire: An Anthology of African American Feminist Thought*. e-book ed., The New Press, 1995.

Sidler, Michelle. "Playing Scavenger and Gazer with Scientific Discourse: Opportunities and Ethics for Online Research." *Digital Writing Research: Technologies, Methodologies, and Ethical Issues*, edited by Heidi McKee and Dànielle Nicole DeVoss, Hampton Press, 2007, pp. 71–88.

Taylor, Keila D. "Rejecting Objectivity: Reflections of a Black Feminist Researcher Interviewing Black Women." *Auto/biography Studies*, vol. 33, no. 3, 2018, pp. 721–26.

Walls, Douglas M., and Stephanie Vie., editors. *Social Writing/Social Media: Publics, Presentations, and Pedagogies*. The WAC Clearinghouse/UP of Colorado, 2018, https://doi.org/10.37514/PER-B.2017.0063.

Chapter 11. Toward a Feminist Ethic of Self-Care and Protection When Researching Digital Aggression

Erika M. Sparby
Illinois State University

Land Acknowledgment. The land on which this chapter was written is the traditional territory the Bodéwadmiakiwen (Potawatomi), Kiikaapoi (Kickapoo), Miami, Očeti Šakówiŋ (Sioux), Peoria, Sauk, and Meskwaki Tribal nations. We must not only learn and understand the history of their genocide and forced removal from these lands, but we must also resist the erasure of their knowledges and cultures.

Content warning. Due to the malicious nature of digital aggression, readers should be prepared to encounter narratives about and references to sexism and misogyny, homophobia, transphobia, and racism, with specific references to violent actions such as death and murder, bodily injury, harm, and assault (particularly to women's (cis and trans) bodies), stalking, doxing, and swatting.

Digital aggression has become a growing focus in digital rhetorics. L. Cagle recently analyzed "strangershots"—or nonconsensual photos taken of strangers and posted online—as violations of privacy. Kaitlin Clinnin and Katie Manthey acknowledge the pervasiveness of vitriolic comments and posit a technofeminist framework for approaching them. Jessica Reyman and I edited a collection of fourteen chapters that addressed a range of topics in digital aggression studies, including design and policy, academic labor, video games, and pedagogy, among others. I have also previously published a study on 4chan and how anonymous spaces develop uncritical memetic behaviors and influence users, as well as one on how woman YouTubers must develop tactics for addressing aggression in their comments sections. This is a small sampling of the digital rhetoric scholarship beginning to address the many facets of digital aggression, and they show that new approaches are required to meet the unique challenges of studying hostile spaces.

Bridget Gelms points to a large issue in this burgeoning subfield: we often foreground participant care and protection because, traditionally, researchers are not put in precarious positions by their research. Similarly, when I studied 4chan's /b/ board[1] in 2015 for my own dissertation, not only was I ill-equipped

---

1. 4chan is a multi-forum imageboard known widely as "the asshole of the internet."

for the mental exhaustion and dispirit I would experience while collecting data from a digital space that at its very core sees me—a queer, (at the time) femme-presenting, and feminist academic researcher—as "subhuman," but I was also unprepared for what would happen when the community I studied found my work post-publication. I argue that it is an ethical obligation for us to protect ourselves as researchers and humans, and so in this chapter I use my experiences studying aggression coupled with others to posit a feminist ethic of self-care and protection that researchers can incorporate into their methods and methodologies when building a research plan involving digital aggression.

The Need for A Feminist Ethic of Self-Care and Protection

An ethic is a set of guiding principles for action, and as such I see this ethic as a framework that can help researchers begin to conceptualize and prepare for the risks and dangers they may face as they begin a research project on digital aggression. I want to begin this section with a series of stories and experiences that demonstrate why a feminist ethic of self-care and protection is necessary to build early in a research plan and to refer to often throughout a research trajectory.

Researching Digital Aggression: The Need for a Feminist Ethic of Self-Care

I researched 4chan's /b/ board in 2015 for my dissertation on rhetoric and aggression in memes and digital spaces.[2] I had spent quite a bit of time on 4chan in my youth, but I'd either forgotten how bad it could be or it had gotten worse over the decade or so since I'd last visited. Alongside general shitposting,[3] 4chan is also renowned for its attempts to shock and offend, which it accomplishes through posts like gore porn, or images and videos of people dying or being killed, being beaten, or suffering extreme bodily injuries. As you can imagine, encountering this kind of content could be quite horrifying. As the study went on, I got better at recognizing and avoiding it, but even still, encountering it was an inevitable part of the study.

While this is true, it's also overly simplistic. There is no central registration (all users are known as "anonymous") and moderation is inconsistent. As a result, there is little accountability for the content posted there, which results in a unique and confusing blend of wholesome, disturbing, and outright aggressive content. While most of the boards follow a set theme, /b/, or Random, is one of the most popular boards, known as a space where anything goes, usually without repercussion.

2. Here's the thing. This book is open access, which means basically anyone with a computer and an internet connection can find and read it. Anons, have fun reading through to make fun of my SJW bullshit and/or call me a feminazi/femoid.

3. Posting content that has no real meaning or point. It is often meant to be funny and ironic but can sometimes be used as a trolling tactic to derail conversations.

4chan also notoriously presents itself as anti-woman and often anti-LGBTQ+.[4] If a woman wants to self-identify in the forum, she's met with the phrase "tits or gtfo," which translates to "show your breasts to prove that you're a woman or leave the site." Posts about women are full of vitriol and misogynistic language. Pornographic images, including creepshots,[5] revenge porn,[6] and other nonconsensual images show up frequently. Sometimes images of women who have been beaten appear, and I have seen video of a trans woman violently attacked outside of a convenience store. Anons—a shortened version of Anonymous by which users on the site identify themselves—categorically reject many LGBTQ+ identity markers, particularly trans*.[7] Additionally, anons regularly use the terms "f*ggot" and the n-word to refer to anyone, regardless of sexual orientation or race, and regularly disparage those who identify as either, let alone both. Although 4chan claims that their content is ironic,[8] as Ryan Milner, Whitney Phillips, and I have each pointed out, recirculating hateful content even in the service of ironic critique—which is not what 4chan is doing—is harmful for normalizing aggressive and marginalizing discourses.

I knew all this going in, but after a few weeks of spending time in this space, I was exhausted and dispirited. I lost sleep, and relationships with my loved ones became strained. This was a space that seemed—even if only ostensibly ironically—to be against the very notion that I should be treated as a human, let alone that I should be allowed to research them.

---

4. As well as racist, but I'm white so, while such content is problematic and toxic, it does not directly challenge my own identity in the same way anti-woman and anti-LGBTQ+ content does.

5. Images taken of women's bodies without their knowledge or consent.

6. Images of nude or mostly nude women who likely consented to the photo but not to its mass circulation in a public space.

7. Defined broadly to include those whose gender identity does not match that which they were assigned at birth, including but not limited to nonbinary, genderqueer, two-spirit, and agender. The irony with this rejection is that many on the board are queer and/or attracted to trans women (sometimes called "traps"). The vitriol directed at these identities appears to be grounded in a weird form of self-hatred that manifests as hate for the larger targeted group. At one point while I was studying 4chan, I observed anons trying to get #transage trending on Twitter, a trolling operation meant to devalue trans* movements by associating them with pedophilia (the core argument was based in a slippery slope fallacy that if someone could identify as another gender, then someone could also identify as another age, meaning an adult should be able to legally have sex with someone underage because they identify as the same age). I also discuss the treatment of trans* identities on 4chan in more detail in "Digital Social Media and Aggression: Memetic Rhetoric on 4chan's /b/ Board."

8. The tagline under the /b/ banner says "The stories and information posted here are artistic works of fiction and falsehood. Only a fool would take anything posted here as fact," but let's not pretend like that isn't a huge copout for not taking responsibility for what they post.

I'm not the only researcher of hostile spaces who has felt this way. Leigh Gruwell and Bridget Gelms[9] are two women-identified scholars of digital rhetoric and online aggression. Gruwell highlights the complications of enacting feminist research values of reflexivity, reciprocity, and transparency on the toxic web. She summarizes her experiences researching these spaces:

> I was surprised by—and thus unprepared for—the intense emotional reactions I experienced after spending hours at a time sorting through hateful, violent, misogynistic language. The process of researching online harassment not only angered me, but made me feel tired and defeated. At its worst, the harassment I was researching got to my core, making me question the value of my worth as a woman and researcher. Most research is draining in one respect or another, but there was something especially taxing about intentionally reading content meant to silence women like me—feminists committed to identifying and resisting sexism, racism, and homophobia online. (Gruwell, "Feminist Research" 92)

In her dissertation on the volatile visibility of women online, Gelms explains, "in conducting inquiry into online harassment, a researcher is likely to expose herself to shocking, depressing, and triggering stories or language" (*Volatile Visibility* 43). She acknowledges that doing research in these spaces can have detrimental effects on researchers, particularly those who are women-identified. In later work, Gelms discusses the effects of seeing digital aggression: "Witnessing or knowing about online harassment can be traumatizing, fear-inducing, and silencing" ("Volatile Visibility" 191). Here she is referring to everyday women-identified users, demonstrating that intentionally observing aggressive content on a regular basis as part of a research study can be detrimental to researchers.

Publishing About Digital Aggression: The Need for an Ethic of Protection

In November 2017—three months after "Digital Social Media and Aggression" was published—I received an email from an anonymous burner account letting me know that my article was being discussed on /sci/, a less active forum on 4chan. I immediately found the thread—which featured a screencap of the abstract—and read it, noticing that the anonymous emailer had even boasted about contacting me. I had intentionally chosen *Computers and Composition* as a venue for my article because it was behind a paywall, and I knew it would be more difficult for aggressors to find. But a well-meaning colleague at another university

---

9. Thank you to Leigh and Bridget for reviewing this piece and helping me contextualize their work accurately and productively.

assigned my article in his graduate digital rhetoric course and linked the PDF on his publicly accessible course website. Once /sci/ got their hands on the abstract, they attempted to discredit it[10] and insult me,[11] despite clearly not having read the whole piece.[12] At one point someone talked about posting it to /b/, a much more active hub of 4chan and the space I had studied; another poster briefly mentioned doxing me.[13] It was a tense few days before the thread fell inactive and slipped from the main board.

A few years later, Jessica Reyman and I negotiated with Routledge to be able to release three chapters of *Digital Ethics: Rhetoric and Responsibility in Online Aggression* as open access on a professional website. But this also put us in a difficult position to choose which chapters we would post. We wanted to be able to represent the awesome feminist work some of our authors did but doing so would put some authors—mostly women-identified—at risk for being targeted by the communities that they studied. We ultimately decided on a chapter written by two white men and another written by two white men and a woman, although the latter is a bit precarious because it also talks about Milo Yiannopoulos, a former Breitbart writer and alt-righter with a near cult-like following online (although it has dwindled greatly since he was banned from Twitter). As of this writing, the book has been out for just over a year, and to my knowledge none of the authors have yet seen negative repercussions from the communities or publics that they studied. This could be due to our post-publication considerations, the fact that the book is insular to specific academic communities and hasn't been found by aggressors, something else, or some combination of factors.

In their chapters in *Digital Ethics*, Gruwell and Gelms document the ways their work on digital aggression has made them targets. Gruwell faced backlash after her article on Wikipedia was published and then featured on a Twitter account called @RealPeerReview, which incorrectly summarized her article as "Wikipedia is anti-feminist because its editorial policy doesn't allow you to just make things up" (Gruwell, "Feminist Research" 97). She explains, "While most young scholars might be pleased to find their research featured in such a visible platform, it was more than a bit shocking to see my work spotlighted in what was clearly meant to be a derogatory way" (Gruwell, "Feminist Research" 97). Comments on the tweet called her names, insulted her, and even made thinly veiled threats of violence and death.

---

10. Ironically proving my article's argument right in the process.
11. Although at one point an anon called me "basically the feminist final boss," and I consider this a great accolade.
12. A few claimed to, but their summaries of the article were so off the mark that it was hard to believe that they had read it. As for the rest—if you're going to insult my work, at least try to read it.
13. Making someone's private information—potentially including but not limited to legal name, address, phone number, workplace, family members' names, and so on—public to threaten and intimidate them.

When Gelms publicized her research survey on Twitter, she received odd emails and was added to Twitter lists meant to track (and presumably harass) her. In her dissertation she discusses the anxiety and insomnia she experienced after receiving upwards of 30 notifications when she logged into her account: "Each time this happened, I experienced a twinge of nervousness that when I would click on my notifications, I would find that I been [sic] doxxed. Part of me was simply waiting for it to happen" (Gelms, *Volatile Visibility* 41). She details her legitimate fear that someone could show up at her house, or that she could be swatted:[14]

> Thinking about all of the women I read about or met who had been swatted or had men show up at their houses in the middle of the night to threaten or assault them, I popped out of bed to triple check that all of my doors were locked. I went to the sliding glass door off of my dining room, confirmed that it was indeed locked, and idled there staring out into the darkness of my backyard. I imagined what it might look like if a group of law enforcement officers, dressed in all black and carrying rifles, crept across my property in the night on a phony tip that I was, maybe, a bombmaker. (Gelms, Volatile Visibility 42)

Gelms also documents the unwanted attention she received on Twitter about her survey, including sock puppet accounts[15] that were following only her and angry tirades about the value (or, in their opinion, lack thereof) of her research.

Whose Research Is Targeted?

These narratives provide a brief snapshot of a few experiences of what researching and publishing about hostile digital spaces can look like, as well as what some other researchers have reported in their scholarship. Everyone is undoubtedly different, but there is a key similarity: most of us who research digital aggression AND have felt mentally, emotionally, spiritually drained and dispirited by it AND have experienced backlash for our research and publications have been women-identified/interpreted[16] and women-identified/interpreted people of color. This isn't to say that men-identified/interpreted researchers don't also receive

---

14. Calling in to the police to report a false offense worthy of a SWAT response. The danger from this tactic comes when authorities come to your door thinking that you are armed and could potentially mistake a phone or TV remote for a gun or other weapon.

15. Fake accounts created to deceive, often used specifically for aggressive—and in Gelms's case, surveillance—purposes.

16. I am being intentional here in my use of both "identified" and "interpreted." I do not personally know every author that has been cited in digital aggression studies, and so I cannot presume everyone's gender identification. But I use "interpreted" to indicate that I recognize that there are nonbinary researchers whose names code feminine or masculine, which impacts how aggressors interpret their gender and thus how they devise their responses.

harassment for their work on digital aggression—they do, but not to the same extent (Chemaly). Part of this disparity could come from volume: publications and scholarship on digital aggression seem to be produced in higher volume from woman-identified/interpreted authors.

I created a list of 51 authors who have written about digital aggression in the last seven years; I have decided not to include this list here because doing so would be unnecessarily exposing authors doing this kind of work. The list is non-exhaustive, but I generated it from authors that were published in the *Digital Ethics* collection, others who recently published digital aggression research in the field, and the scholars those pieces and my own research have cited. As such, they tend to be situated in the humanities.[17] I classified the names of the authors as woman identified/interpreted, man identified/interpreted, or nonbinary from the perspective of an aggressor attempting to determine their gender since our genders are often central in their discussions about our work:

- Woman identified/interpreted names: 32
- Man identified/interpreted names: 18
- Nonbinary names: 1

Of the woman identified/interpreted names, five have multiple publications on the topic of digital aggression; of the man identified/interpreted names, two do. Further, many of the woman identified/interpreted authors write about aggression that they have faced as researchers; eight of them even use titles directly quoting the vitriol they have received. None of the man identified/interpreted authors address aggression from the perspective of being targets themselves, although some talk about gendered aggression generally.

When talking about researching digital aggression with a feminist ethic of self-care and protection, it is crucial to recognize that all researchers are impacted differently along the axes of their intersecting identities. The list I compiled here focuses on gender presentation through the lens of an aggressor, but many of these authors are also white, which also affords certain levels of power, privilege, and protection. A queer woman of color researcher has the potential to face different challenges to her mental health when researching hostile spaces than a straight white disabled woman; although their identities intersect at their gender, they will each receive and respond differently to hostilities directed toward their sexuality, race, and disability. Likewise, when these same researchers publish their work, depending on the spaces they have studied, they could both be opening themselves up for backlash—and for different reasons based in their different identities—than a straight white man might face, although he may also face some retaliation. Some researchers will face different challenges than others, but it remains crucial that we develop a feminist ethic of self-care and protection early in the research

---

17. But a quick glance at this kind of research in other fields reveals an even wider gender gap; and if I expand this list beyond the past seven years, the quantitative gap gets wider still.

process. This ethic has two distinct parts (self-care and protection) that operate independently of each other but also work together to safeguard the researcher.

A Feminist Ethic of Self-Care

Since the early 1980s, feminist researchers have been theorizing feminist care ethics (Gilligan; Noddings), positing care as an ethical virtue for a just society. Many have written about what this "care" looks like, complicating it from the perspectives of gender, race, class, and disability (Raghuram), showing that it is important to ask who cares for others, who is expected to care for them, who is cared for, who is excluded from care, and what does it mean to care/be cared for? These discussions hinge on relationality to the world around, and while many peripherally mention the importance of self in the larger schema of care and others, few have conceptualized what self-care can really mean, particularly in a professional or academic context.

Teresa Lloro-Bidard and Keri Semenko—environmental education teachers—discuss the importance of a feminist ethic of self-care when teaching dark and heavy topics like climate change. They focus on women, who they point out often "disproportionately bear the emotional costs of teaching" (22). I argue that a feminist ethic of self-care is pressing for researchers of all genders. While women, BIPOC, disabled, and LGBTQ+ researchers have a higher likelihood of encountering aggressive content aimed specifically at their identities, men are also not immune to these discourses; in fact, some of these discourses surrounding gender define certain kinds of masculinities as inferior or superior, which is potentially damaging. While self-care has often been conceptualized as feminine, radical and political self-care by all genders is necessary for dismantling and pushing back against neoliberal institutions that value our productivity over our wellbeing.

Christine Eriksen—a geographer—writes about the need for self-care to be incorporated into researcher ethics training. She regularly studies traumatic events such as bushfires in Australia and notes that she has experienced "vicarious traumatization" as a result of her "exposure to the emotionally and politically charged narratives of disaster survivors" (274). Eriksen notes that part of this vicarious traumatization results from feelings of helplessness and an inability to tangibly help survivors. It strikes me that because digital aggression researchers both bear witness to others' trauma and view aggressive content regularly, they may also experience trauma, vicarious or otherwise.[18] Eriksen calls for

---

18. Little has been written about trauma in online harassment and digital aggression, but Gelms opens up in a recent article about how long after she defended her dissertation, "the trauma of the experience still lingers . . . despite it being four years later" ("Social Media Research" 2). She also refers to "the lasting impact [digital aggression] has on those who experience its most severe forms" ("Social Media Research" 5). This article documents many moments of panic and anxiety that could have turned to trauma.

institutional support in self-care training, but in lieu of such guidance, researchers must consciously develop their own self-care regimes.

Importantly, when I talk about self-care, I am not referring to what I like to call "white lady self-care," which is often grounded in capitalism and privilege. Countless blogs, articles, and thinkpieces talk about self-care as spa days, pedicures, shopping sprees, and other forms of "treating yourself." While I'm sure we could all use some indulgence now and again, not everyone has the resources for this kind of self-care; not all of us have the money to pay for it or the time to spend hours on it. Audre Lorde said that "caring for myself is not self-indulgence, it is self-preservation, and that is an act of political warfare" (228). That is, the very nature of caring for oneself is an active and intentional pushing back against capitalist ideals about the functions of our bodies and minds in a capitalist society. Andre Spicer explains that many marginalized identities, such as LGBTQ+, women, and BIPOC communities, took up this idea as "a way of preserving yourself in a world that was hostile to your identity, your community and your way of life," but modern self-care has made its way to mass market spaces and is largely no longer the act of "political warfare" Lorde had originally intended. Resources such as PEN America's "Online Harassment Manual" (which has a section dedicated to self-care) and Heartmob's "Self Care for People Experiencing Harassment" provide some pertinent advice for enacting self-care while experiencing digital aggression. They acknowledge that go-to "self-care buzzwords [. . . like] eat healthy! Medi[t]ate! Take a relaxing bath!" are largely unhelpful to most (Heartmob), although ensuring that we take time to enjoy things like "head[ing] into nature," "mak[ing]" your bed, and "turn[ing] off your phone" are also little acts of self-care that we can engage in when experiencing harassment[19] (PEN).

However, these guides are largely aimed at the everyday person, and not researchers specifically, so it is crucial to define what we mean by self-care in the context of completing research. When I talk about an ethic of self-care, I mean deliberate acts of caring for ourselves as whole beings, as resisting institutional ideologies of productivity and our worth as scholars and teachers. To this end, an ethic of self-care must also always be feminist; that is, it must always prioritize humans and health over product and production. Sara Ahmed says, "in directing our care towards ourselves we are redirecting care away from its proper objects" (np). If the "proper objects" are our research projects, then self-care is directing our energy, time, and attention away from them, even if only for a brief time. This also means that self-care will look differently for everyone. It can mean stepping away from research to spend time with our families or going for a run to clear our heads and prioritize our physical health. Or it can mean none of those things. It's genuinely up to each of us what "self-care" looks like; we all come to this research with our own positionalities and our own physical, emotional, and spiritual needs.

---

19. And honestly, whenever we're feeling overwhelmed by life in general.

The way I conceptualize it currently, a feminist ethic of self-care for digital aggression research does five things:

1. *It urges researchers to be mindful of their mental and physical health while researching.* The stories highlighted above only represent a small fraction of researchers' experiences studying aggression, and there are certainly more. Eriksen also talks about the psychosomatic effects of her vicarious trauma, noting that without proper outlets her mental turmoil turned into physical pain. It is crucial that researchers check in with ourselves on a regular basis and honestly assess our mental health.
2. *It reminds researchers to step back and take a break when they feel they need to.* As part of these regular mental health check-ins, it is crucial to recognize when we need to step away for a moment. When we recognize that our research is having a negative impact on us, taking a break early and recuperating rather than letting that negativity build is going to help us in the long run. Rather than burning out and being forced to take a break, we can make a conscious effort to keep ourselves healthy.
3. *It encourages researchers to build a flexible research timeline that we can adapt as needed throughout the process.* Because we may need to take these breaks, and because there is no way of knowing how many or for how long, it is crucial that we build flexible timelines that will allow us to do so. We must understand that a digital aggression research project has the potential to take longer than other kinds of projects and create realistic research schedules that will allow us to take the breaks we need. Consider building them into the trajectory intentionally.
4. *It is inherently anti-capitalist and anti-institutional.* Prioritizing our health and safety over productivity means resisting institutional expectations to complete our work by certain milestones. But obviously, we don't live in a world where this is always possible. The tenure clock doesn't stop because our research is difficult; we still have deadlines and productivity quotas to meet. I also recognize the inherent privilege I hold when I say, "take a break when you need to," because some researchers will not have the luxury of prioritizing their health over their productivity every time they need to; for some, powering through to get a job and/or meet tenure requirements is an act of self-care because they need job security and/or a salary raise.
5. *It urges us researchers to create community and belonging with others.* Both in addition to and in lieu of taking breaks, it is crucial for researchers studying digital aggression to talk to each other. This can be a challenge since it is often difficult to talk about our own mental health with others, especially if we do not know them well. But there are a lot of us who have experience and are happy to listen and talk. By the same token, though, these conversations are also emotional labor for both parties, and some of us may not be able to always perform it, and that should be honored as well.

These five aspects of a feminist ethic of self-care are incomplete, and perhaps can never be fully completed since they must be able to adapt to individual needs. They are meant to guide researchers toward developing tactics for protecting their mental health while researching. Importantly, I'm only talking about digital aggression researchers here, but as Eriksen's narrative demonstrates, a feminist ethic of self-care could be useful for a variety of disciplines, fields, and research topics, not only digital aggression research; most researchers experience some level of mental strain and fatigue during the research process, and this ethic could help alleviate some of that.

An Ethic of Protection

Earlier, I highlighted examples of women-identified/interpreted scholars—myself included[20]—who received and/or feared backlash for our research post-publication and the considerations my co-editor and I took to protect the authors in *Digital Ethics*. These instances demonstrate what Bridget Gelms calls "volatile visibility," when women's—especially women of color, LGBTQ+ women, and women with disabilities—very existence in digital spaces makes them more likely to receive digital attacks. As those of us who exist at the intersections of these identities continue to publish on aggressive communities, we will continue to make ourselves more visible. And, as Leigh Gruwell stated during a roundtable on digital aggression hosted by the CFSHRC in December 2020, and as her narrative above shows, feminist scholars who study digital spaces are also at risk by virtue of being both visible and feminist. Importantly, because of the connectedness of our digital world, when we become more visible, our families and friends often also become more visible, and there have been records of aggressors targeting them for hurtful and hateful messages.[21] So, considering this volatile visibility, protecting ourselves as researchers and our family and friends is an ethical obligation.

As I have begun to conceptualize it, an ethic of protection asks us to do six things:

1. *Carefully consider where we publish our work.* When digital aggression researchers publish, we need to think several steps ahead and deeply consider the rhetorical velocity of our work. Who will have access to it? How

---

20. It is perhaps important to note that while I identified as a woman while doing and publishing the research mentioned in this article, I have since come out as trans nonbinary. However, my name continues to code as "woman" for people who do not know that about me.

21. This was demonstrated clearly after the Charlottesville riots in 2018 when ostensible do-gooders took to social media to identify the rioters. While many lost their jobs and reported being ostracized by their communities, an unintended effect was people sending harmful messages to the rioters' friends and family members, many of whom were not involved and did not condone their actions (Ellis; Miller)

and where can it be shared? What are some unintended audiences who could encounter it? With the rise of open access, some scholars are actively seeking to publish in spaces where the public could have easy access to their work, but I am conflicted. If I had published my 4chan article in one of our field's open access journals such as *enculturation* or *Kairos*, would this added visibility have made me more vulnerable to attack? Almost certainly. I chose instead to publish behind a paywall, which unfortunately also limits public consumption of knowledge. And I am taking a measured risk by publishing this chapter in this open access collection, but I hope its visibility will afford more benefit than harm.

2. *Consider adding disclaimers.* This suggestion goes beyond publication to venues like conferences as well. With the rise of live tweeting, some researchers have opened by asking viewers to avoid certain phrases or words, or to even refrain from tweeting altogether, to help them avoid detection from the communities they research. /sci/ found my article on 4chan because it was posted to a public course website, so perhaps disclaimers like these on published work could also be warranted. By the same token, if we find ourselves live tweeting during a talk where the author has asked us to avoid certain words, or if we are distributing course materials for students where the author has asked that we not share it publicly, we should heed the disclaimers.

3. *Consider our fellow researchers in your citation practices.* Importantly, when thinking about protection, it is crucial that we think about ourselves as a network of digital aggression researchers and not just as individuals. When drafting this chapter, I contacted the researchers whose stories I shared above and received permission to quote and cite them. Originally, I was also going to share a third perspective from another researcher, but after talking with them, we decided that citing them in an open access piece could unnecessarily increase their risk. Since the people we cite become more visible through our citation—the volatile visibility Gelms describes—it is necessary to consider our citation practices. Because I was highlighting vulnerable moments from others' work, it seemed necessary to alert them, ask for permission, and allow them to review a draft of the chapter.

4. *Lock down our digital identities.* The threat of doxing looms over many of us who do this work, so we need to make ourselves harder to find on social media and through internet searches. I have begun compiling some resources and tips as part of my involvement with the Digital Aggression Working Group that meets annually at Computers and Writing.[22]

---

22. In "Feminist Research on the Toxic Web," Leigh Gruwell also offers a series of useful questions researchers should ask themselves when developing a feminist research plan for hostile digital spaces.

- Search for your name in white pages databases. These sites often contain public but sensitive information like addresses, phone numbers, and even family members' names. Some of the major sites include Intelius, Radaris, and MyLife, but also check Spokeo, PeopleFinder, Been Verified, White Pages, Pipl, ZabaSearch, TruePeopleSearch, PeekYou, Classmates, FamilyTreeNow, TinEye, and TruthFinder. And don't stop there. Sites like these appear and disappear frequently; they are moving targets. Removing your information can take a long time and involve many emails between you and the site,[23] but it is necessary that you do this.
- Google yourself. Look through as many pages of results as you can and begin the sometimes slow and tedious process of deleting unnecessary items from the internet. This will likely mean contacting various webhosts to manually have your name removed.
- Call your local Circuit Court to have your public records removed from the internet. Your success will vary by state since some will only remove information for judges, law enforcement, and survivors of domestic violence.
- Lock down the privacy settings on your social media. Set your profile to private and make it unsearchable. Make your posts unshareable. Use a nickname/handle/pseudonym that cannot be traced to your own. Also, consider social media sites that you might not have used in a while but still have active profiles; delete them if you don't need them.
- Set up two-factor authentication on as many accounts as you can. This will make it harder for people to hack into your accounts.
- Set unique passwords for every account. Use a password manager if necessary.
- These websites also have some useful resources:
  - **Crash Override Network** (http://www.crashoverridenetwork.com/index.html) CEO Zoe Quinn was the main target of GamerGate in 2014, and she founded this network of experts and survivors to help people experiencing online abuse. Their Resource Center (http://www.crashoverridenetwork.com/resources.html) has links that can help researchers prepare for and deal with aggression. Unfortunately, it seems as if the network has not been active since possibly 2016, although the resources are still useful.
  - **FemTechNet** (http://femtechnet.org) Their Center for Solutions to Online Violence (http://femtechnet.org/csov/) is a wealth of information and resources, with specific links for survivors, educators, and journalists as well as tips for how to lock down your digital identity.

---

23. I have been in a back-and-forth with MyLife for over a year now. They refuse to take down my information, but other aggression researchers have had better success.

- **Hollaback** (https://www.ihollaback.org) This website provides resources for bystander training in workplaces, in the streets, and online. In particular, their online harassment guide (https://www.ihollaback.org/resources/) includes ways to engage in counterspeech without escalating, how to protect yourself against harassment, a comprehensive list of supportive organizations (https://iheartmob.org/resources/supportive_organizations) and other important resources.
- **PEN America** (https://pen.org/online-harassment/) This organization has developed an Online Harassment Field Manual (https://onlineharassmentfieldmanual.pen.org) that is one of the best resources I have found. It walks users through how to prepare and respond to aggression and includes information on legal rights and self-care.

5. *Consider notifying our employers.* Our institutional faculty pages are often one of the first results in an internet search for our names. These pages often include our faculty email addresses, phone numbers, and office and classroom locations,[24] and they of course easily link to our employers, including department chairs, college deans, and university provosts. I recommend that you alert your employers when publishing something that could receive aggressive backlash. One way that aggressive attacks have been carried out against researchers involves emailing higher ups (in the case of academia, this could be administrators such as the chair, dean, provost, or even the president of the institution) to attempt to smear the target's reputation and/or to make physical threats. At the same time, our administrators have likely never had to deal with anything like this before, and almost certainly do not know how to.[25]

When my 4chan article began receiving negative attention in Fall 2017 (my first semester in my tenure-track position), I emailed both my department chair and college dean with a list of advice and resources for what they

---

24. Consider asking if this information—including classroom meeting locations and times—can be taken down from public areas of your institution's website. It is likely that it will not be since this information needs to be readily available to students, but it is worth a try.

25. L. D. Burnett's recent piece in *The Chronicle of Higher Education* documents her experience being attacked by right-wing aggressors. She emailed her dean and briefed them on what to expect, and she copied her president on some of her replies to aggressors. The president emailed an all-faculty listserv about the incident and, in a PR move meant to save face, ultimately blamed Burnett for her own harassment. Burnett made all the right moves, but her college president was ill-prepared to handle the situation. Her experience demonstrates the importance of educating our administrators on the proper ways to respond when something like this happens.

should do if aggressors began contacting them. Thankfully, I'd had prior conversations with both and alerted them to this possibility shortly after I began teaching there. I include the full text here as a template should anyone want to use it:

Hello Dean ***,

I want to inform you that my article on 4chan is currently the subject of a discussion on a 4chan board that has included potential intent to dox or harass me outside of the forum. We talked at lunch last month about how this is a risk of my kind of scholarship. Nothing has happened yet (and hopefully won't), but I have been preparing for it just in case. Since you are the dean of the college, I want to give you a heads up on what this might entail and how you or the university might be involved. I also sent a version of this to ***, the chair of the English department.

The most likely harassments would be emails to you and/or *** that attempt to discredit me. Ways that this might happen could include crude insults, photoshopped images, or "proof" that my scholarship is invalid.

In rarer cases, aggressors like these have sent threats to departments or universities. Things like "Fire [him/her] or [something bad will happen]." As I said, these instances are much rarer and never has anything come of them.

- Do not respond to any of them. Even one response proves that you are listening and will instigate more.
- Do not believe any of them. Their goal is shock, not truth.
- Tell me what's going on and keep the lines of communication open between me and any other recipients (i.e.: ***, etc).

The American Association of University Professors has a statement on "Targeted Online Harassment" that includes two recommendations, the first of which would be most relevant to this situation (it also has some other general information about faculty intimidation): https://www.aaup.org/news/targeted-online-harassment-faculty

Here are some other instances of faculty who have been targets and how universities have handled it (often, quite frankly, very poorly) (many of these examples are also linked to politics, but I would expect the kinds of harassment to be similar if it happens to me):

- https://academeblog.org/2017/08/29/online-harassment-of-faculty-continues-administrators-capitulate/
- https://www.insidehighered.com/news/2017/06/26/professors-are-often-political-lightning-rods-now-are-facing-new-threats-over-their

- https://www.insidehighered.com/news/2017/02/02/aaup-says-colleges-should-defend-professors-targeted-online-harassment-due-political
- http://www.syracuse.com/su-news/index.ssf/2017/06/syracuse_university_chancellor_defends_prof_after_tweet_sets_off_right-wing_back.html

Statements of solidarity are also common in these situations, usually with the intent of protecting the target's employment:

- https://academeblog.org/2017/06/19/statement-of-solidarity-with-professor-dana-cloud/

As of right now, the conversation is tame and has not turned toward any concrete plans (although they also might not necessarily talk about it before doing it), and my hope and suspicion is that it will stay this way. I only send you this email preemptively, but with the hope that it will prove unnecessary.

I am of course willing to meet with you and talk about this at greater length if you would like.

Cheers,

Erika

However, I also want to acknowledge that alerting employers and administrators has the potential to backfire depending on how much you feel you can trust your department to offer protection and support. In my experience, transparency has led to both, but for some, mentioning any kind of risk could put them in a (more) vulnerable position. As such, I recommend that you trust your instincts about when/how/if you will contact employers and/or administrators.

6. *Consider alerting local authorities.* Swatting is also a risk of doing this kind of research, so it might be wise to alert local authorities to the work you do and the potential for this risk. However, two caveats: 1) Getting them to understand can be tricky because many law enforcement agencies do not have the tools or knowledge to deal with digital aggression. 2) Some researchers do not have the privilege of being able to trust law enforcement. Again, trust your instincts.

Conclusion: A Feminist Ethic of Self-Care and Protection in Action

At this point in the chapter, I recognize that I have potentially made researching digital aggression sound overly dangerous or scary. It's not, but researchers do have to be careful. While this work is exhausting and dispiriting in many ways,

I also personally find it rewarding and inspiring. What's more, this work is necessary, and it's especially necessary for those of us with some level of privilege to do it. With the rise of alt-right aggressors in all facets of digital life, alongside the seemingly more innocuous trolls who are aggressive "for the lulz," digital spaces are increasingly fraught for a range of marginalized and multiply marginalized identities. My research often highlights moments of rupture, or moments when a response tactic against aggression can effectively combat it, providing space for more diverse voices (Sparby, "Reading Mean Comments"). Others perform similar research, often looking at how to improve platform design, moderation practices, and other proactive approaches (such as the chapters in the *Digital Ethics* collection). Many of us share one important thing: we are looking at moments of triumph against aggression. While it may be difficult to find those moments, uncovering and bringing them to light, to me, makes this kind of work extremely worthwhile. Gelms argues "rather than simply avoiding online harassment research projects, we should determine what we can do methodologically to acknowledge this difficulty and plan for it" ("Social Media Research"). Gelms, Gruwell, and I have worked to develop some of these methodologies to work toward ensuring researcher safety, although there is much more to be done.

What's more, the kinds of attacks being perpetrated against us for what we research are also carried out against us for what we teach and say on social media. Turning Point USA has a "Professor Watchlist" with the names of professors across institutions who they accuse of discriminating against conservative students on college and university campuses. NPR did an exposé that highlights the stakes of what it means to be a professor doing social justice and antiracist work and includes snapshots of several professor's experiences with backlash from what they published (All Things Considered). These examples and others show what is at stake when it comes to digital aggression against researchers and teachers: academic freedom. It is crucial that we learn how to disrupt aggressive discourses and develop response tactics so that they can become spaces that recognize and honor multitudes of identities, perspectives, and ways of knowing. How can we claim to value diversity and inclusion in university settings when many of us who teach from anti-racist, pro-LGBTQ+, and other social justice approaches are concerned that what we say or do in a classroom could result in being doxed or attacked in digital spaces? Simply put, we can't.

I want to close by offering some suggestions of what a feminist ethic of self-care and protection can look like in action by explaining what I wish I had done when studying and publishing on 4chan. As with anything, the way you develop your own ethical guidelines will likely be unique to you, your situation, and your project.

First, a feminist ethic of self-care recognizes that hostile digital spaces can cause exhaustion and emotional distress. I collected most of my data over the span of three months. At one point, I was spending upwards of seven hours a day, at least four days a week, on /b/ watching threads and collecting screencaps.

That was a lot of time to be in such a hostile space, and it took a toll on me. If I would have known the impact it would have had on my mental health, I would have built a longer timeline for data collection and analysis into my research plan, with deliberate breaks to take care of myself. I also wish I would have been able to connect with others doing this kind of research so we could talk about our experiences, but I didn't know many other people in the field at the time and didn't know how to reach out. Including this framework in a research methodology gives the researcher permission to step away and regroup before continuing research while also encouraging them to reach out to friends, family, and supportive colleagues.

Second, an ethic of protection recognizes that personal safety is paramount. It urges researchers to consciously think about the repercussions of their work post-publication and to lock down their digital identities. I have noticed an uptick in digital aggression researchers asking audiences at conferences to refrain from live-tweeting or using certain words and hashtags, which is something I wish I would have done when I presented my preliminary 4chan research at Cs in 2016. I also wish I would have added a disclaimer asking that my article not be reposted in public or semi-public venues. Obviously, I do not mean to prevent sharing articles with students as course readings or research; I mean not putting them on public course websites or other highly visible spaces, which is where mine was found. Doing either or both things could have lowered my visibility to 4chan. Making these kinds of considerations early in research projects helps the researcher conceptualize the afterlife and publicity of their work and prepare them for any backlash they may face.

Finally, I began the title of this chapter with the word "toward" because this is by no means a comprehensive approach to self-care and protection when studying digital aggression. It is largely based on what has worked for me and what I wish I would have done. While being a queer nonbinary person in some ways puts me in a vulnerable position when I do this research, I also recognize that as a white and able-bodied researcher on the tenure track, I have a lot of privilege that likely shields me from seeing a fuller picture of what a feminist ethic of self-care would look like for others in different positionalities. What does it look like for a disabled researcher? What about a queer Indigenous researcher? Or a non-tenure track Black man researcher? These are important questions to ask moving forward as we all develop our own self-care and protection ethics for our research projects.

Works Cited

Ahmed, Sara. "Selfcare as Warfare." *feministkilljoys*, 2014, https://feministkilljoys.com/2014/08/25/selfcare-as-warfare/.

All Things Considered. "Professors Are Targets in Online Culture Wars; Some Fight Back." *NPR*, 2018, https://www.npr.org/sections/ed/2018/04/04/590928008/professor-harassment.

Burnett, L. D. "Right-Wing Trolls Attacked Me. My Administration Buckled." *The Chronicle of Higher Education*, 2020, https://www.chronicle.com/article/right-wing-trolls-attacked-me-my-administration-buckled.

Cagle, Lauren E. "Surveilling Strangers: The Disciplinary Biopower of Digital Genre Assemblages." *Computers and Composition*, vol. 52, 2019, pp. 67–78.

Chemaly, Soraya. "There's No Comparing Male and Female Harassment Online." *Time*, 2014, http://time.com/3305466/male-female-harassment-online/.

Clinnin, Kaitlin and Katie Manthey. "How Not to Be a Troll: Practicing Rhetorical Technofeminism in Online Comments." *Computers and Composition*, vol. 51, 2019, pp. 31–42.

Crash Override Network, http://www.crashoverridenetwork.com/index.html.

Ellis, Emma G. "Whatever Your Side, Doxing in a Perilous Form of Justice." *Wired*, 2017, https://www.wired.com/story/doxing-charlottesville/.

Eriksen, Christine. "Research Ethics, Trauma and Self-care: Reflections on Disaster Geographies." *Australian Geographer*, vol. 48, no. 2, 2017, pp. 273–78.

FemTechNet, 2020, http://femtechnet.org.

Gelms, Bridget. "Social Media Research and the Methodological Problem of Harassment: Foregrounding Researcher Safety." *Computers and Composition*, vol. 59, 2021, pp. 1–12.

———. "Volatile Visibility: The Effects of Online Harassment on Feminist Circulation and Public Discourse." 2018. Miami U, dissertation.

———. "Volatile Visibility: How Online Harassment Makes Women Disappear." *Digital Ethics: Rhetoric and Responsibility in Online Aggression*. edited by Jessica Reyman and Erika M. Sparby, Routledge, 2020, pp. 179–94.

Gilligan, Carol. *In a Different Voice: Psychological Theories and Women's Development*. Harvard UP, 1982.

Gruwell, Leigh. "Feminist Research on the Toxic Web: The Ethics of Access, Affective Labor, and Harassment." *Digital Ethics: Rhetoric and Responsibility in Online Aggression*. edited by Jessica Reyman and Erika M. Sparby, Routledge, 2020, pp. 87–103.

Heartmob. "Self Care for People Experiencing Harassment." *Heartmob*, 2020, https://iheartmob.org/resources/self_care.

hollaback!, 2020, https://www.ihollaback.org.

Lloro-Bidart, Teresa, and Keri Semenko. "Toward a Feminist Ethic of Self Care for Environmental Educators." *The Journal of Environmental Education*, vol. 48, no. 1, 2017, pp. 18–25.

Lorde, Audre. *A Burst of Light and Other Essays*. e-book ed., Ixia P, 2017.

Miller, Leila. "How We Identified White Supremacists After Charlottesville." *Frontline*, 2018, https://www.pbs.org/wgbh/frontline/article/how-we-identified-white-supremacists-after-charlottesville/.

Milner, Ryan M. "Hacking the Social: Internet Memes, Identity Antagonism, and the Logic of Lulz." *The Fibreculture Journal*, vol. 22, 2013, pp. 62–92.

Noddings, Nel. *Caring: A Feminine Approach to Ethics and Moral Education*. U of California P, 1984.

PEN America. "Online Harassment Field Manual." *PEN America*, 2020, https://onlineharassmentfieldmanual.pen.org.

Phillips, Whitney. *This is Why We Can't Have Nice Things: Mapping the Relationship Between Online Trolling and Mainstream Culture*. MIT P, 2015.

Raghuram, Parvati. "Race and Feminist Care Ethics: Intersectionality as Method." *Gender, Place, and Culture*, vol. 26, no. 5, 2019, pp. 613–37.

Reyman, Jessica, and Erika M. Sparby, editors. *Digital Ethics: Rhetoric and Responsibility in Online Aggression*. Routledge, 2020.

Sparby, Erika M. "Memes, and 4chan, and Haters, Oh My! Rhetoric, Identity, and Online Aggression." 2017. Northern Illinois U, dissertation.

———. "Digital Social Media and Aggression: Memetic Rhetoric in 4chan's Collective Identity." *Computers and Composition*, vol. 45, 2017, pp. 85–97.

———. "Reading Mean Comments to Subvert Gendered Hate on YouTube: Toward a Spectrum of Digital Aggression Response." *Enculturation: A Journal of Rhetoric, Writing, and Culture*, 2021, https://www.enculturation.net/readingmeancomments.

Spicer, André. "'Self-Care': How a Radical Feminist Idea Was Stripped of Politics for the Mass Market." *The Guardian*, 2019, https://www.theguardian.com/commentisfree/2019/aug/21/self-care-radical-feminist-idea-mass-market.

Chapter 12. Reflections on a Hip-Hop DJ Methodology

Eric A. House
New Mexico State University

What are Black digital writing practices? What does it mean to center on Black digital writing epistemologies when engaging within discourses of writing? These two questions serve as the foundation to my research portfolio and have at their core the desire to participate in the conversations held by scholars such as Adam J. Banks and Regina Duthely in claiming that Black culture has a history of remixing and reimagining writing practices technologically, digitally, and aesthetically, and such remixes and reimaginings are worth our serious attention. But what does it mean to take Black digital writing seriously? What does it mean to center on Black digital writing methodologies in institutions that are not often receptive to the same Blackness in which these methodologies and methods originate? My wager is that serious attention to Black digital methodologies and methods requires a commitment to praxis; it demands a relationship where Black theories and critiques are reflexively remixed and realized through Black practices and actions. It is my hope that by the end of this chapter, readers join me in thinking about the ways in which a Black digital writing methodology might live out its beautiful Black destiny by building space for further Black intellectual activity to impact further digital writing scholarship and participation.

In this chapter, I reflect on my experiences utilizing a Hip-Hop based methodology within research situated on the intersections of race and digital writing to explore issues of ethics and visibility when conducting culturally sensitive digital writing scholarship. Specifically, I consider the complexities of a DJ-based Hip-Hop methodology within a project that analyzes writing studies discourses and argues that the Hip-Hop DJ offers a culturally attentive position from which we might continue realizing digital writing practices. I first investigate Hip-Hop as a methodology within digital writing scholarship, noting what types of questions the culture seeks to address as well as situate myself within Hip-Hop to illustrate my proximity to the culture. I then reflect on the practice of theorizing through the Hip-Hop DJ to define and unpack mixing, remixing, and sampling as digital writing research methods. I end the chapter with implications for considering Hip-Hop DJ digital writing practices as valuable sites of inquiry, thinking specifically about the DJ's potential to transform digital writing pedagogy and digital writing research ethics.

Hip-Hop as Methodology Within Digital Writing

My dissertation, *Breaks, Samples, and Sites for Cyphers: Remixing the Administration of Writing*, sought to exist alongside scholarship that defines Hip-Hop as an entry point to rhetoric and digital writing as I argued for Hip-Hop methodologies by looking towards the Hip-Hop DJ as a model for administering writing. Specifically, I argued that the field should seriously consider DJing as a type of writing as it demands that writing practices be theorized, taught, and practiced through technology and identity. My main task was to uncover the field's mishandling of technology and identity through assumptions of what one might call "neutral" writing systems that ignore the impacts of the bodies and technologies involved, when Hip-Hop specifically demands an embodied definition of writing.

To get a little more specific, my project utilized what I called a Hip-Hop discourse analysis, a remixed research method realized through the analytical and performative functions of the Hip-Hop DJ to both analyze the relationship between identity and technology within a text and extend the analysis to imagine new opportunities and new possibilities. My analyses also centered on practices that resist hegemony and called for continual recognition of and resistance towards the power relations that inform institutional identities, interpretations of spacious programmatic definitions of writing, and articulations of writing curricula that are critical and inclusive. Rather than focusing on a relationship between writing, identity, and technology that is rooted in a view of education as a tool that prepares bodies to be commodities for production, my project looked towards the aesthetic nature of Hip-Hop, described by Emery Petchauer to be, "the emic sensibilities, cultural logics, and habits of body and mind that are at work in hip-hop expressions and practitioners" (6), as a potential site to remix and redefine that relationship, ultimately demanding that we change the roles, responsibilities, and practices of and within writing pedagogy and writing scholarship.

This project was imagined out of dissonance; since the way I experienced the field of rhetoric and writing studies was messy and often clouded. The definitions of writing provided by the discipline seemed incomplete, which led to conversations about writing feeling hollow. So, my project was partly one of healing, as I knew that I felt a connection to writing spaces, but my identity within those spaces was fractured. The dissertation became an opportunity to set some of those fractures to see what the whole frame might be. The same forms and functions that the field gave to writing also existed in other aspects of my life, but those aspects did not have the same presence in scholarly discourses. My work simultaneously became a bridge to connect those areas that I was disciplined to believe were separate. Black culture largely, and Hip-Hop culture specifically were the spaces that were disconnected from conversations of rhetoric and writing, and I was grateful for scholars in our field such as Elaine Richardson, Gwendolyn Pough, Kermit E. Campbell, David Green, and Todd Craig who have done the work of exploring the connections between Hip-Hop and rhetoric as it acted as a blueprint, informing me that such connections can exist. My mission was to then find, name, and bridge some of the specific aspects of my own Hip-Hop identity to my connections with rhetoric and writing. The first task in realizing those connections through my research was to plot out and argue for methodologies that originated from the cultures I identified with. An especially important task, since a main purpose was to recover and reclaim the logics and practices within Black culture as already intellectual and already complex. So, I started by researching, remixing, and unpacking a Hip-Hop methodology.

As I just mentioned, our field has amazing Hip-Hop scholars of whom I'm indebted to since they laid the foundation for many aspiring Hip-Hop rhet/comp scholars like myself, but I'm of the opinion that scholars in education have a little more Hip-Hop methodology swag from which our field can learn from when thinking about Hip-Hop's transformative potential in the classroom. Many conversations I've had or witnessed that try to think through Hip-Hop and writing within our field often slip into the realm created when curious teachers and scholars ask the famous "what does this look like in my classroom" question, which assumes Hip-Hop can be neatly placed within current writing curricula, but I love how some Hip-Hop Based Education (HHBE) scholars disrupt those ideals. HHBE scholars center on Hip-Hop's potential to transform the foundational and fundamental aspects of academia, most of which stems from an understanding that Hip-Hop's aesthetics can speak to students' life experiences and cultural logics (Hill; Hill and Petchauer; Love; Jennings and Petchauer). A turn to the aesthetic recognizes that Hip-Hop is more than a culture that produces texts to be analyzed according to the logics of other epistemologies (Hill and Petchauer). Rather, Hip-Hop itself is a methodological force from which practices are informed and through which knowledges are built.

In utilizing Hip-Hop as a methodology, I had to acknowledge and work through popular definitions. Hip-Hop has a global appeal and every clash and interaction inevitably changes the culture. But my methodology had to acknowledge the lived realities of the Black and Brown youth who first imagined and realized the culture. To do that, I had to focus once again on what an aesthetic approach to Hip-Hop scholarship means by directly challenging popular definitions of the culture.

Rap music has historically stood out as the metonym for Hip-Hop culture within the academy (Hill and Petchauer). While it has undoubtedly been the most marketable aspect of the culture, which would then make it the easiest accessed aspect of the culture and in turn make it a window in which a larger public might view Hip-Hop, rap is only one aspect that has its own idiosyncrasies. As Hill and Petchauer argue, this narrow view of Hip-Hop overlooks the role of knowledge within the culture and limits insights on the ways in which the culture's boundaries are continually challenged and expanded (2). The move towards an aesthetic understanding of Hip-Hop thus challenges scholars to move beyond literary analysis of rap songs and into spaces where, for example, we might question what the logics and stylistics of rap itself suggest about processes of identification and location within social structures (Petchauer). Continuing this example, rather than focus exclusively on the *narrative* of urban Black adolescence presented in Kendrick Lamar's "GOOD Kid, MAAD City," an aesthetic emphasis asks that we engage the Black tonal semantics layered within the album to investigate aural aspects within verses that extend from legacies of Black rhetorical practice. This type of emphasis can highlight a compelling story or social statement while simultaneously creating a sonic landscape for listeners to inhabit, both of which are then accomplished according to the logics and practices of the culture that created the content.

H. Samy Alim's discussion of emic practices within Hip-Hop studies also cannot be ignored within conversations of a Hip-Hop methodology. In referencing James G. Spady's term hiphopography, Alim calls for Hip-Hop scholarship from an emic perspective to ensure scholarship that is for the advancement and edification of the culture (970). For Alim, scholarship strictly from an etic perspective is harmful to the culture's sense of identity through its over-simplification and reduced complexities (970). As such, a necessary practice in utilizing a Hip-Hop methodology is to state where exactly I fit in within hip-hop in order to illustrate my positionality in the culture.

Hip-Hop has always been a part of my home life ecology, starting back to my pops always playing west-coast rap records like Dr. Dre and Above The Law when I was young. Those younger years would also include some immersion into the likes of artists such as A Tribe Called Quest, Wu-Tang Clan, Outkast, Nas, and Jay-Z by way of my older cousin and brothers, but it wasn't until the high school and college years that I was able to start making personal connections. The lyrics would start to hit a little harder, and the tempos seemed to sync with my heartbeat more often. But I never really had the opportunity to claim that I was a practitioner in the way that I wanted to. I've written rhymes before, freestyled with friends, been involved in a few informal dance offs, but couldn't really say that I was a practitioner. H. Samy Alim does note that participants do not always have to own a traditional role of artist since the majority of those who interact with Hip-Hop, and in those interactions continually (re)create Hip-Hop, do so as they go about their everyday lives (Alim). Alim's statement sums up my location within Hip-Hop, yet I still was eager to deepen my engagement. Call it intellectual curiosity, or simply just a desire to do more.

Fortunately, situations led to an opportunity to learn the craft of the DJing, initiating the occasion to further explore my location and identity within hip-hop. My first official interaction with DJing then began:

> The turntables are set up in a back room, walls painted dark blue. Records fill up most of the space. Of the records, I only recognize a few. That speaks to the depth of DJ Alias's collection, but also to the limit of my own knowledge. DJ Alias is a

local DJ who spins for my cousin, a local artist emcee, Big Meridox. Meridox introduced us, and Alias was gracious enough to introduce me to the art form. Throughout my time, we reviewed turntable vocabulary such as the platter, slipmats, headshells, cartridges, and stylus, then talk through the vocabulary of the mixer, such as faders, treble, bass, and cue settings. The first task is juggling, which is looping to the same part of a record back and forth between the two turntables, all while keeping in the appropriate cadence.

DJ Alias picks a song I'm familiar with, Method Man's "Bring the Pain," and I officially take my first step in DJing. I try to match the cadence each time I juggle, but I lack dexterity on the turntable and occasionally bump the record when I should be gliding. The bumps mess up the stylus placement. I get frustrated and turn everything off to reset. That's when DJ Alias gives me some of the most important advice when it comes to DJing, "Regardless of what happens, you have to keep the party going."

I still have yet to go public with my DJing, but my time spent learning the craft was and continues to be informative and influential in imagining the potentials for digital writing when realized and practiced through Hip-Hop. It is from this experience of learning the craft that my methodology for digital writing comes to life. It is the moment where my relationships with both Hip-Hop and writing scholarship collide, positioning me in a sort of liminal space; I was raised in Hip-Hop, but I was disciplined through the academy. Rather than choose one over the other, the methodology had to be one of synthesizing and mixing.

A Hip-Hop methodology, one that centers on process of identification through methods that are sensitive to social locations, thus asks us to synthesize and reimagine. It asks that we think digitally by going beyond conceptions of Hip-Hop as a trendy lesson or set of practices for surface-level interrogations about writing definitions and programmatic articulations and into spaces of networks, mixes, and assemblages. Through this methodology, my goal was to explore what happens when we ask writing to play in time with the beat established from cultural difference. I ask, what happens when you throw some 808 beats with classical music and see if that mixing can change our conceptions of how writers participate and interact with the mix. How would "Canon in D" sound if we looped the intro a couple of times, sped the tempo up and threw in some boom-bap? How might that change what we know about writing? How might that change what we know about discipline and race? How might that change what we know about culture and digital writing?

A Hip-Hop methodology offers an opportunity to explore these sorts of questions. This approach to methodology allows a specific type of leeway that often isn't granted through other approaches in that Hip-Hop has historically favored purposeful selection. We give credit where credit is due, and I attempted to do my due diligence in the naming and analyzing, but the ultimate test in whether my methodology is sound rests in the same way anyone measures Hip-Hop performances and productions: Was it dope, or nah? Did it give me life, or did I barely recognize it? Does it inspire, or will it be forgotten?

Theorizing the Practices of the DJ: A Definition of the Mix, the Remix, and the Sample

> The moment when the dancers really got wild was in a song's short instrumental break, when the band would drop out and the rhythm section would get elemental. Forget melody, chorus, songs—it was all about the groove, building it, keeping it going. Like a string theorist, Herc zeroed in on the fundamental vibrating loop at the heart of the record, the break.
>
> *– Chang (79)*

My Hip-Hop methodology demanded that my approach to rhetoric and writing studies place the concept of digital writing as a point of entry into all discussions of rhetoric and writing, rather than considering digital writing as a derivative or a subsection to a larger Writing studies (emphasis on the capital W). Heavily influenced by Adam J. Banks' *Digital Griots*, my work considers DJing as writing,[1] which recognizes that conceptions of writing should "consider what the DJ offers ... when we move beyond a few mentions of individual writing practices completely lifted from context, from tradition, from social, cultural, political, and technological networks" (153). Banks' argument for DJing as writing recognizes that our scholarly and pedagogical pursuits are already taking place in a multimedia age, and to talk of rhetoric and writing without considering the impacts of the technological and multimodal would be to decontextualize our work. Considering DJing as writing is to acknowledge the realities of our multimedia world, and that demands that we take seriously the writing practices that have already been theorizing and practicing through the digital, through multimodality, and through technology. Like Banks' work, my usage of a Hip-Hop methodology suggests that Black and Brown people *been* doing the work of digital writing, and it's about time the rest of the field catch up and pay attention to lessons that our elders have been teaching us.

After having established the questions that a larger Hip-Hop methodology is seeking to unpack, as well as establishing a Hip-Hop methodology as a

---

1. Banks uses the phrase "DJing as writing AND writing as DJing" to illustrate a conflation of the two. My research purposely only uses DJing as writing in recognition of my history as being disciplined as a writing scholar before learning the language of the turntable. I will return to this point when considering the implications for my research.

necessary and legitimate approach to research in digital writing, my next task was to illustrate how Hip-Hop DJ practice and methods do the work previously mentioned. All of what I argued about a Hip-Hop methodology came from a cyclical relationship between practice and theory; I sampled, mixed, and remixed a Hip-Hop methodology through my own practices learning the craft of DJing, through attending DJ sets in my community, and through immersing myself in scholarship invested in DJ logics. When I practiced and developed my own DJ skills, I would sit and reflect on the ways in which I try to work my way into a mix, think about my process for finding a break and consider how those sorts of logics synthesized or disrupted what I thought about writing. While at DJ sets, I would pay attention to the energy emitted in each mix, scratch, sample, and think about the ways in which DJs made the mix accessible to all the participants. And when working through scholarship, I would try to find the language and images to help me make sense of it all. And through these steps, I found strong connections to notions of the mix and the sample as concepts to help realize my bridge between Hip-Hop and rhetoric and writing.

A brief note answering the question why DJs and not any other Hip-Hop practitioner: while a variety of Hip-Hop identities offer critical insights into rhetorical practices and composing processes, I was more interested in the Hip-Hop DJ's functions as writing facilitator and manager. DJs present spacious definitions of writing and foster interactive writing situations where a multitude of people might collaborate and create, a practice which might make the act of administering, teaching, and researching writing more critical of difference. These specific functions also provide occasions to craft strong arguments about the ways in which DJs approach texts as non-linear and networked, approaches necessary when discussing writing in our digital worlds.

While DJs share logics and purposes across genres, it is the *practice* of Hip-Hop DJs situated within Black rhetorical tradition that sets them apart from other genres. The ways in which they enter each writing/composition occasion and the manners in which they interact with the crowd differ from other styles; those practices are worth emphasizing as they have social and political implications that cannot be assumed of every type of DJ. But as I mentioned, two specific practices of the Hip-Hop DJ, the mix and the sample, set them apart from their contemporaries, and unpacking those two practices not only illustrated the nuance of the Hip-Hop DJ, but also provided some moments to think more critically about DJing as writing.

Defining the Mix & Remix

One of the central assumptions within my research is that the practices of the DJ offer a critical position to reconsider the cultural and racial implications within digital writing. Hip-Hop's origin story offers plenty of insights as to how legacies of racialized oppression led to the creation of the culture, in which case

Hip-Hop itself might be defined as an embodiment of racialized resistance. But, like Joseph Schloss, my work argued that the historical emphasis of Hip-Hop that highlights oppression is just one part of the story. While the social and political situation undoubtedly was the catalyst from which the culture was realized, it is also important to note the ways in which the methods and practices themselves reflect an evolution of digital writing practices originating from Black and Latinx rhetorical legacies, practices which themselves have rich rhetorical histories.

One such discussion of a practice originating within Black rhetorical production suggests that the location of the Hip-Hop DJ exhibits complex mediation practices known as mixing and remixing, critical digital writing practices based in Black rhetorical practice that are necessary to question hegemonic ideologies. As a part of my purpose was to forward the histories of Black digital writing practices, my initial step in working through and understanding of mixing was to see what scholarship had to say to ground and contextualize. Through an investigation of Black cultural production and sound technologies, Alexander Weheliye theorizes the concept of "the mix" as a model of Black temporality and cultural practice, claiming that DJs manage a duality that is found in both the more concrete mixing of sonic information and in the mixing of DJ's expectations and practices with those of the audience (89). It is within the managing of this duality that DJs illustrate tactics to bring together competing-yet-complementary beats as their weaving together of separate sonic material creates a location in which all associated identities might interact (92). For Weheliye, this mixing act challenges discourses of Western modernity in a Bhabhaian sense through disrupting grand narratives of reason and progress by adding marginalized cultures back into the mix, an act that then forces us to rethink the (im)possibility of universal and homogenizing discourses (23).

I want to emphasize here that the definition of mixing presented by Weheliye doesn't ask for or produce some new, never seen or heard of type of writing practice. My work seeks to push back against the idea that conversations of digital writing must always be fresh and new, and instead I argue that Black and Brown rhetorical histories and legacies *been* doing the digital writing work. It is more so to say that we should take the practice of mixing seriously as a type of writing, understanding that mixing forces us to rethink linearity within texts. It asks us to pay attention to the competing-yet-complimentary as we write for a purpose of creating interactive locations. These are the sorts of lessons that we might unpack when we take mixing seriously as a digital writing practice.

The term "remix" is utilized in various ways and for multiple purposes both within and outside of Hip-Hop, and for that reason it was necessary to clarify how exactly I thought through the term in the context of my project. As one who relates to Hip-Hop from the 2000s, my understanding of remix was heavily influenced by Diddy and the Bad Boy Family who presented records that relied on knowledge of the original track or previous mix in order to deeply engage with the remix. I'm thinking specifically of the "Special Delivery," "Bad Boys for

Life," and "I Need a Girl Parts 1 & 2," remixes, where part of the experience was in both valuing what was done before and dissecting what was new, all while staying within the same plane in which both records reside. Diddy and the Bad Boy family were able to mainstream and make "remix" into a product that is accessible to a larger audience, but my work is more so fascinated with the process that precedes. For these remixes to be visible and accessible to a larger public, there must be some form of analysis that breaks down and makes visible the energy that defines the track in the first place. Once that energy is known, options and opportunities follow. Expanding on that energy to imagine spacious and inclusive definitions of writing is the goal of the Hip-Hop-based analysis presented in my investigation of digital writing.

Defining the Sample

Joseph Schloss presents one of the more comprehensive investigations of the process of sampling and beat-making practices that are foundational to DJ culture. While Schloss is more so interested in the practices of Hip-Hop producers, his investigations do note that practices of Hip-Hop producers' stem from the logics and legacies of the DJ, in which case most of what producers do is informed by DJ practices (37). The biggest difference is found in the context; Hip-Hop producers similarly sample, loop, and mix sounds in the creation of a track to be recorded, while DJs utilize the same techniques for live functions. Schloss names four specific aesthetic values that guide the process of sampling: understanding the structure of a beat, naming the internal characteristics of individual samples, thinking through the relationships of samples when they are juxtaposed, and understanding the shared assumptions and context cues that imbue any sample choice with significance.

As rhythm is arguably one of the most important aspects within Hip-Hop, the practice of understanding beat structuring stands as a foundational requirement in DJ practice. Schloss suggests that Hip-Hop compositions are often cyclical, in which case practitioners would make use of looping to repeat aspects of sampled tracks for an intended effect (136). The loop then defines the underlying rhythmic structure from which any sort of movement or deviations must interact (136). Schloss also highlights looping within the legacy of African American rhetorical practice, naming it to be a form of signifying.[2] Looping as a practice that helps realize underlying structure thus also reflects a rhetorical prominence through its extension to Black rhetoric (138).

The next two aesthetic values (naming internal characteristics of samples and thinking through samples relationships when juxtaposed) build off each other

---

2. Mitchell-Kernan (qtd. in Alim) defines signifying as the practice of encoding messages or meanings within natural conversations, typically through elements of indirections.

through a recognition of interactivity. Schloss connects the interactivity of samples to legacies of and affinities for collage within African American art practices. Within these practices, the vibe of the beat begins to unfold as the DJ or producer adds in parts. Schloss quotes collage artist Romare Bearden to make parallels between collaging and sampling, as Bearden states, "You have to begin somewhere . . . so you put something down. Then you put something else with it, and then you see how that works . . . Once you get going . . . all sorts of things begin to pop up. Sometimes something just falls into place, like piano keys that every now and then just seem to be right where your fingers happen to come down" (153). Sampling, like collaging, recognizes a unique form of textual agency by disrupting ideas of the subject as the sole creator from which discourse flows. Instead, it recognizes a reciprocal relationship where samples inform the mix just as much as they are informed by the mix.

Lastly, a definition of sampling must take into consideration the context in which a beat will exist. Schloss mentions that the choices of producers, and their successes or failures, is dependent on a complex mixing of variables. On one hand, the beat-making process is competitive; producers want to flaunt their skill as they participate in Hip-Hop's legacies of toasting and dueling. On the other hand, they want to make sure their compositions are digestible for audiences who may not be as interested in the aural battles between producers. The act of sampling might then be described as highly rhetorical in that it requires recognition and negotiation across contexts through understanding that one choice cannot satisfy all parties, yet each choice should be purposeful.

The Hip-Hop DJ can set themselves apart from other styles of DJing through practices that are rooted in Black and African tradition. Almost every DJ is involved in some aspect of mixing, but Hip-Hop DJs, as Weheliye mentions, ask us to rethink the (im)possibility of universal discourses through their play with time and audience expectation. Sampling is not unique to Hip-Hop DJs, but the way in which Hip-Hop DJs transform sampling into an art is reminiscent of African and African American collaging practices, all of which are founded within a Black rhetorical excellence. As a practice placed in a Black cultural tradition, my discussion on Hip-Hop DJ methodology argued that Hip-Hop DJing is an illustration of digital writing that has the capacity to critique discourses of whiteness and cultural exclusion since it was created within the very discourses in which it seeks to be critical.

Tying it all Together: DJing as Writing/ DJing as Digital Research Methods

My research was a practice in digital writing informed by the logics of Hip-Hop; it placed the DJ as a writer, turned writing theory and scholarship into tracks, and allowed for the logics of the turntable to analyze, mix and remix in order to forward different findings, conclusions, and implications. My goal was to place competing-yet-complementary tracks on separate turntables, mixing them all together to create a space where multiple identities can participate and interact. I wanted to find and sample the proverbial break within the scholarship, looping it and adding it to the mix. And I wanted to utilize a Hip-Hop based digital writing practice to illustrate the value in digital writing practices rooted in Black rhetoric.

The results of these methods had some interesting takeaways that I wish to unpack. I first want to acknowledge and highlight a research methods connection within this type of digital writing scholarship. The methods of sampling, mixing, and remixing position the Hip-Hop DJ as a discourse analyst as they often take note of the ways in which bodies are informed by and in turn inform the discourses that surround them. The discourse analysis operates through the DJ's presence as digital writers with the notions of sampling, mixing, and remixing suggesting that words exist across time and space, and the logics of the turntable and the mixer invite words and ideas to "become a series of interwoven networks [and a] mixture of fragments used to create a new whole" (Duthely 352). Based on this connection, I label my method Hip-Hop discourse analysis, and recognize it as a digital research method due its guiding logics and practices based in DJ practice.

I also want to acknowledge that my Hip-Hop and digital writing inspired read and remix is just one type of intervention situated within a specific culture that operates within its own negotiated logics and practices. But Hip-Hop is complex, and the way I utilize it cannot be the same way that everyone within the culture understands it. For one, my analysis and remix operated almost exclusively from DJ logics when Hip-Hop has a mixing and blending of styles, practices, and performances that all embody the culture. An analysis situated within emcee practices or graffiti logics all share Hip-Hop as a guiding discourse, but the specifics of the methods would have to change, which might then lead to differences in the outcomes (Hoch). I consider that to be a potential, instead of a weakness as it suggests that even Hip-Hop as the guiding force for this intervention has a multitude of possibilities that rely on one's positionality within the culture.

It is also important to reiterate that I am not a master DJ by any means; it would be more accurate to say that I'm still a beginner learning the fundamentals as I continually develop my own DJ identity. And while I loved Hip-Hop prior to becoming a scholar, I was disciplined in rhetoric and writing before I started learning to administer the mix. As a result, and as I've previously stated, my theories very much operate from the position of DJing as writing, rather than writing as DJing, an important distinction I think necessary to make clear. I agree with Adam J. Banks that DJing as writing and writing as DJing can be interchangeable when we focus on the practical application of the two (153). My distinction of DJing as writing instead of writing as DJing is only to signal that my reading and analysis comes from the acknowledgment that I've been disciplined in writing studies before learning the language of the turntable. As a result, my approach to this research places writing as the dependent variable.

The Complexity of Digital Writing in Pedagogy

An important finding that my DJ analysis uncovered within current writing pedagogy discourse is the need for a more critical handling of digital writing when considering the complexities of identity and technology. My analysis illustrated that what is often imagined within the writing classroom is a disembodied and static definition of composition, one that originates with the letter and is now evolving toward the digital realm, with "digital" only signifying the screen. To compose would then be to constantly move towards either the printed page or the screen with a specific affinity for the alphanumeric.

However, the practices of the DJ suggest that writing is a little more complex than that since it involves a constant mediation between identity and technology. Duthely suggests that hip-hop culture rejects a linear model of writing, instead arguing that Hip-Hop's handling of multimodality might give us much to reconsider when we talk about the creative potential of digital writing techniques (352). Banks and Weheliye talk through DJs as illustrating this complexity, claiming that they recreate discourses of culture and technology through their composing practices, becoming a model of multimedia writing grounded in rhetorical excellence (28–29; 23). Banks specifically emphasizes the stakes for Black students as he notes that an emphasis of the DJ's culturally based multimedia writing practices might help develop approaches in, "composition theory and practice that no longer consigns [B]lack students, writers, or scholars to token 'colored day at the carnival' status nor consigns digital theory, rhetoric, and writing as [W]hite by default . . ." (27). As we continue to think of and theorize through digital writing methodologies, I argue that we take Banks' purpose seriously for the sake of those students who, through being subjected to homogeneous writing definitions and applications, are forced to culturally repress when discussions of digital writing could be an invitation for theory and exploration.

Further, I find it important that this implication is not forwarding Hip-Hop as the final solution. I rather am arguing against totalizing solutions, acknowledging that any one cultural location cannot account for the intersecting identities that inhabit digital writing definitions and applications. Both Banks and Weheliye's theories of the DJ as cultural and technological composer may think through Black cultural tradition and production, but neither are exclusively Hip-Hop. DJing as a writing practice shifts when its cultural location shifts, illustrating a need for more DJ writing theory to understand how identity and culture impact writing practices. However, my explorations of DJ practice suggest that the cultural locations of those involved in the mix matters, especially those that have historically been denied access and visibility, and each needs the ability to positively impact the overall vibe. To that end, digital writing scholarship would do well to continue thinking through the complexities of culture and location in defining and articulating the parameters for writing.

A Question of Ethics

And then there's the conversation of ethics. There is a common practice in Black culture to be guarded and protective of what it is that we build and what aspects we choose to share out. And those practices are well-founded and well-understood when one considers histories of colonization and appropriation. It makes sense when we acknowledge that Black culture is loved more than the Black people who've created it and the Black bodies who continually live it. So, the questions arise as to whether it is even possible or responsible to bring in Hip-Hop and Blackness when trying to imagine digital writing scholarship when there remains the constant threat of cultural erasure and appropriation. We can make the argument that we must do better to serve Black and Brown students who are not imagined or represented in digital writing scholarship, or that we must call out white supremacy as a guiding logic in research and scholarship in rhetoric and writing. I would argue those are valid and immediate reasons. But my work has taught me that I must also pay attention to the effects and not just the intention. When sharing this work, it is almost always met with positivity and what I would call a generative curiosity, but it always falls to this question: "This sounds fun, but how can I use this in my classroom?"

The issue that I have with that question is that I often translate it to mean "how can I seem like I'm doing this type of work while still upholding my homogeneous view of writing?" Or, potentially worse, it translates to "how can I colonize your cultural approach and add it to my toolkit, repurposing it in ways that I see fit?" I'm not suggesting that anyone who has ever asked that question had a colonizing mentality; some ask that question with a genuine desire to forward non-marginalizing and anti-racist scholarly and pedagogical practices. But the effect often treats these Black intellectual endeavors as a subsection to the main field, or as an additive to foundational conversations. I argue we should do better.

And I think that's the beauty of centering on Black methodologies. It provides the occasion to center on Black scholarship by remixing the knowledge bases from which we justify our methods and draw our conclusions. It makes plain the claim that Blackness is intellectual. It suggests that claims of validity can be justified according to Black means, and that we should resist the need to acknowledge Black methods and methodologies as only visible and legitimate once they pass the test for white intellectual visibility and validity.

But the question remains, considering how deeply committed and engrained academia is in whiteness, is it still ethical to bring in Black culture when there is the constant threat of appropriation and erasure? Black culture and Black people are already there. And I have learned that a major issue is trying to pretend as if the oppressive boundaries that academia created and continue to uphold are normal and natural. My research has given me opportunities to rethink the sorts of methodology we utilize to explain and justify our work, and I would argue that the field has been assuming neutrality in methodology. Our cultural orientations suggest that there are so many ways to have these conversations, and all these methods have within them justifications and ideals that, if we pay serious attention to, will not only shift the way we conduct our research, but also transform what we can even imagine as being a purpose of that research in the first place.

Final Thoughts

Black digital writing practices and methods have the potential for reflection and invitation; they ask that we pay close attention to how our bodies enact and are interpellated by our physical and social realities, and they encourage us to write and perform through those observations. They invite us to understand writing processes through networks and assemblages and recognize the opening and remixing of those networks as valuable intellectual endeavors. They demand that we research through the spaces and locations we inhabit, and demand that we acknowledge the differences that inevitably exist in our locations. Lastly, they unapologetically name Blackness, Black culture, and Black bodies as intellectual, visible, valuable, and beautiful.

Works Cited

Alim, H. Samy. "'The Natti Ain't No Punk City': Emic Views of Hip Hop Cultures." *Callaloo*, vol. 29, no. 3, 2006, pp. 969–90.
Banks, Adam J. *Digital Griots: African American Rhetoric in a Multimedia Age*. Southern Illinois UP, 2011.
Campbell, Kermit E. *Gettin' Our Groove On: Rhetoric, Language, and Literacy for the Hip Hop Generation*. Wayne State UP, 2005.
Chang, Jeff. *Can't Stop Won't Stop: A History of the Hip-Hop Generation*. Ebury Press, 2005.
———, editor. *Total Chaos: That Art and Aesthetics of Hip-Hop*. Basic Civitas, 2006.
Craig, Todd. "'Makin' Somethin' Outta Little-to-Nufin' Racism, Revision and Rotating Records- The Hip-Hop DJ in Composition Praxis." *Changing English*, vol. 22, no. 4, 2017, pp. 349–64.
Craig, Todd, and Carmen Kynard. "Sista Girl Rock: Women of Colour and Hip-Hop Deejaying as Raced/Gendered Knowledge and Language." *Changing English*, vol. 22, no. 4, 2017, pp. 143–58.
Duthely, Regina. "Hip-Hop Rhetoric and Multimodal Digital Writing." *The Routledge Handbook of Digital Writing and Rhetoric*, edited by Jonathan Alexander and Jacqueline Rhodes, Routledge, 2018, pp. 352–60.
Green, David. "Changing English Studies in Culture and Education Flow as a Metaphor for Changing Composition Practices Flow as a Metaphor for Changing Composition Practices." *Changing English*, vol. 24, no. 2, 2017, pp. 175–85.
Hill, Marc Lamont. *Beats Rhymes and Classroom Life: Hip-Hop Pedagogy and The Politics of Identity*. Teachers College P, 2009.

Hill, Marc Lamont and Emery Petchauer. *Schooling Hip-Hop: Expanding Hip-Hop Based Education Across the Curriculum*. Teachers College P, 2013.

Hoch, Danny. "Toward a Hip Hop Aesthetic: A Manifesto for the Hip Hop Arts Movement." *Total Chaos: Art and Aesthetics of Hip Hop*, edited by Jeff Chang, Basic Civitas, 2006, pp. 349–64.

House, Eric. "Breaks, Samples, and Sites for Cyphers: Remixing the Administration of Writing." 2019. University of Arizona, dissertation.

Jennings, Kyesha and Emery Petchauer. "Changing English Studies in Culture and Education Teaching in the Mix: Turntablism, DJ Aesthetics and African American Literature." *Changing English*, vol. 24, no. 2, 2017, pp. 216–28.

Lamar, Kendrick. *Good Kid, M.A.A.D. City*. Top Dawg Entertainment, 2012.

Love, Bettina L. "What Is Hip-Hop-Based Education Doing in Nice Fields Such as Early Childhood and Elementary Education?" *Urban Education*, vol. 50, no. 1, 2015, pp. 106–31.

Pachelbel, Johann. "Canon In D Major for Strings and Continuo: Partia No. VI in B-Flat Major." *Musicalische Ergötzung; Partie in G Major*, Musical Heritage Society, 1970.

Petchauer, Emery. *Hip-Hop Culture in College Student's Lives*. Routledge, 2012.

Pough, Gwendolyn D. *Check It While I Wreck It: Black Womanhood, Hip-hop Culture, and the Public Sphere*. Northeastern UP, 2004.

Pough, Gwendolyn D., Elaine Richardson, Aisha Durham, and Rachel Raimist, editors. *Home Girls Make Some Noise: Hip Hop Feminism Anthology*. Parker Publishing, 2007.

Richardson, Elaine. *Hiphop Literacies*. Routledge, 2006.

Rose, Tricia. *Black Noise: Rap Music and Black Culture in Contemporary America*. Wesleyan UP, 1994.

Schloss, Joseph. *Making Beats: The Art of Sample-Based Hip-Hop*. Wesleyan UP, 2004.

———. "Sampling Ethics." *That's The Joint: The Hip-Hop Studies Reader*. 2nd ed., edited by Murray Forman and Mark Anthony Neal, Routledge, 2011, pp. 609–30.

Smitherman, Geneva. *Talkin and Testifyin: The Language of Black America*. Wayne State UP, 1986.

Weheliye, Alexander G. *Phonographies: Grooves in Sonic Afro-Modernity*. Duke UP, 2005.

Chapter 13. Trauma-Informed Scholarship in Digital Research and Design

Shannon Kelly
MICHIGAN STATE UNIVERSITY

Eric Rodriguez
PORTLAND STATE UNIVERSITY

Stuart Blythe
MICHIGAN STATE UNIVERSITY

Ben Lauren
UNIVERSITY OF MIAMI

We begin this chapter with a short vignette to set the stage for our discussion about trauma-informed (TI) digital research and design in the context of rhetoric and writing. The vignette is about a transformational moment in a project that involved a collaboration between community members participating in a homelessness speakers bureau and faculty and students at an R1 institution in the Midwest. The goal of the collaboration was to help raise awareness about homelessness and housing insecurity by producing eight original audio compositions that combined spoken word stories about homelessness set to original music composed to accompany each story.[1] The narrator of the following vignette is Ben Lauren, who was one of the project organizers. In the vignette, Ben discusses a moment where he listened to one of the stories for the first time.

> At one key moment, the storyteller's voice wavered when they talked about surviving homelessness. I could hear the storyteller swallow the weight of the memory as they took slow, full breaths. I suddenly realized this traumatic moment from this person's life was now documented by an audio recording and anyone could encounter the re-telling in multiple settings. How would other people respond to the story? How would the storyteller feel about others' responses?

---

1. The MI Homeless Voice stories are available here: https://soundcloud.com/mi-homeless-voice. The site belongs to the community group, and the storytellers have the choice to take down their story if they change their mind about sharing online. As such, the site may not always exist.

We believe this vignette communicates a clear exigence for our chapter: digital projects can engage and/or amplify the trauma of people in sometimes unpredictable or unforeseen ways. In short, digital projects have the very real potential to retraumatize people. More, and perhaps more unnerving, we won't always realize that we've retraumatized someone we are working with. In this chapter, we don't specifically talk about trauma-informed work as a digital method, but as a philosophical grounding for developing, thinking through, and sustaining digital work in accountable, responsible, and caring ways. It is our contention that nearly all scholarly projects have digital elements today—from making activities with digital tools (e.g., phones, video camera, or screencasting software), to research projects that involve different kinds of software (e.g., Google Drive or NVIVO), to systems we use to communicate and coordinate with one another (e.g., Slack, Teams, email, etc.). We argue that a trauma-informed mindset can (and should) provide foundational guidance for how digital scholars and artists develop, sustain, and curate work, and how we approach our participants and collaborators in just and equitable ways. To help illustrate this argument, later in this chapter we provide accounts of how we used trauma-informed approaches for two different projects that included significant digital elements. We describe how a set of trauma-informed considerations helped us approach the digital work of these projects. As a result, we start this chapter by asking value-based questions such as these: What is our responsibility to respond to trauma and be aware of its impact as researchers and as collaborators? How can we design our projects anticipating the potential impacts of trauma and retraumatization? Our answers to these questions are, in part, what this chapter is about. It is likely clear to readers at this point that we believe that digital writing scholars need a better understanding of trauma and its pervasive impact on people who we collaborate with and invite to participate in our research projects.

In this chapter, we offer a rhetorically grounded methodology for incorporating TI approaches to digital writing scholarship. Importantly, we do not exclusively focus on providing a prescribed checklist of how to be TI in digital work. In our work together, we learned that developing a TI approach is more complicated than that. Instead, we offer readers a way to begin evaluating their own work through a TI lens to help guide project development, protocols, and (potential) responses to trauma. What follows, then, is a brief discussion of trauma, existing scholarship on trauma in writing studies, our approach to a rhetorically grounded TI methodology, a reflection on two TI digital projects, and the implications of our TI work for the field.

The Complexity of Trauma

Given that much of the collaborative work of the projects we focus on in this chapter was completed with people whose training is in social work, we intentionally draw from scholarship in social work to help us understand and describe trauma. The Institute on Trauma and Trauma-Informed Care (ITTIC) defines trauma as contingent upon a person's reaction to an event or circumstance (16). It is, to a significant extent, an individual's perception that determines whether an event or circumstance is traumatic. Trauma is thus "conceptualized by considering the events/circumstances that occur, the characteristics of those events/circumstances and the negative effect(s) they have on the individual's well-being" (SAMHSA, qtd. in ITTIC 16). Under this definition, there is a difference between adversity (the experience of negative events) and trauma (people's reactions to such experiences). Not only can trauma be the result of one event, but it can also be ongoing, as may be the case with physically or emotionally abusive relationships, homelessness, or racism.[2] However, even though trauma is contingent upon an individual's perception, it has a universal sense in that a particular adverse event would likely be traumatic for anyone who experienced it, as is recognized by the International Classification of Diseases (ICD-10, qtd. in Stein et al.). In acknowledging that trauma is based on perception to a significant degree, trauma is not an experience one can just "get over" by having a "better attitude."

Although there is no checkbox of criteria that definitively qualifies an experience as traumatic, clinicians point to a series of indicators of maladaptive responses to adverse events. Stein et al. note that a common response is avoidance of situations or circumstances. Vincent Felitti et al. demonstrate that trauma response has a direct impact on risky health behavior and negative health outcomes throughout one's life.[3] Rothschild and van der Kolk also describe the psychophysiological impacts of trauma, with van der Kolk particularly noting the physiological changes in the brain resulting from trauma. Recent research has also taught us that trauma might be passed down through generations of families or groups in their genes in ways that impact health outcomes over the long term (Costa, Yetter, and DeSomer).

Guidelines for trauma-informed (TI) care have been developed to improve clinical practice (Harris and Fallot) and have been adapted to implement TI organizational design (ITTIC) and TI pedagogy (Carello and Butler; Day). Trauma-informed care has two primary goals: to reduce the possibility of traumatization and/or retraumatization in how spaces, systems, studies, classrooms, etc. are designed and implemented; and, to provide care if someone experiences trauma. Regarding the first goal, universal precaution is an important element of TI

---

2. For a helpful discussion of racial trauma, see Dara Winley's (2020) blog here: https://www.psychologytoday.com/us/blog/take-care-black-women/202006/racial-trauma-is-public-health-emergency.

3. We also wish to note, in addition to the 61% percent of adults who had experienced one Adverse Childhood Experience (ACE), nearly 1 in 6 respondents reported that they had experienced four or more types of ACEs (CDC "Vital Signs").". Regarding higher education, Carello and Butler provide similar numbers in explaining that by the time young people reach college, "66%–85% report lifetime traumatic event exposure and many report multiple event exposure" (157).

practice. Arising from medical practice, universal precaution refers to approaching individual with the same intention "to reduce the possibility of triggering or re-traumatizing" (ITTIC Manual 15). A practitioner who operationalizes universal precaution in medical practice refers to always using the same safety precautions for handling blood or bodily fluids (e.g., wearing gloves and personal-protective equipment). Extended to organizational or research design, TI universal precaution involves "putting on metaphorical gloves (changing our interactions, policies, etc.) to prevent the possibility of re-traumatization" (ITTIC Manual 10). We believe universal precaution calls our attention as writing scholars to the assumptions we make about our participants' or collaborators' background and positionality, including their response to project work and motivations for collaborating or participating. Universal precaution suggests that we approach each participant as if they have experienced trauma to ensure just and equitable forms of safety, choice, and empowerment to build trust when contributing to scholarly work. We also recognize our ability to support participants may be limited because of our own identity, positionality, and background or experiences as well.

The second goal of trauma-informed care acknowledges that trauma can be ongoing, which means that projects and classrooms should be designed in such a way that makes care available for survivors of trauma (Carello and Butler 156). This also means that designing a TI environment cannot be done in isolation. A researcher or teacher trained in rhetoric and writing cannot, indeed should not, expect to be able to care for someone experiencing trauma. Nor should a traumatized individual be made responsible for designing a less traumatizing space for them to navigate (because that can be particularly triggering). We believe, in the context of rhetoric and writing, TI care requires teams of people with complementary skill sets and different backgrounds.

Discussions of Trauma in Writing Studies

While in the previous section we intentionally noted working from scholarship in social work, we also want to situate ourselves as rhetoric and writing scholars using TI approaches. Writing studies, as Michelle Day notes, has drawn its understanding of trauma largely from the humanities-based field of trauma studies, where the focus has been on writing about traumatic experiences and the use of difficult literary texts (4). Throughout the early 2000s, this humanities-based influence (as opposed to clinical research in social work and counseling) meant that trauma was approached through pedagogy intended to heal trauma with writing (Berman; Borrowman; Bishop and Hodges). Such a pedagogical focus on trauma is something that Janice Carello and Lisa Butler have named "potentially perilous pedagogies" that may teach trauma via assigned texts and assignments without being trauma-informed pedagogies (155). The pedagogies are perilous in part because they may retraumatize students by asking them to write about past events but also in part because most writing instructors are not prepared to respond in such instances. A trauma-informed approach is very different from encouraging students to heal trauma through writing.[4] More recently in writing studies, though, Black feminist approaches, cultural rhetorics, and feminist care ethics have addressed trauma in storytelling methodologies, research design, and care-based practices.

Black feminist epistemology calls for reconceiving theory from the margins, for centering and protecting the most vulnerable, and valuing experiential and lived realities (Walton, Moore, and Jones). We also see important contributions to care-based, ethical research practices from Constance Haywood's and Cecilia Shelton's recent presentations during the Black Technical and Professional Communication panel hosted by Virginia Tech. During her talk, Shelton defined a "key criteria of 'good' work to be asking: does it enrich the lives of participants?" and Haywood forwarded a Black feminist methodology to avoid harm and work toward liberation, reminding viewers that research ethics—which are never neutral or objective—tell us how to work, and who and what are valued. Haywood also called for more care regarding consent practices, noting that for too long Black participants and communities were not able to consent to their own representations. Black feminist practices are central to continuing conversations on care-based, action oriented social justice work in the field.

Care-based research is another area in writing studies that overlaps with TI approaches. In their article "Research as Care," Maria Novotny and John Gagnon describe the unexpected challenges that surfaced doing research with participants who have experienced trauma. Based on their research experiences, Novotny and Gagnon offer a methodological toolkit that community-engaged scholars can adapt to their own projects. The concepts provided are not so much a checklist as a series of considerations: "1) mediating academic use, 2) responsivity to reliving trauma, 3) recognizing participant motivations, 4) collaborative meaning-making, and 5) accounting for identity evolution" (71). Each of these considerations seeks to develop a collaborative, reciprocal relationship with research participants that works against the hierarchical roles that scholars and participants too often inhabit (intentionally or unintentionally).

In a subsequent article, "Revisiting Research as Care," Novotny and Gagnon call for adopting decolonial approaches to trauma work to better enact care-based research (487). While we do not necessarily describe our work as decolonial, our TI approach worked from care-based practices in terms of eschewing normative institutional practices regarding data collection and engaging in a methodology

---

4. While important work has been done to expand TI care beyond a focus on harm to more healing-centered approaches (Ginwright), for our audience and purpose here, we have chosen to use TI practice. We find 'trauma-informed' important in that it specifically names trauma. In doing so, we aim to expand awareness about the pervasiveness of trauma across many different lived experiences, regardless of whether one is specifically studying trauma.

of visiting; one where our time as a research group was not entirely quantifiable. Metis scholar Dylan AT Miner describes this kind of "visiting" as being attuned to the doing, making, and being in the "quotidian spaces of teaching/learning" (Miner 132) where being in the presence of others is a necessary rejection of Western institutional norms about how time should be spent while doing research. While working as a research group on the MI Homeless Voice project, for example, sharing a meal together and prioritizing unstructured time for eating and visiting were integral aspects of every group session. These sorts of relationship building activities helped make our digital work together more trusting and collaborative. So, while our research still operates within Western paradigms of academic scholarship and institutions, Gagnon and Novotony's approach to care-based methods is a means to working within and resisting harmful institutional expectations.

Here, it's important for researchers to grapple more with the idea and practice of care: who is receiving care? Who is being asked to do the caring? What does care mean within a research project used for academic promotion or degree completion? While a researcher may be considered the primary beneficiary, Novotony and Gagnon's work offers important considerations for constructing research protocols that represent a caring approach. One example of a caring approach is ongoing consent throughout a project. In our work with the MI Homeless Voice project, ongoing consent meant that participants could choose to remove their work at any time during and after the project. To implement caring approaches that respond to specific participant and project needs, it's necessary to build relationships between everyone involved with the research that will lead to ongoing dialogue about a project and caring interactions.

Novotny and Gagnon's article demonstrates how scholarship that works from trauma-informed practice simultaneously engages in cultural rhetorical practice. While cultural rhetorics (CR) does not have a monopoly on storytelling or "intersectional, community-engaged approach[es]" that are "ideal for promoting dissemination and implementation of contextually relevant research" (McCauley et al.), these methods have helped shape TI approaches in our field. Two central practices in CR that inform TI-care are empathy and accountability. In CR, these two practices shape its embodied, methodological orientation that requires scholars "be willing to build meaningful theoretical frames from inside the particular culture in which they are situating their work" (Bratta and Powell). Empathy, in CR, requires that boundaries and borders between beliefs and identities be deconstructed to situate oneself in a place of openness. As such, this means that scholars build knowledge *with* a community, understanding how research is a "constellative practice" which emphasizes that "knowledge is never built by individuals but is, instead, accumulated through collective practices within specific communities" (Bratta and Powell). This situatedness is about accountability to redefining ontological orientations between the researcher and "researched." In other words, these practices forward research that is not extractive from a community and acknowledges culture as a means of understanding rhetorical practice. While some CR and TI terminology differs, both traditions focus on creating an academic culture where scholars approach care-based research methods from a project's outset.

Care is also an important element of feminist scholarship, and since the 1980s in a variety of social science fields, feminist researchers have theorized care ethics (Noddings; Gilligan; Ruddick; Tronto). These oft-cited texts shaped ethics of care theories that argued for care beyond the private sphere to shape politics and culture, and to reject "us versus them" thinking and instead extend a wider network of caring relations (Held). More, in writing studies, feminist care ethics have been discussed in composition research in collaborating on research design and implementation with participants (Kirsch and Ritchie), care as a methodological approach in medical rhetorics (Novotny and Opel), and care as a praxis for developing feminist pedagogy around issues of surveillance (Hutchinson and Novotny). The range in how feminist care ethics have been taken up both within and outside writing studies attests to the need for care in our relations and research design. There are important echoes between feminist care ethics and how care-based methods have influenced our TI approach. Conversations regarding care and the need for care to look different depending on the project and research group were important in informing our TI approach given that our design must be flexible and responsive to participant, situation, positionality, and purpose. In this way, both care-based and TI practices are deeply rhetorical.

Trauma-Informed Practice is Rhetorical Practice

As writing studies scholars, we see our contribution to developing TI methods as twofold in terms of communication and attending to emergence. In writing studies, we work in collaboration to shape, design, and create communication. At the same time, shifting to a focus on language and communication does not mean distancing from the material effects of trauma or attention to bodies. In addition to studying what language does in the world, as rhetoricians we are also invested in how language attunes us to being—or not—in relationships and in communities. In this way, we see our contribution to TI work as one with rhetorical and material implications for how we experience the world, and how we interpret and take up TI practice.

As we have stated, trauma is an ongoing experience. New and different circumstances can cause trauma responses that may be unexpected even for the person experiencing the event. Thus, a rhetorical orientation to trauma as an emergent experience is necessary. In this way, the concept of universal precaution suggests that scholars implement TI design from a project's outset and approach all participants as if they have experienced trauma in order to prepare for potential trauma response. Trauma responses can be unpredictable because triggers are not universal—they are unique to the individual and circumstance. For example, something as mundane as a song or even a television show might elicit happiness in one person but might trigger a trauma response in another. Or someone may have been working through their traumatic experience for some time but sharing that story with a new audience can trigger a trauma response. Healing is not a linear process, and because of trauma's psychobiological (i.e., embodied) effects, reliving trauma can undoubtedly be felt by and communicated through the body. As such, TI practices need to be attentive to bodies, situation, audience, and circumstance.

Because trauma is an ongoing phenomenon, it is important to invite expertise into the room to have someone trained in observing trauma responses who can respond accordingly to need and circumstance. We are not suggesting that rhetoricians must also be trained social workers or clinical specialists, but we are calling for more collaboration between researchers and trained clinicians to practice TI care appropriately. This is a call to *stay in our lane*, while not allowing *our lane* to become a reason not to engage in TI methods. For example, one collaborative possibility is to consult with TI experts on interview protocols or survey questions before conducting research, or to invite an expert from counseling services or a trusted member of the community to attend focus groups or other research meetings and in certain circumstances to lead a debrief session for participants after the meeting. In other words, we believe that TI care must go beyond only providing a resource list for someone experiencing trauma to seek out on their own.

An important topic just under the surface in this conversation is agency. In TI practices, we cannot control whether someone has a trauma response, but we can control how we approach the possibility that such a response can occur during scholarly work, and we can plan to be responsive to it if it does[5]. One way to ensure participants can act with agency is to allow them to shape their participation, and to shape the research design when possible. As Day explains, "the power to make choices about what constitutes safety and empowerment must also include participants/audiences/students, not just researchers/teachers." Although we cannot control a situation to eliminate trauma responses, we can be part of creating relations and community within a research group to have TI conversations specific to the group that extend care to one another and enable every member to determine their involvement and contribution.

Distinguishing between Research Ethics and TI Practice

Intending to avoid harm is not the same thing as actively building a trauma-informed process that offers support and care if harm occurs. From our work in creative community engaged projects, we've noticed important differences

---

5. While not the focus of our chapter, we believe that researchers can also pay attention to secondary trauma response in themselves when engaging in a scholarly project.

between what our Institutional Review Board (IRB) requires for ethical research with human subjects, and what has surfaced as ethical in trauma-informed, care-based methods.[6] Here we briefly sketch out differences between IRB requirements and what we have come to learn from working in a sometimes-interstitial space with arts-based or creative-community projects that do not always require IRB approval, yet still have the potential to cause harm to participants.

An IRB's purpose as a regulating authority and partner in doing "human subjects" research is to ensure research complies with university, state, and federal regulations to protect human subjects. IRBs are likely to require special review for human subjects research with vulnerable populations, but they do not necessarily require TI approaches.[7] Rather, IRBs focus on the consenting process, which appears to be TI, but does not necessarily require ongoing support structures. The 1979 Belmont Report describes the values undergirding IRB protocol: highlighting beneficence, respect for persons, and justice as core principles. Additionally, the report names necessary research design as informed consent, assessment of risks and benefits, and selection of subjects. The guiding principle of "do no harm" is especially salient for the legacy of abusive research the Belmont Report and university IRB offices were responding to in the 1970s. While these guiding principles can be aligned with TI practice, it is ultimately a researcher's decision to develop TI protocol. In other words, just because a research project is approved by the IRB does not automatically mean it qualifies as TI.

In rhetoric and writing, there are a range of projects that do not always require IRB review, even though the work includes participants and is sometimes participant driven. The very concept of human subjects research does not include work in oral history, documentary filmmaking, and some other arts-based projects. The MI Homeless Voice project, for instance, was a creative project more akin to documentary filmmaking than the systemic inquiry that defines "human subjects research." The gap between what counts as human subjects research according to regulating authorities and creative projects transfers a great deal of ethical decisions to scholars. Of course, oral historians, community-based researchers, and internet researchers working in sometimes ambiguous spaces have developed various ethical stances and practices to help create uniformity around ethical choices. For example, the Oral History Association's (OHA) Statement of Ethics describes a "web of mutual responsibility" made up of everyone involved in the research who work to "ensure that the narrator's perspective, dignity, privacy, and safety are respected." OHA ethics design includes informed consent, interviewee review and approval of recorded materials, and expressly calls for researcher care

---

6. We wish to note that each Institutional Review Board has its own requirements, so our discussion is limited to the regulating authorities we've worked with over our scholarly careers.

7. Although, we wish to note the IRB for the Essential Needs project used a TI approach and was approved by the IRB without any issue.

not to make promises that cannot be kept regarding research use, circulation, or preserving participant anonymity.

Community Based Participatory Research (CBPR) emerged in the early aughts as a methodology that encouraged shared ownership of research to redress the vast disparities in resources between universities and community participants. CBPR works by first collaborating with a community on a topic or issue of concern to the community "with the aim of combining knowledge and action for social change to improve community health and eliminate health disparities" (Minkler and Wallerstein 4). CBPR methods urge scholars to acknowledge "historic or current positions of power" with community partners to build relationships where "each person and stakeholder group feels valued" and to create research spaces that value lived experience (Wallerstein and Duran). And the Association of Internet Researchers (AoIR) produces current and developing guidelines for online research that might not be considered human subject specific but can still include research on and with internet users even if not institutionally considered human subject research. These approaches sketch out "a web" of ethical responses and methods that are specific and flexible to community-based and people-centered situations not always explicitly addressed through IRB review or exemption.

The differences in the previous approaches also exemplify how every project offers its own unique set of circumstances that ethical statements do not always cover or that are discovered along the way that require researcher action. One such practice that emerged during our work on MI Homeless Voice was building in ongoing moments of consent rather than a single consent form signed at the project's beginning. These multiple moments of consent meant that participants always retained ownership over their story and could choose to withdraw their story or change their participation at any time during and after the project. Of course, this level of ongoing consent can conflict with research tied to the academic calendar and/or needed to fulfill requirements for degree completion or promotion. But for the MI Homeless Voice project, ongoing consent was a practice that surfaced in collaboration with speakers during the project and remained necessary throughout. As discussed in the previous section, TI as rhetorical practice requires modification to new situations, and so, what worked for MI Homeless Voice will not translate exactly to other communities and projects. TI methods require continually attending to specificity as an ongoing process.

Toward a TI Heuristic for Writing Studies

The work of Patricia Sullivan offers a compelling argument for adapting research ethics *in situ*. (See, for example, Sullivan "Beckon, Encounter"; Lauer and Sullivan "Validity and Reliability"; Sullivan and Spilka "Qualitative Research"; and Sullivan "Beyond.") Sullivan has long advocated an approach to methodology as a flexible heuristic that produces situated knowledge as opposed to generalizable knowledge, which is more akin to how the IRB approaches research. In TI work, before a project even begins, the researcher needs to be in dialogue with their collaborators and participants determining whether, how, and to what extent their research needs to incorporate TI methods. This means that to be TI is best approached as a practice rather than as a goal to be accomplished.

Following the work of Sullivan, we offer a set of flexible, relational heuristics for TI approaches to scholarship in rhetoric and writing. We do so, however, all too aware of Euro-Western rhetoric's "impulse to taxonomize and collate, to force together various culturally distinct practices of communication or knowledge-making into a singular system or tradition" (Banks), which in turn emphasizes and reaffirms institutional barriers that complicate the building of relationships. In other words, we understand that heuristics are both useful and dangerous. They are useful because they provide scholars with a set of clear concepts and ideas that they can use for guidance in a general sense (e.g., the Belmont report describes the importance of respect, beneficence, and justice). Yet, heuristics are also dangerous because they can too easily categorize and conflate complexity in ways that diminishes critical thinking and reflection. To be effective, we believe heuristics must be positioned in conversation with other rhetorical considerations, such as institutional context, research group dynamics, inclusion of participants, collaborator needs, research topic, community, and project-specific exigencies, etc.

To caution readers, what we offer is a way of thinking about TI scholarship that should be carefully and critically utilized, and differently adapted based on a specific project and setting. Drawing from these ideas will not automatically qualify a scholarly project as TI given that trauma is incredibly complex and particular to the individual and context. That said, in our work we've found the concepts of Safety, Choice, Empowerment, Trustworthiness, Collaboration, and Cultural, Historical, and Gender/Sexuality Awareness have helped us to design, deploy, and evaluate TI practices within our research groups, and with participants. We modified the framework in Table 13.1 from the ITTIC's "Trauma Informed Organizational Change Manual" except for Inclusivity, which we added to their framework. The manual's express purpose is to help organizations adapt trauma-informed practices that may or may not involve medical care. The authors note that "similarly to how we worked with systems to adapt TIC (trauma-informed care) to TI-EP (trauma-informed educational practices) or TIM (trauma-informed medicine), the language in this manual can be adapted to your specific system" (14). The flexibility to develop and revise this TI heuristic accounts for specificity of situation and adaptation. For example, in a specific situation, one approach might be prioritized over another. These practices are meant to work in tandem, but also depend on the situation and are not hierarchically ordered. Our definitions are also intended to be developed for different contexts, depending on how, when, and for whom they're practiced. In Table 13.1, we offer a definition of each of these considerations.

In the next section of this chapter, we provide project examples to describe how our work made use of these heuristics in two very different settings. The goal is to provide readers with these descriptions to give further guidance in terms of developing and implementing rhetorically grounded and flexible methods. Each table demonstrates how we implemented our trauma-informed heuristic and provides a summary and overview of the two projects. In the paragraphs that follow the table, we expand on each of these considerations during the project's lifecycle in more detail.

Table 13.1. TI Heuristics

Heuristic	Definition
Safety	Pertains to the physical and emotional well-being of all research participants (e.g., ensuring a sense of bodily safety in a space; being attentive to signs of discomfort during research; following up with participants).
Trustworthiness	Includes providing multiple sources of information to participants about what will take place during the data collection or collaboration, how the research or what is created will be used, why, when, and under what circumstances (e.g., developing clear, ongoing consent processes; prioritizing privacy and confidentiality; responding to feedback).
Choice	Involves how much agency participants have in terms of determining how their data and contributions will be used in the research, and how they participate in the research (e.g., how much control the project grants participants over their data, story, and how these are used).
Collaboration	Approaches doing scholarly work with rather than for or on participants and works toward reciprocity and away from extractive research (e.g., eliciting feedback from all participants, checking-in and debriefing throughout the research process, and following up with participants and providing any helpful resources depending on the context and response/feedback).
Empowerment	Recognizes and builds on individual strengths and skills and fosters a scholarly atmosphere that allows participants to feel validated and affirmed during collaboration (e.g., intentionally creates productive and caring relationships so participants can contribute and participate based on their strengths and desires).
Inclusivity	Avoids language and research design approaches that directly state or assume and/or harmfully generalize cultural, familial, historical, and gender/sexuality experiences, backgrounds, and/or identities (e.g., sharing and using specified gender pronouns, inclusive language, and anti-racist practices).

Project 1: MI Homeless Voice

Navigating the work of MI Homeless Voice was uniquely rewarding and challenging. The project involved creative collaboration and did not qualify as systematic inquiry as defined by regulating authorities. In other words, we were not studying participant making practices, but instead were collaborating on creating original music compositions together to amplify the stories of people too often ignored in society. The scholarly outcome of the project was the audio composition itself, which was, in its simplest form, a digital artifact. The goal for our collaboration was to contribute to the mission of the speakers bureau by producing materials that would work to reduce the social stigma associated with experiencing homelessness and to raise awareness in our community. How we approached the project was similar to how songwriting circles or writing workshops function. That is, we were always collaborating and sharing ownership—perhaps a contested concept in this project—over what was made.[8] What was perhaps different about our collaboration is that the storytellers had ultimate creative control. They could approve or disapprove of story edits, accompanying music, artwork, and etc. (and many did exercise this choice to make sure their story was amplified in the way they wanted, particularly from a cultural perspective).

At the beginning of this chapter, Ben described listening to a story for the first time and realizing that an unforeseen exigence of the project emerged: the project was not just about recording audio stories—it was also about people who had experienced trauma, and who felt compelled to tell their stories even though doing so was sometimes difficult. What happened next in the project is that Ben brought this discovery back to the organizer of the speakers bureau to talk through a plan for working through how to keep people safe during the project work. The plan that emerged was also informed by a dialogue with colleagues who had previously done community-engaged work, and from readings about collaborating with survivors of trauma (especially impactful were Novotny and Gagnon; and Mathieu, Parks, and Rousculp).[9] The plan in some ways remained the same and in several ways its focus shifted to adopt a more TI approach moving forward. What follows isn't the entire story of the project, but a snapshot to detail how a TI approach was intentionally foundational to this digital project.

Project Plan

The original plan was to move through recording and composing quickly so that the project would be complete within 3–6 months (to record, write music, and complete the eight tracks). We would have a few meetings on campus to host

---

8. While we do not wish to muddy the waters with a more indepth discussion of ownership here, we do wish to point out that ownership has both legal and ethical conceptualizations, particularly in academic contexts and in songwriting circles.

9. Particularly, Ben would like to thank Trixie Smith for sharing experiences and resources that helped to reimagine the work of MI Homeless Voice. And Paul Feigenbaum, Mark Sullivan, and Jeff Grabill for debriefing about the project work in general.

recording activities. Then, individual music composers would reach out to storytellers via email to work on compositions. There were a few reasons for this more distributed approach. First, we committed to fund every trip the speakers would take to campus so that the project didn't cost them money (albeit it did cost each participant time). Second, many of the storytellers had jobs, and getting time off from work could be difficult. Third, modes of transportation were not always dependable or available for each participant, who lived in different parts of the state. As well, we believed moving quickly would be best for our collaborators who wanted to work on the project, as we knew they had busy schedules and lives. When we brought the project plan to our collaborators, everyone seemed to agree with the pace.

What changed, however, was the project plan slowed down so that the group could build relationships and support each other through the work outlined in the previous paragraph. We started a discussion about supporting each other, and we then asked the organizer of the speakers bureau to discuss what kind of support system they might need in place for members of the group who felt raw after telling their story or hearing someone else's. Importantly, this person was not an outsider to the community, but someone they felt could take on the role. As a result, the group selected a member of their community to run a debrief at the end of meetings and then to also check-in with people after meetings. Additionally, the group was asked if more meetings and time together would be of interest, and while some were worried about the time and cost (rightfully so), most everyone did want to come together and listen to the work as a group in support of each other more often. As a result, the budget of the project needed to change to accommodate paying for several trips to campus, in addition to paying for studio time for recording, mixing, and mastering the work.

Consent

One thing promised at the beginning that stayed the same was the consent process, which mirrored the Oral History Association's ethics guidelines to ask for consent at each step of the project. Our consent process drew considerably from the heuristics of safety, choice, and trustworthiness. The consent process explained that each person could stop collaborating at any moment without penalty or choose to re-engage after a break. To illustrate, a storyteller could record their story and decide to stop collaborating at that moment. If so, they would still receive the recorded story and they would own the rights to those files, and no one would work on developing them anymore unless additional consent was given. This consent process was intentional from the beginning of the project, as our foundational approach to the work was that at no point would ownership of each story be transferred to others (this is contrast to research studies where once data is collected, even if it is incomplete, scholars may use it to inform their study, which we believe is an extractive approach that can quickly become harmful to people who have experienced trauma). Consent continues even now that the project has ended. The storytellers choose where, when, and how to share their stories (i.e., digital files) with people. Some have made them public on a shared SoundCloud account, while others have chosen to share them in certain instances. Those who chose to make their stories public may choose to eventually make them private again.

Table 13.2. TI Heuristics applied to MI Homeless Voice.

Heuristic	Examples from MI Homeless Voice
Safety	debrief sessions at the end of meetings
	listening to story recordings together
	check-ins after particularly difficult collaboration sessions
	meeting in private spaces like conference rooms, rather than open spaces
Trustworthiness	on-going consent procedures that involve describing in detail how stories might be used at conferences, in publications, or other speaking events, and documenting these descriptions in writing
	honoring and soliciting participant feedback about the project
Choice	consent procedures that make it easy for participants to opt out of sharing their story during or after scholarly activity concludes
	creating structures that allow for artistic direction and depiction of their stories
Collaboration	giving and receiving feedback on artistic direction and/or consent procedures
	carefully invite expertise to engage in the project so that no one person fulfills too many or all the roles
	identify roles early in the project to help build community and clarify relationships
	honoring the norms that emerge from working together and name them in some way
Empowerment	asking for permission, not forgiveness
	editing out certain moments of the story that the participant later decided against including
	recomposing music if a participant felt it didn't amplify their story in a way conducive to the message
Inclusivity	spent a great deal of time listening, learning, and believing each other
	avoiding assumptions about editing out embodied sounds, including not editing stories for correctness (i.e., white supremacist language practices)
	intentionally schedule time for building relationships (such as eating together without an agenda)
	leveraging institutional resources and support to make space for people who are often ignored to tell their stories

To manage the consent and sharing process, we ended the project by writing an agreement about how stories could be used.[10] What we made were digital artifacts—original story and music compositions. Such artifacts travel all too easily in digital spaces, and so our agreement outlined appropriate ways for sharing each other's stories, including describing the kind of risks involved with doing so. The goal was to outline a set of circumstances where how people encountered the stories would speak to the project's original goals, and to preview the ways copyright holders might protect themselves in cases of abuse or misuse. The agreement attempted to help assure, in part, that we were not inadvertently objectifying homelessness as an issue.

Meetings

Our meetings became co-working sessions, and we met nearly once a month during the project for between 2–4 hours. Often, we would eat together at the start of our meetings—just to make sure there were times for us to connect as people without necessarily focusing on our project goals (for more on this method, see Miner). During these meetings, we would also engage in activities like listening to story recordings and drafts of music. When we would do that work, our goal would be to offer feedback, but also to be together and offer support while listening and responding to each other's impressions. In many ways, our meetings acted like a writing workshop in that people had opportunities to give and receive feedback. However, giving feedback was not a requirement of being together, and neither was sharing your story. In other words, people could choose not to share their stories. Or the group could choose to talk through a story, music, or another element of the project in more depth. As a result, it was important to have an agenda for our meetings that was flexible. To be clear, we would set an agenda of items to accomplish, but then we knew that we might adjust these goals depending on what emerged during our meetings. The goal was to be responsive to emergent needs and concerns, and in doing so, to build trusting relationships by making space for people to speak up when they felt comfortable doing so. The flexible structure of our meetings became something that was dependable. In other words, if any issue surfaced about the project, the meeting spaces were one avenue for bringing attention to these situations to the whole group. As well, responding to emergent needs allowed others to lead at times, particularly when it came to questions about a speakers bureau event outside of the MI Homeless Voice project.

Project 2: Designing for Supporting Equity in Essential Needs

This project began in the spring of 2018 as a learning community with student success stakeholders ranging from student services and housing, faculty members

---

10. Importantly, Bump Halbritter helped to inform the idea of writing an agreement among members of the group.

and graduate students, and other resource offices distributed across our campus. We wanted to understand what resources were available for students experiencing acute and chronic basic needs issues, and how they would access these resources. From this initial campus networking, we learned that there are a variety of resources available to students, but accessing resources often came down to knowing the right person in the right office of our large, decentralized campus.

And to find the right person in the right office, students need to repeat their story to multiple people which can be both a detriment to seeking out help and potentially retraumatizing. Our research group coalesced from these early conversations and included two faculty members and a graduate student in rhetoric and writing, the director of the Student Parent Resource Center, a master's in social-work graduate student, a research consultant hired through the provost's office, and our initiative was hosted by our campus's interdisciplinary research hub. We set out to answer: how can the student experience of accessing support services for chronic and acute basic needs issues be equitable, without stigma, private, and express values of compassion, kindness, and universal access? The research group, which was partially geographically distributed, took on several projects that involved digital elements, including the development of a web portal that would assemble all the basic needs resources available to campus. As well, interviews and focus groups were run, partially due to COVID-19, using digital tools like Zoom.

Project Planning

Our collaboration was open to anyone who had attended the learning community conversations or were interested in contributing to the project. We had consistent bi-monthly meetings, but every participant could determine their involvement and defined their role over time as the work developed. For example, one graduate student in the group attended a lot of the early meetings to observe the research design, how the group chose who to interview, and how to work on a project across a huge university campus. As we continued working together, people would take on different roles, and no single person defined the vision, or determined what others would contribute.

After conducting and transcribing seventeen interviews with different campus offices (e.g., housing and dining services, the Office of International Student Services, financial aid, the registrar's office, the graduate school, campus mental health and counseling services, the campus food bank, campus police—to name just a few), we determined that developing an online portal would provide a centralized access point to make resources currently available more apparent and accessible to students, staff, and faculty. In addition to connecting people with resources, this portal would also educate the campus community about what essential needs are and raise awareness in order to reduce social stigma about essential needs services.

Table 13.3. TI Heuristics applied to Essential Needs

Heuristic	Examples from Essential Needs
Safety	conducted focus groups confidentially on Zoom (gave people instructions to temporarily change their names to pseudonyms and to keep their cameras off)
	invited a mental health counselor to participate in focus group sessions to serve as a resource
	developed protocol that avoids prompting people to re-live their trauma
Trustworthiness	establishing team norms and relationships through regular meetings and sharing in project labor
	discussing support resources available with team members and participants if/when working on projects related to trauma can cause secondary trauma
	communicating with participants about what to expect before, during, and after focus groups regarding their participation and interactions with the team
Choice	consent procedures that make it easy to opt out at any time
	sending research questions and other protocol to participants prior to consent procedures to see if they feel comfortable answering the questions or engaging the research tasks
	reminding participants explicitly and implicitly that discussing their own experiences is not a requirement of the research
Collaboration	working with trauma-informed clinical experts on campus developing interview and focus group protocols
	establishing, from the beginning of a project, to make clear the choices people could make to do research or participate in ways that suited their own individual goals and needs
	schedule a collaborative data analysis session with participants
	carefully invite expertise to engage in the project so that no one person fulfills too many or all the roles
Empowerment	invite research team and participants to take breaks from the project work
	sharing de-identified reports with participants, and sharing data in general
	discuss with participants how the data will be used
	establish team norms around how data might be used outside of the research team
	focus group facilitation techniques that ask participants if they want to share, but do not require they do
Inclusivity	use research to advocate for and elucidate the impact of trauma experiences on campus, particularly its systemic impact on students
	highlight discriminatory and other harmful practices tied to race, gender, relationship violence, etc.
	demonstrate how to improve or add on to existing support systems and resources

In working across university systems, we took a systemic approach to basic needs issues. That is, people face acute and chronic need issues because of systematic inequality tied to race, gender, sexuality and sometimes cultural identity and background not because of "personal failure." We began researching basic needs resources available at universities across the country. This was a moment when a member of our research group encouraged us to move to the language of *essential* needs, and away from basic and connotations of deficiency, or remediation. *Essential*, on the other hand, suggests essence; something essential is a *sine qua non*. Without it, nothing else matters. And so, we adopted the language of "Spartan essentials" in designing our online resource portal.

Research Protocols

In developing our IRB protocols, as a group we wrote our interview questions, focus group protocols, and pre-and-post focus group surveys collaboratively to draw from our collective positions and knowledge to think through different possible responses. After our initial drafts, we sought out feedback from TI scholars in psychology to revise accordingly. Following this feedback and revision, we then submitted our TI protocols to the IRB for review and subsequent approval. In addition to collaborating with TI experts, our group also engaged in doing research on TI approaches to think through adapting them to our work in intentional ways.

Doing the Research

We had planned to conduct focus groups on campus with different combinations of one faculty or staff member, one graduate student from our research group, and a licensed counselor. But these plans then needed to be adapted due to COVID-19, which meant the focus groups moved to Zoom. However, shifting the focus groups to Zoom allowed students to participate anonymously since they were given instructions regarding how to change their display name in Zoom to a pseudonym and had a choice not turn on their video. This focus group design ended up more fully protecting participant identity and ensuring confidentiality as a result. Additionally, our focus group sorting survey asked participants if they had requests for who was in the focus group with them, to help them shape the focus group session in important ways.

Emphasizing Care

In our work together, we explicitly discussed how doing work around trauma can affect researchers. Every time a new person joined our group, like when we hired two undergraduate students to work on designing the online portal, part of the group onboarding was to discuss what trauma is, and how to recognize secondary-trauma responses that might occur. Everyone on the team was encouraged to take time away from the project if they needed to, and our deadlines were flexible to accommodate any need that arose. We built-in regular check-ins at the beginning of our meetings to share how we were doing with the work. It was not required that anyone share, but we made sure to begin our time on-the-clock with conversation and any feedback regarding how the work was going. We added a counselor to project work in key moments to help provide additional support as well.

Conclusion: Trauma-Informed Practice as Rhetorical Methodology

We wish to remind readers that there is no checklist that can ensure something is TI for every participant in every situation. However, working from universal precaution—approaching every participant as if they have experienced trauma to ensure equitable forms of safety, choice, and empowerment to build trust when contributing to scholarly work—means that researchers approach all of their work as TI from the outset rather than as an ad hoc consideration. While most projects in writing studies contain digital methods, we have tried to illustrate that TI research practices are not about a single method or moment, but that universal precaution needs to undergird research design from the beginning of a project and inform every interaction and follow-up between collaborators. The reason why it's difficult to isolate specific methods as TI is because trauma is emergent, and specific to an individual. While we cannot predict what's potentially traumatic for every participant, as researchers and collaborators, we can be sensitive to the possibility of trauma responses, and then respond with support and care. Furthermore, we must be aware how our positionalities as individuals and as researchers might impact our ability to sense trauma responses. As a result, we see universal precaution as the important first step toward being TI, and that our heuristic provides a flexible approach to structure and implement TI practices throughout a project.

In our work, we have experienced how digital projects can engage and/or amplify trauma in unpredictable ways: a long intake of breath captured in an audio file, a glassy-eyed pause in a video file, a music track that triggers a painful memory. Given such possibilities, digital writing scholars must understand the potential for trauma response in and to their work. But we cannot assume that an institution's research review protocols were designed to fully mitigate such potential. And so, we have argued here that digital writing scholars must work collaboratively with participants and with professionals trained to address potential trauma responses. What we hope to have offered in this chapter is a heuristic that promotes a sense of safety and trust among all participants by ensuring that everyone can exert control over their contributions and feel themselves to be an integral part of a project, rather than merely an object of study or an outcome of a project.

Note

We wish to acknowledge the intellectual contributions of SEEN team members Kimberly Steed-Page, Reggie Noto, Kaitlyn Nguyen, and Bill Heinrich for impacting the work of the Spartan Essentials project. We also thank the Michigan State University's (MSU) Hub for Innovation in Learning and Technology; MSU Provost's Office, MSU Office of Student Affairs and Services; the MSU College of Arts and Letters; and, Orbis, Mindset, all of whom financially supported our work, but had no role in the design of the study, the analysis and interpretation of the data or the writing of, nor the decision to publish the manuscript.

Works Cited

Banks, Will. "Rhetorics for All of Us." *Cultural Rhetorics Consortium*, http://cultrhetconsortium.org/#:~:text=Cultural%20rhetorics%20is%20the%20study,an%20collaboration%20with%20each%20other. Accessed 16 July 2020.

Belmont Report: Ethical Principles and Guidelines for the Protection of Human Subjects of Research. Department of Health, Education, and Welfare. 18 Apr. 1979, https://www.hhs.gov/ohrp/sites/default/files/the-belmont-report-508c_FINAL.pdf.

Berman, Jeffrey. *Risky Writing: Self-Disclosure and Self-Transformation in the Classroom*. U of Massachusetts P, 2001.

Bishop, Wendy, and Amy Hodges. "Loss and Letter Writing." *Trauma and the Teaching of Writing*, edited by Shane Borrowman, SUNY P, 2005, pp. 141–56.

Borrowman, Shane, editor. *Trauma and the Teaching of Writing*. SUNY P, 2005.

Bratta, Phil, and Malea Powell. "Introduction to the Special Issue: Entering the Cultural Rhetorics Conversations." *Enculturation: A Journal of Rhetoric, Writing, and Culture*, vol. 21, no. 1, 2016.

Carello, Janice, and Lisa D. Butler. "Potentially Perilous Pedagogies: Teaching Trauma is not the same as Trauma-Informed Teaching." *Journal of Trauma and Dissociation*, vol. 15, no. 2 2014, pp. 153–68.

Costa, Dora L., Noelle Yetter, and Heather DeSomer. "Intergenerational Transmission of Paternal Trauma Among US Civil War ex-POWs." *Proceedings of the National Academy of Sciences*, vol. 115, no. 44, 2018, https://doi.org/10.1073/pnas.1803630115.

Day, Michelle. "On Trauma and Safety: Toward Trauma-Informed Research Methods." *Making Future Matters*, edited by Rita Wysocki and Mary P. Sheridan, Computers and Composition Digital Press; Utah State UP, 2018, http://ccdigitalpress.org/makingfuturematters

———. "Wounds and Writing: Building Trauma-Informed Approaches to Writing Pedagogy." 2019. University of Louisville, dissertation, https://doi.org/10.18297/etd/3178.

Felitti, Vincent J., Robert F. Anda, Dale Nordenberg, David F. Williamson, Alison M. Spitz, Valerie Edwards, Mary P. Koss, and James S. Marks. "The Relationship of Childhood Abuse and Household Dysfunction to Many of the Leading Causes of Death in Adults." *American Journal of Preventive Medicine*, vol. 14, no. 4, 1998, pp. 245–58.

Ginwright, Shawn. "The Future of Healing: Shifting from Trauma Informed Care to Healing Centered Engagement." *Medium*, 31 May 2018, https://medium.com/@ginwright/the-future-of-healing-shifting-from-trauma-informed-care-to-healing-centered-engagement-634f557ce69c

Gagnon, John T., and Maria Novotny. "Revisiting Research as Care: A Call to Decolonize Narratives of Trauma." *Rhetoric Review*, vol. 39, no. 4, 2020, pp. 486–501.

Gilligan, Carol. *In a Different Voice: Psychological Theories and Women's Development*. Harvard UP, 1982.

Harris, Maxine Ed, and Roger D. Fallot. *Using Trauma Theory to Design Service Systems*. Jossey-Bass, 2001.

Haywood, Constance, panelist. Panel discussion. "Black Research Methodologies, Methods, and Ethics." Black Technical and Professional Communication Task Force Virtual Panel, 30, Nov. 2020, hosted by Virginia Tech.

Held, Virginia. Interview by Richard Marshall. *3:AM Magazine*, 20 Mar. 2013, https://philosophy.commons.gc.cuny.edu/virginia-held-interviewed-at-3am-the-ethics-of-care/.

Hutchinson, Les, and Maria Novotony. "Teaching a Critical Digital Literacy of Wearables: A Feminist Surveillance of Care Pedagogy." *Computers and Composition*, vol. 50, 2018, pp. 105–20.

Kirsch, Gesa E., and Joy S. Ritchie. "Beyond the Personal: Theorizing a Politics of Location in Composition Research." *College Composition and Communication*, vol. 46, no. 1, 1995, pp. 7–29.

Lauer, Janice M., and Patricia Sullivan. "Validity and Reliability as Social Constructions." *Professional Communication: The Social Perspective*, edited by Nancy Roundy Blyler and Charlotte Thralls, Sage, 1993, pp. 163–76.

Mathieu, Paul, Steven J. Parks, and Tiffany Rousculp, editors. *Circulating Communities: The Tactics and Strategies of Community Publishing*. Lexington Books, 2011.

McCauley, Heather, Rebecca Campbell, NiCole Buchanan, and Carrie Moylan. "Advancing Theory, Methods, and Dissemination in Sexual Violence Research to Build a More Equitable Future: An Intersectional, Community-Engaged Approach." *Violence Against Women*, vol. 25, no. 16, 2019, pp. 1906–1931, https://doi.org/10.1177/1077801219875823.

Minkler, Meredith and Nina Wallerstein, editors. *Community Based Participatory Research in Health*. Jossey-Bass, 2003.

Miner, D. A. "Mawadisidiwag Miinawaa Wiidanokiindiwag // They Visit and Work Together." *Makers, Crafters, Educators: Working for Cultural Change*, edited by E. Garber, L. Hochtritt, and M. Sharma, Routledge, 2019, pp. 131–34.

Noddings, Nel. *Caring: A Feminine Approach to Ethics and Moral Education*. U of California P, 1984.

Novotny, Maria, and Dawn S. Opel. "Situating Care as Feminist Rhetorical Action in Two Community-Engaged Health Projects." *Peitho*, vol. 22, no. 1, 2019, https://cfshrc.org/article/situating-care-as-feminist-rhetorical-action-in-two-community-engaged-health-projects/

Novotny, Maria, and John T. Gagnon. "Research as Care: A Shared Ownership Approach to Rhetorical Research in Trauma Communities." *Reflections*, vol. 18, no. 1, 2018, pp. 71–101.

Rothschild, Babette, and Bessel A. van der Kolk. "Utilizing EMDR and DBT Techniques in Trauma and Abuse Recovery Groups." *EMDR Solutions: Pathways to Healing*, edited by Robin Shapiro, W.W. Norton, 2005, pp. 263–82.

Ruddick, Sara. *Maternal Thinking: Toward a Politics of Peace*. Beacon Press, 1989.

Shelton, Cecilia, panelist. Panel Discussion "Black Activists as Technical Communicators." Black Technical and Professional Communication Task Force Virtual Panel, 30 Nov. 2020, hosted by Virginia Tech.

Stein, Dan M., et al. "DSM-5 and ICD-11 Definitons of Posttraumatic Stress Disorder: Investigating 'Narrow' and 'Broad' Approaches." *Depression and Anxiety*, vol. 31, no. 6, 2014, pp. 494–50, https://doi.org/10.1002/da.22279.

Sullivan, Patricia. "Beckon, Encounter, Experience: The Danger of Control and the Promise of Encounters in the Study of User Experience." *Rhetoric and Experience Architecture*, edited by Liza Potts and Michael Salvo, Parlor Press, 2017, pp. 17–40.

———. "Beyond a Narrow Conception of Usability Testing." *IEEE Transactions on Professional Communication* vol. 32, no. 4, 1989, pp. 256–64.

Sullivan, Patricia, and Rachel Spilka. "Qualitative Research in Technical Communication: Issues of Value, Identity, and Use." *Technical Communication*, vol. 39, no. 4, 1992, pp. 592–606.

Trauma-Informed Organizational Change Manual. The Institute on Trauma and Trauma-Informed Care Buffalo Center for Social Research, 2019, https://socialwork.buffalo.edu/social-research/institutes-centers/institute-on-trauma-and-trauma-informed-care/Trauma-Informed-Organizational-Change-Manualo.html.

Tronto, Joan C. *Moral Boundaries: A Political Argument for an Ethic of Care*. Routledge, 1993.

Violence Prevention: About the CDC-Kaiser ACE Study. Centers for Disease Control and Prevention, 13 Apr. 2020, https://www.cdc.gov/violenceprevention/acestudy/about.html

Wallerstein, Nina, and Bonnie Duran. "Using Community-Based Participatory Research to Address Health Disparities." *Health Promotion Practice*, vol. 7, no. 3, 2006, pp. 312–23, https://doi.org/10.1177/1524839906289376.

Walton, Rebecca, Kristen Moore, and Natasha Jones. *Technical Communication after the Social Justice Turn: Building Coalitions for Action*. Routledge, 2019.

# Chapter 14. Considerations for Internet Participant Selection: Algorithms, Power Users, Overload, Conventionalization, and Participant Protection

John R. Gallagher
UNIVERSITY OF ILLINOIS

> Purposeful [participant] selection, though, is more than a technique to access data; our selection choices frame who and what matters as data (Freeman, 2000). These choices interface the other methods in a study to ultimately become the stories that are told. Consider, for example, the intersection of participant selection and interview analysis. The participant's story is embedded in a matrix of researcher choices: research questions, selection criteria, interview style, analysis technique, and countless other choices. Thus, purposeful selection is a mechanism for making meaning, not just uncovering it. From this perspective, purposeful selection is epistemological; researchers construct versions of reality grounded in their selection choices. (700)
>
> – Earl Reybold, Jill Lammert, and Stacia Stribling

Theorizing participant selection needs to account for a small number of users who are responsible for a large amount of internet activity. Influencers and celebrities dominate Twitter, thereby creating misperceptions about how often the "average" Twitter user participates. Users who participate frequently and have influence on other users often have different perceptions and habits than those who are lurkers or users who participate less often. In terms of methodology, these "power users" may skew dataset averages because data collected about them are not representative. Recruiting power users is but one key consideration when selecting participants.

This chapter addresses five challenges for participant selection with respect to internet research. These challenges are 1) algorithms, 2) power users, 3) overload of possible participants, 4) conventionalization of experiences, and 5) participant protection from online toxic communities. In doing so, I advocate for active reflection on the ways participant selection processes shape an empirical internet-based study. Reflecting on participant research helps to "question our own assumptions" to "actively" and "progressively" change our own habits (Agboka 299). In turn, this questioning can begin to address cultural hegemony in academic research (Agboka 299).

First Challenge: Algorithms May Invisibly Shape Participant Selection

Algorithms can shape how participants are selected. Algorithms spotlight, often invisibly, atypical users, such as power users. Algorithms are mathematical expressions used to scale up human-based decisions. If we critique algorithmic bias, then we critique human bias that has been transformed into *automated routines*. One aspect that separates algorithms from their programmers and designers, however, is their ability to make decisions without human input. From this perspective, algorithms possess a sense of agency that is akin to human agency but is still dependent on human agency. Algorithms have been around since ancient times. For example, Babylonians used algorithms for factorization. For the past several decades, grocery store companies have used algorithms to determine the items customers are likely to buy based on their shopping history. Web crawlers, such as Google, index the internet via algorithms that use keywords and other variables to systematically make the world wide web searchable. With the rise of vast, real-time social media networks and the scale of digital infrastructure, algorithms display, collate, and filter users that researchers can see.

Considering how algorithms shape participant selection is a key challenge for internet researchers. We need to account for the degree to which our access to participants is determined by algorithms or other models that sort users automatically. What we encounter as researchers on our own web pages or social media feeds is not what all users encounter. This issue is not a post-modern or post-structuralist concern either: web pages are literally different depending on the algorithms used to tailor web pages based on user activity, account history, and tracking data.

Algorithms typically use some form of reach, or what we might colloquially call popularity, to sort users into various "bins." Some bins are easily viewed whereas others fall into obscurity. These differences lead to websites literally appearing differently to different users. A concrete example of this algorithmic differentiation is algorithmic price discrimination. Synthesizing multiple studies, law professor Oren Bar-Gill writes the following:

> Uber, Amazon, Staples, and the online video game store Steam were found to vary price by geographic location and, in Uber's case, also by the time of day. B&Q, a British multinational company, tested in its brick-and-mortar stores digital price tags that interfaced with customers' phones and adjusted the displayed price based on the customer's loyalty cards data and spending habits. Grocery stores are experimenting with digitized and personalized pricing using e-coupons. Allstate was criticized for optimizing prices based on its calculated likelihood that

individual users would comparison-shop before purchasing insurance. (218)

Price discrimination presents methodological concerns for internet researchers: web pages are not only interactive ("Web 2.0"), but they are also customized. When researchers recruit internet users to interview, survey, and observe, those participants may likely experience different web pages. To be clear, this algorithmic price discrimination and other algorithmic determinations are not simply a matter of different interfaces due to accessing websites via mobile or desktop technologies; this issue can be identified by asking participants how they access the internet. Rather, algorithmic determinations are less identifiable because they function in the background of web pages, often taking innumerable variables into account. Consider that social media networks such as Facebook, Instagram, LinkedIn, TikTok, Twitter, and YouTube use thousands of variables to determine social networks newsfeeds, i.e., who sees what posts.

Accounting for what participants view on their web pages clarifies selection criteria by making those criteria explicit rather than assumed. It leads to transparent research procedures and consistency for comparison across participants. I have found three ways to account for algorithms when recruiting participants. First, I ask participants about the advertisements they see on their respective digital accounts. Second, I request some screenshots from participants. These images can help researchers determine how participants' view of web pages differ from our own. Screenshots can also help researchers more clearly determine differences between power users and non-power users by documenting how notifications and other interfaces shape participants' viewpoints and perspectives. For example, power users are likely to get many notifications. Third, before formally recruiting participants, I ask potential participants about their perspectives about algorithms and the degree to which algorithms play an active role in their activity. I usually do this over email. This third consideration helps me to understand participants' own metacognition about how they are sorted by algorithms.

Second Challenge: Power Users

The second challenge to participant selection, as I've alluded to, is to identify "power users" to understand how selection will shape research findings. The term "power" does not imply that power users are good or bad. I also want to avoid a conflation of the term with Foucauldian notions of power. Rather, "power" users possess an ability to hold influence over other users and generate a larger amount of activity when compared to typical users. I use power to invoke the concept of power laws, or that idea that the functional relationship of one variable changes in proportion to the other. Long tail functions are one example of power laws. An anecdotal example of power laws is the "1 percent rule of Web 2.0 culture" wherein one percent of users are responsible for the content and the rest of users do not produce content.

Internet researchers have found the phenomenon of power users in a variety of contexts and digital spaces. I found it in my research of a Facebook forum (Gallagher *Interactive*; Gallagher "Five") and in the distribution of commenter activity on articles in *The New York Times* (Gallagher et al.). I found that out of ~450,000 comments from *The New York Times*, the top 0.49 percent of commenters account for approximately 17.2 percent of all comments (163). Technical communication scholars Liza Potts, Rebekah Small, and Michael Trice found a similar pattern in that nine users (out of tens of thousands) were responsible for 20 percent of posts on reddit (359). Communications scholars Todd Graham and Scott Wright found an even more radical distribution of what they call superparticipants, wherein .4 percent of users were responsible for 47 percent of a forum's activity (631). Brian Weeks, Alberto Ardevol-Abreu, and Homero Gil de Zúñiga performed a survey of opinion leaders, determining that "power users" (my term) can leverage their active participation into real influence on other users and for online forums themselves.

Attending to powers users is important because I worry that my own work is guilty of recruiting power users and not more representative of typical users on their specific platform. This worry is informed by my personal life: I am married to an engineer who performs cutting-edge research in the area of cavitation rheology as well as cutting of soft materials (think here of cutting polymers). This engineer consistently challenges my research, calling into question many unstated assumptions. Also called into question are issues of generalization: how can I make decisions and conclusions based on just a few case studies? I need to clarify and reflect on my choices not only in my scholarship but also in my daily life whenever I discuss my research in a domestic setting.

Understanding how a power user can impact data was, for me, a useful lesson on how to learn of the importance of power users' participation (and whether to recruit them or not). In my dissertation, I conducted observations of a private Facebook group because I was interested in how writers develop strategies for incubating participation in a closed group. The group discussed politics, often in heated fashion. I obtained IRB access and consent from the administrator, Tracy Monroe (pseudonym), and the members themselves. I had a hunch that Monroe was not only administering the group (deciding who could join and who needed to be removed) but also actively managing the group. Monroe set rules and told me that she tried to model behavior for the group by posing questions and initiating posts.

My hunch about what was happening with Monroe's case, however, was not enough to indicate the *degree* to which Monroe was managing the group. I had many *assertions* about Monroe's activity, but my engineering spouse asked me to defend my claims with data-driven methods. For this reason, I web-scraped the entire forum (August 1, 2012–August 1, 2013), which resulted in 5622 total posts and comments. Monroe was responsible for ~28 percent of all posts and ~26 percent of all comments. The average character length of her posts was 377 characters whereas the average character length of the rest of the entire group was 250. Given that the forum had 129 members at that time, these numbers demonstrated that Monroe was a power user. She was the most frequent group member, and her posts were the longest. She exerted a great amount of influence on the group.

This large dataset helped me to contextualize and describe Monroe's activity as a power user and to describe other group members as more or less typical. For instance, when Monroe wrote short posts or comments, I could consequently describe this behavior as atypical for Monroe's own activity, but these shorter posts reflected the activities of the typical member of the Facebook group under study. Without the general trends of the group, I would have had no broader context to fall back upon when describing forum members' individual posts or Monroe's activity.

Monroe's case study helped prepare me for being careful about participant selection and performing a lot of contextual work *before* contacting possible participants. In this sense, it was a crucial experience for what I call "selection context" or what Reybold, Lammert, and Stribling call "subjective focus" (701). For them, selection is more than a rote set of choices. They write:

> Selection as method requires researchers to be aware that choosing sites and participants for our research is more than a technical process. As Peshkin (2001) reminded us, these choices are the 'selection and choice of what to perceive' (p. 251). How we perceive the research issue impacts who we perceive to be at the core of that issue and thereby what we hope to learn from those whom we have identified. (703)

With this perspective, Reybold, Lammert, and Stribling advocate for selection as an extension of researchers' ". . . theoretical and conceptual framework" (702). From Monroe's case, I learned I needed to call my own assumptions as well as my participants' assumptions about their digital activity into question because the scale of internet research makes it difficult to determine how different users view such networks. For example, as Kristin Arola ("Design") argues, digital technologies that use standardized interfaces ascribe behaviors to users, thereby engendering normative, often colonizing, behaviors. These behaviors can simultaneously lead users to perceive that other users are having similar experiences to their own. But as Arola ("Land-Based") has demonstrated, there are a variety of digital designs possible to users, which can produce a litany of possible experiences—possibly overloading researchers with too many participants to address.

Third Challenge: Overload

For internet research, the sheer volume and variety of participants presents practical considerations. In many ways, internet research inverts typical participant selection: the problem isn't a lack of willing participants but too many possible participants. Recruitment thus becomes less about finding participants and more about developing detailed selection criteria for participant recruitment and winnowing down possible pools of participants for sampling.

Selection procedures are the most important step for researchers (internet or not) to develop because they help researchers identify who should or could be included in a research design. We need to identify and interrogate our 1) own research inquiries, 2) the tools we have at our disposal, and 3) our methodological and epistemological commitments. I avoid the phrase "research questions" in the previous sentence because we often cannot formulate our inquiries into formalized questions until we have identified tools, conducted background research, and thoroughly consulted relevant literature. From this standpoint, selection procedures (not yet principles of selection) are an iterative, non-linear, and recursive process. In this way, selection procedures generate principles of selection, or the categories and elements that help me to determine who I should ask to participate in my research projects.

When I am beginning a new project, I initially sketch out these three elements on a blank piece of paper. I usually make three columns. I prefer unlined paper because I can draw arrows to generate connections between my inquiries, tools, and commitments. I try to avoid using the screen because I have ADHD and screens tend to overstimulate my thought process and my eyes. However, developing a personalized process is part of the research process. I have found this personally rewarding too, as it helps me to think iteratively through my own perspectives while I formulate questions. Upon developing these procedures, I consider the *principles of selection* that determine the types of people I aim to recruit.

Principles of selection allow internet researchers to grapple with overload in coherent ways. With the development of circulation studies (Gries; Edwards "Circulation"; Eyman) and spreadable media (Jenkins), data, discourse, and messages are on multiple platforms simultaneously, often with contradictory audience reception and varying amplifications. By amplification, I mean different messages can be increased or decreased depending on discourse producer, audience reception, platform, and interface. Due to this overwhelming amount of information, we need reflexive, detailed principles of selection that use some form of real-time analysis or note-taking.

Sara Riddick has offered one such approach through what she calls "digital drifting" or where researchers take notes on the affective nature of real-time events that are streamed through social media platforms. Riddick's approach calls for researchers to observe the live reactions used on Facebook or YouTube video to gauge how audiences receive a particular message, which in Riddick's case are political speeches. Riddick's approach can be leveraged effectively as a tool for selecting participants because researchers can find audiences who are reacting to discourses and attempt to recruit those users.

More broadly, principles of selection encourage us to inculcate higher awareness of sampling techniques and approaches. All researchers should aim to limit under/over sampling and eliminate sample bias.[1] Under and over sampling involves taking too many or too few datapoints, respectively, from a dataset. For participant selection, that dataset is potential participants. To be clear, principles of selection may focus on a particular group, leading researchers to focus on one class or group of participants (this focus is not sample bias but researcher selection). Oversampling, in qualitative human subjects research, occurs less frequently due to the labor involved. Under sampling, conversely, occurs frequently due to the labor-intensive process of in-depth qualitative research, such as ethnographies that require time intensive participant observations and interviews.

I have found the following principles of selection to be especially useful: accessibility, time frame(s), and participant's knowledge about research inquiries. For internet research specifically, however, other principles might need to be considered. Platform usage, audience reception (for example, comments), and likes/retweets/views and other qualitative affordances (Tarsa) are three such principles of selection. One principle of selection I found useful in my work was to reorient principles of selection to include users who had large amounts of audience reception, in other words, lots of comments. These users, who often were power users themselves, could thus speak about considering audiences after their texts were published, thereby enabling me to determine the activities writers engage after the publication of their work. Another principle of selection could include whether (and to what degree) digital writers respond to their audiences. These two principles could be applied to non-internet research, but they are both especially important for internet researchers who aim to account for digital writers and content producers who circulate their work on platforms such as TikTok, Twitter, Snapchat, Reddit, and Facebook.

Fourth Challenge: Conventionalization of Experiences

Conventionalization is an expectation of regularized and routinized patterns of behaviors. Conventionalization is a key issue with respect to participant selection. Internet researchers need to be aware how and to what extent the participant responses they receive are manufactured not by experiences but by technological templates, cultural norms, and individual memories. Derek Edwards and Neil Mercer, in a study of classroom conventionalization, describe the concept as a "cultural basis of thinking and remembering, especially with the process of 'conventionalization,' through which cultural symbols, signs, and texts, and the mental schemata that used them, took on their recognized properties" (92). Digital networks because they use prefabricated, standardized templates (Arola "Design"), encourage users to conventionalize their experiences. These

---

1. Sample bias is different than researcher bias. Researcher bias is inescapable, largely due the methodological and epistemological commitments researchers bring to their projects.

standardized interfaces enable possible participants to extrapolate their experiences to the general user or the culture of the internet platform or digital space.

For example, I am likely to encounter dramatically different conventionalization if I recruit participants on Reddit who identify as women versus those who identify as men. Alternatively, if I recruited power users, these participants are likely to conventionalize and routinize replying as a norm of the forum or space whereas typical users would report replying less frequently. In my own research, I try to limit making cultural extrapolations inferences from a single participant or even group of participants unless I have a representative sample that properly samples the population under study.

In my experience, conventionalization is difficult to identify until a large pool of participants has been recruited. Once a sample has been identified and recruited, I tend to rethink my recruitment procedures because my current participants may be warping (in good or bad ways) the data I have been collecting and analyzing. I attempt to account for conventionalization via this reconceptualization process. But, as with all naturalized routines and habits, conventionalization is simply an important element that researchers must be aware of when they select participants.

Fifth Challenge: Participant Protection from Toxic Communities

The final challenge I address in this chapter is considering how to protect participants' identities as *part of the recruitment process*. Internet-based participants face a greater threat from their participation in academic research because the scale of possible threats and harm is greater than if they were an offline participant. It's also important to remember this harm is also possible for researchers who identify as women, something that researchers Erika Sparby, Adrienne Massanari, and Whitney Phillips have addressed in their scholarship. Identifying possible publication venues and what happens to scholarship after it is published is vital to protecting participants. For example, considering where articles are stored, such as public venues, should be considered when participants are recruited. Related, testing participants' activity through online search and determining if participants are at-risk for coming up in easy-to-access searches could be an element in participant selection.

With respect to this latter element, my personal preference is to search online for participants' identities and activities before recruiting them as a participant. I tend to collect numerous texts from a potential participant, usually via an automated process called web-scraping. After I collect those texts, I plug in different sentences, phrases, and "turn of phrases" from the participant to determine if those texts come up in a Google search. This prevents future participants from being targeted by toxic online communities if that community accesses my research.

Conclusion: Granularity as a Response to Scale

All researchers engaged in qualitative human subject's research need to develop metacognition about participant selection. It's an important step but can be overlooked as an uncomplicated one. It is even more critical for internet researchers due to the scale of digital networks. While this chapter has addressed five challenges for participant selection, there are many that remain unaddressed. All these issues grapple in some way with the idea of scale—because the internet is, after all, a massive network.

While computer scientists and engineers try to model massive network behaviors and address scale in their research, *granularity* is an alternative answer to the question of the internet's massive scale for qualitative researchers. And it's one that writing studies and other qualitatively oriented fields are equipped to address. The stories of participants, told in detail, help to make the internet more than a set of websites driven by corporate profit and user data. How, why, what, and when user-participants communicate, write, inscribe all points to the granular detail needed for internet research. When selecting participants, then, I advocate for finding participants who can narrate their digital experiences in detail and who have extensive records of their digital lives. More importantly, internet researchers need to dwell in the spaces of their participants, likely even before recruiting them. I believe, then, that determining why each participant is selected makes for good practice. Being considerate about each participant's narrative could push a research project forward helps to be deliberate about how and why participants are selected.

Works Cited

Agboka, Godwin Y. "Decolonial Methodologies: Social Justice Perspectives in Intercultural Technical Communication Research." *Journal of Technical Writing and Communication*, vol. 44, no. 3, 2014, pp. 297–327, https://doi.org/10.2190/TW.44.3.e.

Arola, Kristin L. "A Land-Based Digital Design Rhetoric." *Routledge Companion to Digital Writing and Rhetoric*, edited by Jonathan Alexander and Jacqueline Rhodes, Routledge, 2018, pp. 199–213.

———. "The Design of Web 2.0: The Rise of the Template, The Fall of Design." *Computers and Composition*, vol. 27, no. 1, Mar. 2010, pp. 4–14.

Bar-Gill, Oren. "Algorithmic Price Discrimination When Demand Is a Function of Both Preferences and (Mis)Perceptions." *The University of Chicago Law Review*, vol. 86, no. 2, 2019, pp. 217–54.

Edwards, Derek, and Neil Mercer. "Reconstructing Context: The Conventionalization of Classroom Knowledge." *Discourse Processes*, vol. 12, no. 1, 1989, pp. 91–104, https://doi.org/10.1080/01638538909544720.

Edwards, Dustin W. "Circulation Gatekeepers: Unbundling the Platform Politics of YouTube's Content ID." *Computers and Composition*, vol. 47, 2018, pp. 61–74, https://doi.org/10.1016/j.compcom.2017.12.001.

Eyman, Douglas. *Digital Rhetoric: Theory, Method, Practice*. U of Michigan P, 2015, https://doi.org/10.3998/dh.13030181.0001.001.

Gallagher, John R. "Five Strategies Internet Writers Use to 'Continue the Conversation.'" *Written Communication*, vol. 32, no. 4, 2015, pp. 396–425, https://doi.org/10.1177/0741088315601006.

———. "Interactive Audience and the Internet." 2014, U of Massachusetts-Amherst, dissertation, https://scholarworks.umass.edu/dissertations_2/190/.

Gallagher, John R., Yinyin Chen, Kyle Wagner, Xuan Wang, Jingyi Zeng, and Alyssa Lingyi Kong. "Peering at the Internet Abyss: Using Big Data Audience Analysis to Understand Online Comments." *Technical Communication Quarterly*, vol. 29, no. 2, 2020, pp. 155–73, https://doi.org/10.1080/10572252.2019.1634766.

Graham, Todd, and Scott Wright. "Discursive Equality and Everyday Talk Online: The Impact of 'Superparticipants.'" *Journal of Computer-Mediated Communication*, vol. 19, no. 3, 2014, pp. 625–42, https://doi.org/10.1111/jcc4.12016.

Gries, Laurie. *Still Life with Rhetoric: A New Materialist Approach for Visual Rhetorics*. Utah State UP, 2015.

Jenkins, Henry. *Spreadable Media: Creating Value and Meaning in a Networked Culture*. New York UP, 2013.

Massanari, Adrienne. "# Gamergate and The Fappening: How Reddit's Algorithm, Governance, and Culture Support Toxic Technocultures." *New Media & Society*, vol. 19, no. 3, 2017, pp. 329–46.

Phillips, Whitney. *This is Why We Wan't Have Nice Things: Mapping the Relationship Between Online Trolling and mainstream culture*. MIT Press, 2015.

Potts, Liza, et al. "Boycotting the Knowledge Makers: How Reddit Demonstrates the Rise of Media Blacklists and Source Rejection in Online Communities." *IEEE Transactions on Professional Communication*, vol. 62, no. 4, 2019, pp. 351–63, https://doi.org/10.1109/TPC.2019.2946942.

Reybold, L. Earle, Lammert, Jill and Stribling, Stacia. "Participant Selection as a Conscious Research Method: Thinking Forward and the Deliberation of 'Emergent' Findings." *Qualitative Research*, vol. 13, no. 6, 2013, pp. 699–716, https://doi.org/10.1177/1468794112465634.

Riddick, Sarah A. "Deliberative Drifting: A Rhetorical Field Method for Audience Studies on Social Media." *Computers and Composition*, vol. 54, 2019, pp. 1–27.

Sparby, Erika M. "Digital social media and aggression: Memetic rhetoric in 4chan's collective identity." *Computers and Composition*, vol. 45, 2017, pp. 85–97.

Tarsa, Rebecca. "Upvoting the Exordium: Literacy Practices of the Digital Interface." *College English*, vol. 78, no. 1, 2015, pp. 12–34.

Weeks, Brian E., Alberto Ardèvol-Abreu, and Homero Gil de Zúñiga. "Online Influence? Social Media Use, Opinion Leadership, and Political Persuasion." *International Journal of Public Opinion Research*, vol. 29, no. 2, 2017, pp. 214–39, https://doi.org/10.1093/ijpor/edv050.

Section 4. Digital Tools for Understanding Discourse, Process, and Writing: Languaging Across Modalities

Chapter 15. Studying Unknown Unknowns: Lessons from Critical Making on Twitter

Whitney Lew James
UNIVERSITY OF NOTRE DAME

In June 2020, SARS-CoV-2, the novel coronavirus that caused a global pandemic, had been known to the medical and scientific community for approximately six months. There were still many unanswered questions about COVID-19, but the American public was highly divided on what little concrete information was available as well as the credibility of information sources. The Pew Research Center reported that between April and June 2020, Republicans and Democrats became increasingly divided on several issues related to the pandemic ("Republicans, Democrats Move Even Further Apart"). Another Pew poll indicated that both Republicans and Democrats felt the CDC and other public health organizations were most likely to get COVID facts correct; however, 54% of Republicans felt Trump and his administration reported accurate information compared to only 9% of Democrats (Mitchell et al.). Why were Americans becoming increasingly divided about what is scientifically factual and who provides accurate information?

While many factors are responsible for divisions among the American public, one likely contributing factor is information echo chambers on online news sources, particularly on social media platforms, where 52% of Americans get most of their news (Suciu). Echo chambers, also known as filter bubbles, occur when individuals are exposed to information and ideas that reinforce their existing views—creating an echo and amplification of their own ideas—while suppressing alternative perspectives (Sunstein). While the existence of echo chambers remains debated in scholarly circles, evidence suggests that both Twitter and Facebook are "dominated by echo chambers" (Cinelli et al. 6). Although studies suggest that the tendency to seek out information that confirms pre-existing opinions is particularly strong in content consumption on online social media (Del Vicario et al.; Garimella et al.), this phenomenon does not only occur in online spaces. Social media echo chambers are simply the latest iteration of the homophily principle, or the human tendency to interact with like-minded peers. Content curation and recommendation algorithms on social media platforms are specifically designed to support homophily, further exacerbating the likelihood of social media echo chambers.

The ways that recommendation algorithms—nonhuman, rhetorical agents that provide personalized recommendations based on aggregated user behavior data—contribute to echo chambers is of great concern to digital rhetoricians. As John Gallagher, Estee Beck, and Annette Vee, among others, have argued, computer code and predictive algorithms are rhetorical agents that must be studied within our field and incorporated into our pedagogy. What makes this type of research incredibly difficult is that both echo chambers and the recommendation algorithms that appear to contribute to their existence are opaque. The predictive algorithms used by recommendation systems are proprietary "products" that social media companies fiercely guard. In this sense, predictive algorithms are "unknown unknowns"—objects of study that researchers do not know what they don't know about (Brunton and Nissenbaum). Studying unknown unknowns is highly difficult and relevant given the increasing influence of predictive algorithms on all facets of life and requires innovative and non-traditional research methods.

In 2019, I conducted a live study of Twitter's recommendation system, Who to Follow or WTF, using a series of Twitter bots, small bits of code that automatically perform specific functions, to understand how recommendation algorithms may contribute to the echo chambers phenomenon. Because I wanted to learn about and critique Twitter, using the platform itself seemed like the best method for accomplishing both goals. I chose to learn about algorithms by creating my own simple algorithm and to display my critique of predictive technology on the very platform I studied. From March to November 2019, I created eight Twitter accounts that used WTF's account recommendations to follow content aligned with a specific lifestyle, ideological, or demographic group. Each of these accounts was then connected with a bot that automatically retweeted the account's feed making the contents of the individual Twitter feeds visible to the public. In essence, I used bot automation to critique recommendation automation. Twitter terminated the project by suspending all the accounts associated with my study—as well as my personal Twitter account and the account of a former employer—for "platform manipulation and spamming." Ironically, the suspension of my access to Twitter gives insight into how the company silences critique while their own algorithms appear to be designed to propagate the uneven spread of information that I was accused of committing. Over the course of the study, I not only learned about recommendation algorithms and echo chambers, but also about the challenges of conducting research on a live social media platform.

This chapter will discuss why and how I used Twitter bots as an activist research method to study predictive algorithms as well as the major obstacles I faced. To begin, I briefly discuss the difficulty of studying predictive algorithms as well as the urgent need to address the inequality produced by these proprietary computer programs. Using critical making as a methodological framework, I argue that Twitter bots are a useful research method for digital rhetoricians studying predictive algorithms. At the heart of this chapter, I describe my personal use of Twitter bots and discuss my difficulty exporting Twitter data for analysis, connecting my experience with the issues of data ownership on the platform. I make no definitive claims about the best or most effective methodology or methods for studying unknown unknowns; instead, I encourage others to adopt a flexible and activist approach to critiquing power structures on social media and other algorithmically mediated digital spaces using my project as inspiration for future work.

Unknown Unknowns of Who to Follow

Twitter's recommendation algorithm—WTF—is a predictive algorithm that curates the types of accounts Twitter users follow and, in turn, information that users are exposed to and speed with which users receive information. The WTF "product," as it is referred to by Twitter, provides highly personalized account recommendations to users with the goal of "maintaining and expanding the active user population" by helping users "discover connections" (Gupta et al.). In 2015, a team of Twitter engineers reported that WTF was directly responsible for more than 500 million new connections each month and produced billions of recommendations a year (Goel et al. 106). At the time, WTF was directly responsible for one-eighth of all connections made on Twitter, not to mention the connections that eventually developed based on initial recommendations (Goel et al. 106). While additional information about WTF's influence has not been released since 2015, WTF is certainly a powerful actor in the Twitterverse.[1]

Although the engineers of WTF have described the general principles of the recommendation algorithm, Twitter users and independent researchers remain in the dark about exactly how the algorithm functions. At the International World Wide Web Conference, the designers responsible for WTF described the recommendation process: using a large-scale snapshot of Twitter's entire network of connections, referred to as an "interest graph," WTF identifies accounts that are "similar to" the user and, from that calculation, accounts the user might be "interested in" (Gupta et al.). Both sets are recommended to the user as potential accounts to follow. And yet, many unknown unknowns remain. For example, how is the "interest graph" developed? How exactly are "similar to" and "interested in" accounts identified? What user data beyond the "interest graph" is used to make recommendations? Is data about user interactions with WTF gathered? Does the algorithm account for the difference in "organic" follows versus "recommended" follows? This lack of information about WTF, as with all other proprietary predictive and recommendation algorithms, results in what Finn Brunton

---

1. Twitter's WTF is just one of many increasingly influential recommendation algorithms. In their contribution to *The Routledge Handbook of Digital Writing and Rhetoric*, Mihaela Popescu and Lemi Baruh discuss the norming effects of recommendation systems on cultural fields and products. As rhetoric and composition scholars continue to study predictive algorithms, more research focused specifically on the rhetoricity of recommendation systems is needed.

and Helen Nissenbaum refer to as information asymmetry: "when data about us are collected in circumstances we may not understand, for purposes we may not understand, and are used in ways we may not understand" (1–2). Twitter has untold information about our personal lives and lifestyles gathered from sources we do not know about, used in ways we do not know, and results in recommendations that we may not understand.

Studies of both recommendation systems like WTF, it raised red flags about the homogenizing and potentially oppressive effects of the recommendation algorithm. In a study of live recommendation systems, like WTF, researchers found that feedback loops can develop "when a platform attempts to model user behavior without accounting for recommendations" (Chaney et al.). Researchers have also found that recommendation systems using collaborative filtering, as WTF does, are "susceptible to *biases* that may appear in input data," which amplify existing biases and reinforce stereotypes (Tsintzo et al. 1, emphasis in original). Studies of WTF found that the algorithm "disproportionately accelerated the growth of already popular users" likely "altering the diversity of information users consume on the platform" (Su et al.); "further exacerbate[d] the majority-minority gap" by limiting the spread of information (Halberstam and Knight); and created a glass ceiling limiting the visibility of women (Nilizadeh et al.; Zhu et al.) and men of color (Messias et al.). Although there is ample evidence to suggest WTF contributes to inequality on the platform, Twitter's engineers seem unaware or unconcerned. In 2014, a team of Twitter researchers published information about the WTF "interest graph" referring to the graph and their research as "a set of authoritative descriptive statistics" on an active social network (Myers et al. 1). However, at no point in the article do they consider how the implementation of WTF in 2010 affected the structure of Twitter's interest graph and/or contributed to the structure of the network.

Because WTF is part of the larger system of highly influential and inequitable predictive algorithms and Twitter does not seem to hold itself accountable for the effects of their recommendation system, digital rhetoricians, among others, need to continue conducting critical analyses of WTF. And yet, humanities researchers may have less access to the vast resources and technological expertise used to create the big data studies cited above. When I decided to research how WTF may contribute to echo chambers as part of my dissertation, I had significantly limited technological access, support, and know-how. Beyond my personal limitations were the issues of the invisibility of echo chambers and unknown unknowns of predictive algorithms. My ideal goal was to make these invisible and unknowable things somehow tangible for myself as a researcher and for the public that is impacted by recommendation algorithms and echo chambers. While I had a clear vision of my research goals, my approach to completing the project was murkier. As a novice both in terms of research and computer algorithms, I required a methodological framework that supported non-traditional research and was flexible enough to deal with a range of constraints.

A Critical Making Framework

Critical making is a methodological framework for exploring the social aspects of technology through the process of making. As a beginning researcher, critical making appealed to me because of its ad-hoc, do it yourself (DIY) approach that incorporates both academic research and activist work on social media, as evidenced in the collection *DIY Citizenship: Critical Making and Social Media* edited by Matt Ratto and Meagan Boler. As a methodological framework, critical making is especially useful for (1) rendering abstract concepts material through the process of making, (2) humanities and social science scholars studying technology, and (3) process-focused, metacognitive research projects.

Matt Ratto, who popularized the term and founded the Critical Making Lab at the University of Toronto, defines critical making as "materially productive, hands-on work intended to uncover and explore conceptual uncertainties, parse the world in ways that language cannot, and disseminate the results of these explorations through embodied, material forms" ("Textual Doppelgangers" 228). Ratto contends that critical making "frames a need to incorporate technical work alongside critical social analysis and makes a claim that doing so can both extend current scholarly critiques and direct them into society in new ways" ("Textual Doppelgangers" 229). Additionally, critical making focuses on the "constructive process as a site for analysis . . . emphasiz[ing] the shared acts of making rather than the evocative object" ("Critical Making," 253). Ratto and Boler argue that "making as a 'critical' activity . . . provides both the possibility to intervene substantively in systems of authority and power and . . . offers an important site for reflecting on how such power is constituted by infrastructures, institutions, communities, and practices" (1). Critical making, then, provides a flexible methodological framework for activist researchers who want to learn new ways to critique existing power structures through collaborative making.

For researchers who want to experience first-hand the power of algorithms on social media, critical making provides a fruitful framework both for approaching the creation of computer code and the study of unknown unknowns. Rachael Graham Lussos has argued that writing Twitter bots from a critical making framework allows the creator to "experience how the hidden writing of social media technologies—the automated programs that enable (or in some cases, disable) use of those technologies—involves a rhetorical analysis." Although Lussos writes about graduate students, students are not the only academics who can learn about the hidden writing and rules of social media through hands-on experimentation with bots—novice and experienced researchers need to find new ways to engage with and study the predictive algorithms that are increasingly impacting our lives. Because researchers will likely never have access to the proprietary algorithms that they wish to study, the most significant results of our work might be the knowledge we develop through actively engaging with predictive algorithms. Because critical making emphasizes the experiential knowledge that comes from the process of engaging with technologies, digital rhetoricians and researchers interested in intangible and inaccessible algorithms can benefit from adopting such a methodological framework.

Twitter Bots as an Activist Research Method

Twitter bots are small pieces of computer code that interact with Twitter's Application Program Interface (API) to perform certain functions automatically. In this sense, Twitter bots themselves are computer algorithms set to tweet, reply, retweet, or message content based on a predefined set of conditions. Like all algorithms, bots are coded by individuals or groups of individuals. While bots and algorithms run without human intervention and have consequences beyond the intentions of the creator, these programs are not inherently bad, good, or otherwise—they are products of the botmaker's work as well as the culture in which the bots were created. Still, bots are often considered nefarious agents spreading misinformation, propping up authoritarian governments, and generally spamming, annoying, and confusing the Twitter public. These charges are not unfounded: ISIS used social bots to spread radicalism, pro-Russia bots drowned out protest through hashtag manipulation, and social media bots triggered actions in automatic stock market trading systems that resulted in a brief but significant "flash [stock market] crash" (Subrahmanian et al.; Ferrara et al.). While Twitter bots have certainly been used for malicious ends and the effects of bots on the social media ecosystem are complex, Twitter bots can also be tools for activism and social critique. Mark Sample theorizes protest bots or "bots of conviction" as the modern version of a protest song: "a computer program that reveals the injustice and inequality of the world and imagines alternatives." Considering the activist possibilities of Twitter bots, I argue that digital rhetoricians should consider their use for research purposes, while recognizing the complexity of the consequences of bots in digital spaces. Twitter bots can be useful research tools for a range of projects because they require little technical expertise, run automatically, and provide anonymity.

Compared to other automated computer programs, Twitter bots require relatively little technical expertise while giving researchers direct experience creating algorithms. As I will demonstrate later in a description of my collaboration to create Twitter bots, not only is there a large and inviting community of botmakers and enthusiasts who provide online tutorials for creating bots, but researchers can consult with more experienced coders and programmers quite easily.[2] While bots require relatively low technical knowledge, the dividends they pay in conceptual knowledge about social media rhetoric, digital literacy, nonhuman rhetoric, computer programming and automation, among other things, are high. For example,

---

2. Twitter bots with specific functionalities can also be created using Google spreadsheets that use code developed by more experienced programmers, as documented by Lussos and Holmes and Lussos.

James R. Brown Jr. created a Twitter bot, @yourletterbot, to "grapple" with the realities of the "robot rhetor" (497). Creating the bot helped Brown Jr. conclude that "computation is a rhetorical medium and that software is within the purview of rhetoric" (497). That is, the act of creating bots gives digital rhetoricians invaluable experiential and affectual insights into rhetoric in digital spaces. Making bots and other automated programs actualizes and concretizes abstract and hidden information and mechanisms. Thus, the research produced through the creation of bots can offer robust insights for digital rhetoricians without requiring extensive programming experience.

By their very nature, bots operate automatically, affording researchers and activists a range of benefits from constant data collection to safety from harmful rhetoric. On a very practical level, the automation of bots allows a research project to continue without constant intervention from an individual. For my own research, automation allowed me to gather the content of eight different Twitter feeds twenty-four hours a day, seven days a week. As I will note below, automation also allowed me the ability to gather and archive certain types of data, which prevented me from losing all my research materials after Twitter suspended my accounts. As a form of social critique, automation can create a deluge of counternarrative posts. Steve Holmes and Rachael Graham Lussos argue in an article about bots and #GamerGate[3] that protest bots—such as their own bot @Dr_Ethics—consistently and constantly injected alternative viewpoints into the one-sided, toxic hashtag stream. Additionally, software engineer Randi Harper used an autoblocking bot to prevent harassment from #GamerGaters before they could even engage with her personal account. Sample considers automation integral to the way bots can protest, as the programs "present society a bill it cannot pay . . . at the rate of once every two minutes." Automation is certainly powerful and can be used in harmful or annoying ways, but these examples also suggest that automation can be a productive and useful tool for activist researchers to gather data, insert counternarratives and critique into social media platforms, and protect themselves from harassment.

Along the same lines of the protective nature of automation, the anonymity afforded by bots can also protect researchers from online harassment. When developing my research project, one of my advisors' main concerns was my personal safety. Indeed, academics—many of whom are from marginalized and oppressed groups—from across the country and a range of disciplines have been subjected to online harassment from both conservative and liberal extremists (Kamenetz). Through the practice of "doxing," publicly releasing personally identifiable information, online harassment becomes offline threats. Rhetoricians Les Hutchinson and Dana Cloud were both doxxed and targeted for their scholarship. Hutchinson was doxxed and received threats against herself and her

---

3. #GamerGate began in August 2014 as a coordinated harassment campaign against women in tech who spoke out about sexism in the video game industry.

family for engaging in Twitter research for her MA thesis in 2012 (Hutchinson). At RSA 2018, Dana Cloud spoke about the harassment and threats she experienced after being doxxed because of her scholarship. Engaging in research with bots can provide a layer of personal protection and anonymity against online and offline harassment and threats allowing activist researchers to continue their critical-making research.

To help distinguish research bots from bots used to suppress or manipulate users, I suggest that researchers be transparent about their work. I clearly indicated that the accounts were bots through the Twitter handles, names, and bios—all of which also noted that they were part of a research project about echo chambers on social media. I also avoided making the accounts appear humanlike by leaving default profile and background images. When my bots followed an account, the profile clearly stated their purpose as research tools. Additionally, as the bot started retweeting content from other users, they could easily remove themselves from the study through blocking the bot. Similarly, researchers who made a Twitter bot to help facilitate social justice organization found that appearing "less human" made the bot more effective in developing connections among users (Savage et al.). Both my bots and Botivist suggest that clearly identifying accounts as bots is not only the most effective method for encouraging user engagement, but also the most ethical.

Critiquing Automation with Automation

While studies suggesting that Who to Follow and other recommendation algorithms have homogenizing and norming effects that are detrimental to minorities further spurred my critical making project, I originally became concerned about echo chambers when I found myself in one. Shortly after joining Twitter in mid-2018, #AsianAugust, which celebrated a historically significant month in Asian American film, began appearing in my feed. While I joined Asian American actors, filmmakers, and fans on Twitter in cheering over the release of *Crazy Rich Asians*, *To All the Boys I've Loved Before*, and *Searching*, my offline friends and colleagues seemed to know little about #AsianAugust. Being part of the #AsianAugust echo chamber disconcerted me on two fronts. First, I was surprised at how distorted my perspective on #AsianAugust was. Because the topic was so popular on my Twitter feed, I assumed it was popular on everyone else's—the issue had been amplified within my Twitter echo chamber. Second, I was dismayed that #AsianAugust was not gaining more widespread attention outside the Asian American community. The hashtag was being suppressed or filtered out of the content feeds of others. When I began designing research projects for my dissertation, I remembered my frustration, alarm, and disbelief about the (lack of) circulation of #AsianAugust.

Although the project was a solo endeavor, I drew on the expertise and guidance of a range of collaborators—online forums, open-source code and applications, online videos, national coding organizations, computer programmers, and a fellow graduate student—to execute this critical-making study. When I conceived of the retweeting bots, I only had a surface-level knowledge of the capability of bots and no experience coding. I found bot enthusiast Stefan Bohacek's Botwiki forum and began watching Daniel Shiffman's "The Code Train" YouTube tutorial series on Twitter bots. I attended a Women Who Code event hosted by the Dallas-Fort Worth chapter where I worked with a local computer programmer who specialized in Node.js. We collaborated not only on writing the Twitter bot code, but also thinking through how the bot would perform the functions I needed to make individual content feeds visible to the public. To set up automated retweeting as well as archive data on a database service, I worked with a fellow graduate student, Sean McCullough, who had more experience in programming. I list the steps for creating a bot not only to document the process for myself and others, but to point to the many types of collaboration I used for this critical making project. While working with a computer programmer and graduate student are traditional modes of collaboration, I also collaborated using open-source code and applications, online tutorials, and virtual forums. These digitally mediated modes of collaboration significantly contributed to my project, just in-person collaboration did.

Through these collaborations, I designed a bot that would gather the last 200 unique tweets that appeared on the account's content feed and retweet every other tweet at a thirty-minute interval. Retweeting at these intervals allowed the bot to consistently retweet content, but not tweet beyond the daily and hourly limits imposed by Twitter ("About Twitter Limits"). When completed, the bots performed three main functions each time the program ran:

1. Gather the last 200 tweets that appeared on the account's content feed
2. Retweet every other gathered tweet to the account's timeline
3. Send retweet data (Twitter handle, date and time, and text-based content, among other unique identifiers) to a database for archiving

From July 1 to November 5, 2019, bots retweeted the content from eight different Twitter feeds and archived data about the tweets.

The process of designing and coding the bots taught me about how algorithms must be intentionally designed, but also how quickly and easily algorithms can be created. Leigh Gruwell has challenged digital rhetoricians to work "within the confines of the platforms they study" to "take advantage of each space's unique affordances" (Gruwell). Twitter created the "retweet" function to encourage user engagement through the recirculation of content. I used this feature of Twitter's architecture because the retweeting function (1) made the content of personalized Twitter feeds publicly visible and (2) allowed me to create an archive of each account's content feed. Without exploiting the retweeting function, I would have been unable to make the content visible or analyzable. My main takeaway from coding the retweeting bot was that any algorithm designer needs to be highly attentive to the unexpected outcomes of their work and consult with many different stakeholders to avoid accidentally and later, automatically harming others.

The process of following accounts using Twitter's WTF recommendation algorithm gave me insight into how individuals experience the creation of a social media echo chamber and how influential WTF is in creating personalized feeds. Because recommendation systems "are a paradigmatic example of the interaction between humans and algorithms in the cultural arena," not only do echo chambers reflect user and algorithm bias, but the Twitter feeds I created needed to account for both (Bressan et al. 745). To begin, I identified highly influential accounts within a given conversation. These accounts would be considered "interested in" accounts that are highly vocal in a particular discussion. After following accounts from highly influential and prominent members of a community, I transitioned to use WTF recommendations, allowing the algorithm to take over the following process. During this phase of following, WTF rapidly served up recommendations, building an archive of data on my preferences and further pushing each Twitter account into groups. I also followed accounts that appeared within the content feed. When an individual reposts content on their timeline, it often appears in the timelines of their followers. While these secondary account follows are not directly coordinated by WTF, they are still influenced by the recommendation algorithm.

Establishing methods for coding Twitter bots and following Twitter accounts took substantial time and thought, but the creation of the personalized content feeds that could be considered echo chambers took very little time. I initially planned on gathering data about the echo chambers over several months, assuming that it would take time for the divisions to appear across the eight different Twitter accounts. However, I was surprised to see just how quickly personalized Twitter feeds that highlighted specific worldviews developed. For each Twitter feed, I followed approximately 100 accounts in less than thirty minutes. With WTF serving up hundreds of new recommendations every second, each account rapidly developed a distinct network of "friendships," the term Twitter uses for accounts a user follows. There was only a small fraction—5.5 percent—of overlap across the eight accounts' "friendships." Although I could only mimic the perspectives of a particular group, the Who to Follow algorithm quickly and efficiently created personalized Twitter feeds reflecting those perspectives.

This small study suggests—and Twitter appears to confirm by terminating my activity—that the platform itself is designed to manipulate and disrupt the exchange of information through the creation of personalized feeds. Twitter relies heavily on user interactions, and feeds that support an individual's pre-existing views are one of the best ways to increase engagement. Feeding people what they want to "like" and recirculate makes perfect sense from a user engagement-focused perspective. Although I had read plenty of research about how WTF contributes to echo chambers and increases inequality, the process of creating personalized feeds representing specific viewpoints made the abstract concept far more concrete and disturbing. I understood from hands-on experience just how quickly people are sorted, categorized, and pigeonholed by the WTF recommendation algorithm.

Data Problems

During the conceptual phases of my critical making study, one of the main concerns was the sheer amount of data that the retweeting bots would generate. With eight accounts potentially tweeting a combined 38,400 tweets a day, the amount of raw data could become unmanageable quickly. However, obtaining usable and analyzable data was the most difficult and unexpected obstacle I encountered during this research project. When all eight Twitter accounts were suspended on November 5, 2019, I immediately lost access to each account's timelines as well as information about the followed and follower accounts. Even before I was shut out of Twitter, I had difficulty gathering data that included media-rich content. The goal of this project was to understand how individuals experience personalized Twitter feeds, so I wanted to qualitatively analyze tweets as they would appear in a Twitter feed, not as decontextualized strings of text-based data best suited for corpus analysis. Gathering qualitatively analyzable data proved the most significant and persistent challenge of this project and speaks to larger issues of data ownership on social media.

Despite my best efforts and consultation with others, I found no method of data exporting that could provide me with media-rich data that was unfiltered by Twitter. ATLAS.ti, qualitative analysis software, was the only platform I found that offered media-rich content, displaying tweets in a way like how they would appear on Twitter. However, the software offers researchers limited ability to know exactly how the imported tweets were chosen; ATLAS.ti data is a selection of 100 "recent" tweets that are mediated by Twitter. ATLAS.ti acknowledges the limitations of their Twitter exports in the user manual: "Note that you only will be able to import tweets from the last week. Further, as the final selection is done by Twitter and not within our control, queries at different times, or on different computers may result in different tweets" (110). To my knowledge, ATLAS.ti's interface is the only way to export tweets easily and quickly in a way that replicates the experience of individual users. Twitter's insistence on filtering the exporting of data replicates the content feed personalization on the platform itself. It remains an unknown unknown how and why any tweet appears on a users' content feed and the same goes for exported tweets on ATLAS.ti.

My difficulty accessing data from Twitter is in line with the platform's Terms of Service that give very little power to users and virtually unlimited power to the tech company. By simply submitting, posting, or displaying content on Twitter, users "grant [the platform] a worldwide, non-exclusive, royalty-free license (with the right to sublicense) to use, copy, reproduce, process, adapt, modify, publish, transmit, display and distribute such Content in any and all media or distribution methods now known or later developed" ("Twitter Terms of Service"). Twitter also retains the right to "suspend or terminate your account or cease providing you with all or part of the Services at any time for any or no reason" ("Twitter Terms of Service"). In other words, Twitter takes an authoritarian approach on its own platform—the company not only wields absolute authority over their proprietary algorithms, but also over content produced by individuals using the platform.

While researchers and individual Twitter users have trouble accessing their own data and knowing how their data is used by the platform, research using bots may raise concerns about contaminating data on social interactions and network connections on Twitter. Because Twitter's recommendation algorithm uses a snapshot of the existing network architecture to calculate recommendations, experimenting with WTF could be contaminating the "interest graph." Even worse, by allowing WTF to prompt me to create echo chambers, some might argue that my project amplifies and reinforces the homogenizing effects of the recommendation algorithm.

These are valid concerns about my project and others that attempt to experiment with live social media platforms. However, I argue that small studies such as mine have very little influence on the overall social structure of social media platforms and, even more importantly, data about social interactions on social media is already compromised by predictive algorithms that feed on and exacerbate implicit bias. Brunton and Nissenbaum argue that "data pollution is unethical only when the integrity of the data flow or data set in question is ethically required" (69). Twitter's use of the WTF recommendation system without accounting for the homogenizing effects of the algorithm already compromises the data set. Additionally, because I studied unknown unknowns from a weak position in the information asymmetry, I would argue that my methods are justifiable. Nevertheless, issues surrounding proprietary algorithms and ownership, management, and contamination of the user data gathered by and fueling these algorithms remains a thorny issue that will not be resolved if tech companies keep the public in the dark.

Conclusion

Studying unknown unknowns can be incredibly frustrating. I hit roadblock after roadblock trying to export data and reinstate suspended Twitter accounts. At the time of writing, my personal Twitter account remains suspended, and Twitter has refused to provide additional information about why I was suspended or how I might be able to return to the platform. With only a list of "friendships" for each account and a handful of tweets filtered by Twitter, I had to work with limited data. However, these frustrations and setbacks have helped me further understand the power dynamics of social media platforms. Twitter quite clearly exerted its power over me as an individual and activist researcher. While I was still able to make insights about how WTF contributes to the creation of echo chambers, experiencing the difficulty of studying unknown unknowns and feeling the full force of Twitter's authority has been the most significant learning experience from this study. Some of the tangible products of my research may have been erased, but the deep experiential knowledge that I developed during this critical making project remains.

For activist researchers interested in adopting a critical making methodological framework, studying unknown unknowns, using automated bots for research, or experimenting on a live social media platform, I offer the following suggestions for designing a research project:

- Look to other academic disciplines and activists for new research methods
- Consider the affordances of your chosen platform of study and incorporate the platform into your critique
- Collaborate in a range of modes when developing your research project
- Document and reflect on the creation process and prototyping phase of any objects or artifacts that you make
- Export data as frequently as possible to multiple platforms, but know that you may need to adjust your research goals and/or results based on the ability to retain analyzable data

If social media platforms like Twitter had their way, independent researchers would never gain access to information about echo chambers or predictive algorithms. The data gathered about individuals and groups is the currency of the internet and any technologies, such as recommendation systems, that increase user engagement or data collection are highly valuable to social media corporations. It is precisely because these unknown unknowns are so securely guarded, profitable, and influential that digital rhetoricians and other academics need to conduct publicly accessible scholarship. Thus, adopting non-traditional, activist research methodologies is imperative to increase public and scholarly knowledge about predictive algorithms, content circulation, and echo chambers.

Works Cited

About Twitter Limits. Twitter, https://help.twitter.com/en/rules-and-policies/twitter-limits. Accessed 22 July 2020.

ATLAS.ti 8 Mac User Manual. ATLAS.ti Scientific Software Development, Berlin, 2019.

Beck, Estee. "Implications of Persuasive Computer Algorithms." *The Routledge Handbook of Digital Writing and Rhetoric*. edited by Jonathon Alexander and Jacqueline Rhodes, Routledge, 2018, pp. 291–300.

Bressan, Marco, et al. "The Limits of Popularity-Based Recommendations, and the Role of Social Ties." KDD Conference, 13–17 Aug. 2016, San Francisco, California.

Brown Jr., James J., "The Machine That Therefore I Am." *Philosophy and Rhetoric*, vol. 47, no. 4, 2014, pp. 494–512.

Brunton, Finn, and Helen Fay Nissenbaum. *Obfuscation: A User's Guide for Privacy and Protest*. MIT Press, 2015.

Chaney, Allison J.B., Brandon M. Stewart, and Barbara E. Engelhardt. "How Algorithmic Confounding in Recommendation Systems Increases Homogeneity and Decreases Utility." ACM Conference on Recommender Systems (RecSys) held at Vancouver, Canada, 2018.

Cinelli, Matteo, Gianmarco De Francisci Morales, Alessandro Galeazzi, Walter Quattrociocchi, and Michele Starnini. "Echo Chambers on Social Media: A Comparative Study." *ArXiv:2004.09603 [Physics]*, Apr. 2020, http://arxiv.org/abs/2004.09603.

Cloud, Dana. "Fighting Back Against the Alt-Right's Higher Education Agenda." *18th Biennial Conference and 50th Anniversary Celebration of the Rhetoric Society of America* held in Minneapolis, Minnesota, 2018.

"The Coding Train." YouTube, https://www.youtube.com/channel/UCvjgXvBlbQiydffZU7m1_aw. Accessed 22 July 2020.

Del Vicario, Michela, Alessandro Bessi, Fabiana Zollo, Fabio Petroni, Antonio Scala, Guido Caldarelli, H. Eugene Stanley, and Walter Quattrociocchi. "The Spreading of Misinformation Online." *Proceedings of the National Academy of Sciences*, vol. 113, no. 3, 2017, pp. 554–59.

@Dr_EthicsGate. May 2017, https://twitter.com/Dr_EthicsGate.

Ferrara, Emilio, Onur Varol, Clayton Davis, Filippo Menczer, and Alessandro Flammini. "The Rise of Social Bots." *Communications of the ACM*, vol. 59, no. 7, July 2014.

Gallagher, John R. "Writing for Algorithmic Audiences." *Computers and Composition*, vol. 45, 2017, pp. 25–35.

Garimella, Kiran, Gianmarco De Francisci Morales, Aristides Gionis, and Michael Mathioudakis. "The Effect of Collective Attention on Controversial Debates on Social Media." *WebSci '17: 9th International ACM Web Science Conference*, 2017, pp. 43–47.

Goel, Ashish, Pankaj Gupta, John Sirois, Dong Wang, Aneesh Sharma, and Siva Gurumurthy. "The Who-To-Follow System at Twitter: Strategy, Algorithms, and Revenue Impact." *INFORMS Journal on Applied Analytics*, vol. 45, no. 1, 2015, pp. 98–107.

Gruwell, Leigh. "Constructing Research, Constructing the Platform: Algorithms and the Rhetoricity of Social Media Research." *Present Tense*, vol. 6, no. 3, 23 Jan. 2018, http://www.presenttensejournal.org/volume-6/constructing-research-constructing-the-platform-algorithms-and-the-rhetoricity-of-social-media-research/.

Gupta, Pankaj, Ashish Goel, Jimmy Lin, Aneesh Sharma, Dong Wang, and Reza Zadeh. "WTF: The Who to Follow Service at Twitter." International World Wide Web Conference Committee, 13–17 May 2013, Rio de Janeiro, Brazil.

Halberstam, Yosh, and Brian Knight. "Homophily, Group Size, and the Diffusion of Political Information in Social Networks: Evidence from Twitter." *Journal of Public Economics*, vol. 143, 2016, pp. 73–88.

Holmes, Steve, and Rachael Graham Lussos. "Cultivating Metanoia in Twitter Publics: Analyzing and Producing Bots of Protest in the #GamerGate Controversy." *Computers and Composition*, vol. 48, June 2018, pp. 118–38.

Hutchinson, Les. "Wielding Power and Doxing Data: How Personal Information Regulates and Controls our Online Selves." *The Routledge Handbook of Digital Writing and Rhetoric*. edited by Jonathan Alexander and Jacqueline Rhodes, Routledge, 2018, pp. 303–16.

Kamenetz, Anya. "Professors Are Targets in Online Culture Wars; Some Fight Back." *NPR.Org*, 4 Apr. 2018, https://www.npr.org/sections/ed/2018/04/04/590928008/professor-harassment.

Lussos, Rachael Graham. "Twitter Bots as Digital Writing Assignments." *PraxisWiki* on *Kairos: Rhetoric, Technology, and Pedagogy*, vol. 22, no. 2, 19 Dec. 2017, http://praxis.technorhetoric.net/tiki-index.php?page=PraxisWiki%3A_%3ATwitterBots#References.

Messias, Johnnatan, Pantelis Vikatos, and Fabrício Benevenuto. "White, Man, and Highly Followed: Gender and Race Inequalities in Twitter." International Conference on Web Intelligence held in Leipzig Germany, 2017.

Mitchell, Amy, Mark Jurkowitz, J. Baxter Oliphant, and Elisa Shearer. "Three Months In, Many Americans See Exaggeration, Conspiracy Theories and Partisanship in COVID-19 News." *Pew Research Center's Journalism Project*, 29 June 2020, https://www.journalism.org/2020/06/29/three-months-in-many-americans-see-exaggeration-conspiracy-theories-and-partisanship-in-covid-19-news/.

Myers, Seth A., Aneesh Sharma, Pankaj Gupta, and Jimmy Lin. "Information Network or Social Network? The Structure of the Twitter Follow Graph." International World Wide Web Conference Committee held in Seoul South Korea, 1–11 Apr. 2014.

New York Supreme Court, Appellate Term—First Department. *The People of the State of New York v. Malcolm Harris and Twitter, Inc.* American Civil Liberties Union, https://www.aclu.org/files/assets/brief-harris-appellateterm.pdf. Accessed 20 July 2020.

Nilizadeh, Shirin, Anne Groggel, Peter Lista, Srijita Das, Yong-Yeol Ahn, Apu Kapadia, and Fabio Rojas. "Twitter's Glass Ceiling: The Effect of Perceived Gender on Online Visibility." AAAI Conference on Web and Social Media held in Cologne Germany, 2016.

Popescu, Mihaela, and Lemi Baruh. "Privacy as Cultural Choice and Resistance in the Age of Recommender Systems." *The Routledge Handbook of Digital Writing and Rhetoric*. edited by Jonathan Alexander and Jacqueline Rhodes, Routledge, 2018, pp. 280–90.

Ratto, Matt. "Critical Making: Conceptual and Material Studies in Technology and Social Life." *The Information Society*, vol. 27, 2011, pp. 252–60.

———. "Textual Doppelgangers: Critical Issues in the Study of Technology." *DIY: Citizenship: Critical Making and Social Media*. edited by Matt Ratto and Megan Boler, MIT Press, 2014, pp. 227–37.

Ratto, Matt and Megan Boler. "Introduction." *DIY: Citizenship: Critical Making and Social Media*. edited by Matt Ratto and Megan Boler. MIT Press, 2014, pp. 1–22.

"Republicans, Democrats Move Even Further Apart in Coronavirus Concerns." *Pew Research Center—U.S. Politics and Policy*, 25 June 2020, https://www.people-press.org/2020/06/25/republicans-democrats-move-even-further-apart-in-coronavirus-concerns/.

Sample, Mark. "A Protest Bot Is a Bot so Specific You Can't Mistake It for Bullshit." *Medium*, 4 Oct. 2015, https://medium.com/@samplereality/a-protest-bot-is-a-bot-so-specific-you-cant-mistake-it-for-bullshit-90fe10b7fbaa.

Savage, Saiph, et al. "Botivist: Calling Volunteers to Action Using Online Bots." *Proceedings of the 19th ACM Conference on Computer-Supported Cooperative Work and Social Computing—CSCW '16*, ACM Press, 2016, pp. 811–20.

Su, Jessica, Aneesh Sharma, and Sharad Goel. "The Effects of Recommendations on Network Structure." World Wide Web Conference 2016 held in Montreal, Canada, 11–15 Apr. 2016.

Subrahmanian, V.S., et al. "The DARPA Twitter Bot Challenge." *Computer*, vol. 49, no. 6, June 2016, pp. 38–46.

Suciu, Peter. "More Americans Are Getting Their News from Social Media." Forbes, 11 Oct. 2019, https://www.forbes.com/sites/petersuciu/2019/10/11/more-americans-are-getting-their-news-from-social-media/.

Sunstein, Cass R. *Republic.Com*. Princeton UP, 2002.

Twitter Terms of Service. Twitter, 18 June 2020, https://twitter.com/en/tos#us. Accessed 14 July 2020.

Vee, Annette. "Understanding Computer Programming as a Literacy." *Literacy in Composition Studies*, vol. 1, no. 2, 2013, pp. 42–64.

@yourletterbot. Aug. 2013, https://twitter.com/yourletterbot. Accessed 5 July 2020.

Zhu, Jane M., Arthur P. Pelullo, Sayed Hassan, Raina M. Merchant, and Rachel M. Werner. "Gender Differences in Twitter Use and Influence Among Health Policy and Health Services Researchers." *JAMA Internal Medicine*, vol. 179, no. 12, Dec. 2019, pp. 1726–29.

Chapter 16. Language Policing to Language Curiosity: Using Corpus Analysis to Foreground Linguistic Diversity

Laura Aull
University of Michigan

Language Acknowledgment. The author acknowledges that this chapter uses English, a language brought to North America and used to overshadow or eclipse hundreds of Native American languages, including ones still used today such as Navajo and Ojibwe and many now extinct such as Yahi and Natchez. This chapter specifically uses standardized written academic English, a dialect of English that has been used, particularly since the 18th century, to establish and maintain racial, socioeconomic, educational, and other forms of inequity by privileging the usage criteria and preferences of a small number of language users at the expense of other dialects which are equally systematic (rule-governed) and meaningful. By offering this language acknowledgment, I strive to raise awareness about and acknowledge my own participation in the linguistic homogeneity of U.S. research and teaching, even as I also hope that the ideas in this chapter offer some alternatives to this long-standing and limiting homogeneity.

The Contradiction

Most college writing courses represent a clear contradiction between theory and practice. In theory, writing instructors believe in diversity and inclusion. We believe diversity extends the limits of what we know and helps us see those very limits. We believe diversity is not only inevitable in higher education but that it makes it stronger, which means that linguistic diversity is inevitable and positive for higher education. For decades, rhetoric and writing scholarship has stressed that supporting students' language diversity supports students' identities and cultures (CCCC "Students' Right to Their Own Language"; CCCC "This Ain't Another Statement! This Is a Demand for Black Linguistic Justice!"; Horner et al.; Inoue; Perryman-Clark "African American Language, Rhetoric, and Students' Writing: New Directions for Srtol"; Smitherman "'Students' Right to Their Own Language': A Retrospective"), and linguistics research has likewise long underscored that all languages consist of multiple, equally systematic dialects (Curzan; McWhorter *Word on the Street: Debunking the Myth of a Pure Standard English*).

From these, we can define linguistic diversity accordingly: the condition of human language as composed of different registers and dialects, which are all linguistically equal but socially differentiated, in other words, equally rule-governed and responsive to community needs but valued differently according to socially constructed hierarchies. This definition highlights that language difference is inherent in language—difference, and dissonance, are common ground (Gonzales). It follows, too, that such linguistic diversity merits critical language awareness, or descriptive analysis informed by awareness of linguistic equity and socially constructed value across different uses of language (see, for example, Shapiro 2022).

In practice, we teach classes and work in educational institutions in which language difference is punished rather than celebrated: language difference is common ground, but the social value attached to different language use is not. Our writing courses almost invariably assess students based on the norms of a single dialect, standardized written academic English (SWAE). Writing instructors and scholars are likewise held to these norms. After their use of SWAE in their own schooling, they write applications, funding proposals, instructional materials, and scholarship in SWAE. It is possible for writing instructors to feature diverse voices in a course reading list and to expect students to write in a homogeneous way in student papers. It is possible for writing instructors to do this without understanding or discussing this contradiction with students. In short, it is common to find writing pedagogies that support diversity in theory while maintaining linguistic homogeneity in practice, a contradiction I have repeatedly participated in and reified myself, first unwittingly and later in the name of access, and still as I write this in SWAE and struggle with the narrow constraints of my ability to express these ideas. Building on the definition of linguistic diversity above, we can define linguistic homogeneity as the privileging of a single register and dialect of human language. At its most common and problematic, linguistic homogeneity suggests a single dialect is linguistically superior without accompanying critical language awareness, or without descriptive analysis with acknowledgment of linguistic equity and socially constructed difference.

There are many reasons for linguistic diversity in theory and linguistic homogeneity in practice. One is that much related scholarship has to date focused more on theory rather than practical strategies for classrooms; another is that many writing courses are taught by instructors trained in English literary studies rather than currently descriptive traditions like linguistics (Hasty et al.; Aull). A related reason is writing instructor and/ or programmatic training that insists that offering access to discourses of power means only assigning and offering feedback on SWAE in conventional genres, rather than a fuller range of student meaning-making strategies (Martín et al.). Even for those who believe in diversity and inclusion, it can be hard to determine how to *do* linguistic diversity in writing classrooms.

This chapter proposes that linguistic analysis helps us escape this contradiction by enacting a paradigm shift from language policing to language curiosity, or a paradigm in which language is a site for descriptive exploration rather than for dialect hierarchies and mastery. The essence of this idea is not new; research reviewed in the next section makes language a subject of critical, reflective inquiry, for instance, in literacy narrative assignment tasks. But this chapter turns to digital approaches to make an additional proposal: that corpus linguistic analysis offers not only a mindset but a methodology for centering our pedagogies on linguistic diversity. It is a method that makes diverse language use an object of analysis versus evaluation. The next section provides context for understanding why this matters, followed by sample corpus tools for use in writing classrooms.

Responses to the Contradiction

Research in rhetoric and writing shows clear concern over the ways that writing classrooms maintain discourses of power while aiming to offer access to them. Two responses include calls for better understanding and acknowledgment of language difference and calls for better understanding of standardized language expectations. Bruce Horner, Min-Zhan Lu, Jacqueline Royster, and John Trimbur call for translingual writing classrooms that critically analyze a range of language choices (Horner et al). Mike Duncan and Star Vanguri call for style studies that "move beyond impressionistic language that is rooted in value judgments and toward specific language that names those features of writing we value" (xiii). Both approaches call for what Horner et al. describe as "*more*, not less, conscious and critical attention to how writers deploy diction, syntax, and style, as well as form, register, and media" (304).

Calls for alternative discourses suggest that including both standardizing and non-standardizing language will help rhetoric and composition studies explore new methods and reach broader publics (Bizzell 12). Geneva Smitherman has for decades drawn on multiple dialects in her scholarly writing (a pertinent example: "See, when you lambast the home language that kids bring to school, you ain just dissent dem, you talking about they mommas!" [Smitherman "Ebonics, King, and Oakland" 99]). Suresh Canagarajah builds on Bruce Horner and John Trimbur's call for multiple languages in composition classrooms by making a case for "think[ing] of English as a plural language that embodies multiple norms and standards" through consideration of multimodal and multilingual literacy traditions (Canagarajah 589, 600). Laura Gonzales underscores translation as multimodal practice, inherent to language fluidity valuable in academic and professional contexts and evidence of the power of instability and constant flux (112).

Michael MacDonald and William DeGenaro outline a basic writing program model that supports a "transcultural ethos" for writing classrooms by making various language practices a subject of critical, reflective inquiry in literacy narrative assignment tasks, joining others who similarly point to literacy narratives as sites for inviting and supporting linguistic diversity in composition classrooms (Lovejoy et al.). Staci Perryman Clark's "African American Language, Rhetoric, and Students' Writing" uses a linguistically informed approach to show how three African American composition students successfully use phonological and syntactical features of Ebonics alongside SWAE to analyze genres and achieve rhetorical goals, including conveying specific cultural ideas and codeswitching for communicative situations.

Calls for fostering awareness focus more on critical analysis of SWAE. Keith Gilyard suggests that "the ascension toward a more perfect democracy" depends on students' ability to "comprehend as completely as possible how discourse operates, which means understanding how the dominant or most powerful discourse serves to regulate and reproduce patterns of privilege" (266). Rhetorical genre studies support this approach by advocating genre awareness, including students' critical analysis of the interplay of constraint and choice in written academic discourse (Devitt *Writing Genres*). Rhetorical genre theory builds specifically on Lloyd Bitzer's notion of rhetorical situations that recur, through which "a form of discourse is not only established but comes to have a power of its own" (13). Genres help reveal students' apprenticeship and socialization through norms of discourse (Miller); a current threshold concept in composition is that genres are enacted by writers and readers through habitual responses to rhetorical situations (Hart-Davidson 39). These ideas theoretically evoke the primacy of discourse or at least a mutually informative relationship between discourse choices (used by individuals and across many individuals) and genre; they suggest that genres not only produce discourse but also socialize attendant ways of thinking and being through recurring discourse (Bawarshi).

Even this brief outline shows that these two responses—calling for alternative discourses and calling for critical awareness—overlap in important ways. They share the goal of fostering students' ability to recognize dominant discourses. They share the idea that there are no innately superior discourses, only discourses that are more and less socially and economically powerful. And they place language at the center of Carol Severino's question for composition courses—*Is the purpose of a composition course to help students fit into society or to convince them to change it?* (74). Too, these responses throw into sharp contrast disjuncture between the freedom we preach and the practices we maintain, a double dealing I participate in by writing this essay in SWAE. With exceptions like Perryman Clark's study, these two responses are also primarily ideological, in that they concern how we think about standardizing English, and they are sociocultural, in that they focus on the social value and implications for its use. These albeit important conversations in composition, in other words, rarely draw systematic attention to language—to the linguistic characteristics of standardizing and non-standardizing language use.

There are some calls for more linguistically informed approaches, not least because assessment usually does focus on language, intentionally or otherwise, by enforcing conventional grammatical and mechanical rules about SWAE. Indeed, many instructors feel very concerned about prescribed mechanical correctness even as research suggests that student success does not depend on it as much as instructors think (Crossley et al.; Freedman; Matsuda). Scholars working in both composition and applied linguistics like Paul Matsuda and Jerry Won Lee emphasize the need for more attention to language and more training in how learners acquire and use it. Matsuda, after calling for an updated understanding of applied linguistics in composition, recommends grammar feedback with metalinguistic commentary based on studies showing the clear value of such feedback for students (Matsuda). To move beyond current discussions about translingual writing, Lee argues we need to "recognize the necessary limitations to any universal assessment criterion" and to support linguistic social justice by "confronting the inequitable discursive economies that afford disproportionate amounts of social capital to certain language practices over others" (184, 177).

In practice, however, it is rare to see systematic attention to language in rhetoric and writing studies because decades of genre-based analysis of student writing has "largely . . . set aside" language or form (Devitt "Re-Fusing Form in Genre Study" 27). Since the "social turn," rhetoric and writing studies have focused especially on individual texts and contexts even as applied linguistics research has examined genre-based discourse patterns (see e.g., Johns; Nesi and Gardner; Staples et al.; Swales). For example, social turn research has examined assignment descriptions and writing habits of small groups of first-year students (e.g., Downs and Wardle; Sullivan), the genre knowledge of students in first-year courses (Rounsaville et al.), or the transfer experiences of a single student or a handful of students throughout undergraduate coursework (e.g., Beaufort; Driscoll and Powell). These studies primarily examine student responses to writing assignments via qualitative and ethnographic methods, focusing on "the interactions of people with texts" in individual cases and contexts (Russell 226), rather than linguistic choices that appear meaningful across contexts and individuals.

These historical developments mean that since the social turn in rhetoric and composition studies, we have gained a more critical and nuanced understanding of individual students and contexts and the myriad challenges associated with transfer across different discourse communities. It means that, research focused on composition classrooms has made the important theoretical case that discourse is a constitutive force in academic genres. It means that many U.S. instructors trained to teach composition have learned the crucial point that language ideologies are embedded and persistent in schooling, and thus those important interventions such as literacy narrative assignments can help students recognize and reflect on those ideologies.

It also means that, while important exceptions appear in research on rhetorical grammar, style, discourse analysis, second language writing, and corpus analysis, contemporary rhetoric and composition largely reflects what Robert Connors called the "erasure of the sentence," what Susan Peck MacDonald called the "erasure of language," and what Matsuda described as "the dismissal of various insights from language studies that can inform the study and teaching of writing"

(Matsuda "Let's Face It" 150). It means that pedagogically, we lack a clear framework for discussing language-level choices with students (Butler); and methodologically, analytic approaches that examine language-level patterns across texts and contexts are rarely used in U.S. writing studies (Lancaster "Academics"; Aull).

Most relevant to the discussion here is that a lack of systematic attention to language in rhetoric and composition studies has left us without a sophisticated understanding of the discursive conditions of SWAE, even as our students and our scholarship are overwhelmingly bound to them. For many instructors, this lack of linguistic understanding can perpetuate standard language ideologies, including that SWAE is normal, natural, non-interfering, and widely accessible for students (Davila). Many rhetoric and writing instructors who are already convinced by ideological critiques of SWAE—convinced that multiple discourses and ways of knowing are valuable—still do not have the tools to make the case that SWAE is not linguistically superior to any other dialect.

In this chapter, I want to suggest that a lack of linguistic understanding makes it harder to recognize what we have internalized and what we value and elide when we use and assign SWAE. It makes it harder to show students what it looks like to approach all language as territory for exploration rather than hierarchies and regulation. Alternatively, I suggest that corpus linguistic analysis helps us shift to a descriptive, critical approach to language use—focused on what language is doing versus what it "should" do—with the help of digital tools. In sum, the social turn and sociocultural emphasis have been invaluable; needed now is a turn in which language itself is seen as a constitutive force and object for analysis. Linguistic analysis, the analysis of word-, phrase-, and sentence-level patterns across examples of language use, supports this turn.

From Language Policing to Language Curiosity

Linguistic analysis of diverse language use with students helps us shift from language policing to exploration in three ways. First, by offering evidence of language use in academic and other registers, it exposes patterns associated with SWAE that help us characterize and challenge its primacy. Second, it allows us to identify patterns in widely circulating alternative uses of English, including in global web-based Englishes, so that there is concerted attention to the linguistic diversity that already characterizes our world and our students' lives. Third, in the very process of inviting students to use linguistic analysis to examine and describe academic and other language use, we shift the focus from evaluation to systematic inquiry. Language becomes a site for exploring what is valued in different contexts, the problems and possibilities of all kinds of language, and students' existing knowledge and curiosity regarding language.

In sum, linguistic analysis across different kinds of writing supports linguistic diversity in practice and in theory. It positions students as analysts of two overlapping ideas: language use is situated and diverse language is correct. These are supported in theory in rhetoric and writing studies, but they are manifest undeniably in practice in corpus linguistic analysis like the following examples which illustrate that language use is social, genre-specific, and responsive to context, purpose, and audience and that students already have language knowledge that is correct, or appropriate, for a variety of rhetorical situations. In the next section, I describe corpus linguistic analysis and example activities that place linguistic diversity at the center of our pedagogies.

Using Corpus Analysis to Explore Registers, Genres, Disciplines

Corpus analysis can be defined as the examination of textual patterns in a selected body of naturally produced texts, usually via computer-aided tools that facilitate searching, sorting, and calculating large-scale textual patterns (Bowker and Pearson). This definition emphasizes textual patterns, which can be lexical or grammatical and are often comparative (e.g., between one corpus and another). The definition also emphasizes naturally produced texts: corpus analysis explores language produced for authentic, real-world purposes. Corpus linguistic analysis offers a way to "zoom out" and look for meaningful patterns—patterns that make authentic language used for genres what it is.

Most writing instructors and students, by contrast, are trained to "zoom in"—to read one text at a time, considering each one vis-à-vis the context of the text such as the purpose, genre, and audience. We learn a great deal this way about the strategies, ideas, and revisions of individual writers or small collections of texts. Informed by a descriptive, non-hierarchical lens, this "zoomed in" way of reading can likewise support linguistic diversity.

Systematic attention to language patterns with the help of corpus analysis can complement this common way of reading, by using the power of digital methods to expose choices that persist across many texts—and in turn, by highlighting the systematicity and sociality of all language use. Since the mid to late-20th century, corpus analysis has commonly served to "support learners' awareness of the textual features of their own writing relative to target (i.e., successful) models" (Hardy and Römer 205). But it can also be a way to descriptively understand different registers, genres, and disciplines, rendering them objects of analysis with knowable patterns that students can explore and making choices about. In other words, corpus analysis employs a set of digital tools—e.g., software and online texts—that allow us to acknowledge and explore linguistic diversity in ways impossible with traditional reading methods alone.

By this I mean that corpus analysis is not only different in terms of quantity, or scale, of analysis. It is also different in quality: corpus analysis does not stop with our intuitions about language use. This is crucial for writing classrooms because it reveals tacit expectations that can remain beneath their conscious awareness (Biber and Gray). It can confirm or disrupt even very popular writing instruction by exposing patterns in actual language use (Lancaster). In other words, it can help us, and our students, see that our perceptions about language can be a lot like stereotypes—ideas based on what we have heard and witnessed in a few examples, but not which we have corroborated by witnessing hundreds or thousands of representations.

Below, I offer two initial activities to illustrate some free corpus tools. These activities likewise provide basic examples of how corpus analysis can help us focus writing courses on exploring language descriptively, positioning students as critical analysts of language use around them. The two examples are organized according to a brief description, steps and reading students do as part of the process, online corpus tools students might use (and what the interface looks like), and observations from exploring language in this way with students.

Slang Analysis

Brief Description and Goals

This slang analysis asks students to explore a slang word or phrase that interests them. They explore the slang expression based on reading about slang and use of the expression by family and friends, in current dictionaries, and in a global corpus of web-based English. The process foregrounds student knowledge of and interest in language and draws explicit attention to language diversity in their lives and across the world. The use of the global English corpus is crucial: it is a digital tool that compiles and facilitates exploration of language use, not according to prescriptive rules but according to authentic uses organized by geographic, cultural spaces—i.e., it offers a tool for meeting the linguistic diversity inherent in language with critical language awareness. As part of those explorations, the process invites critical questions about the role of community, reclamation, and appropriation in language use.

Example Reading

Reading about slang leads to important discussion that inform students' own analyses before they begin. For instance, the first two sources below address issues related to English language usage and rules, as well as their evolution over time. The subsequent sources highlight the important role of non-standardized language vis-à-vis formation, inclusion, and exclusion in social groups, generations, and other communities. The final two sources discuss language appropriation and highlight the role of linguistic capital in different social contexts. All the sources support discussions about how the class can thoughtfully approach the upcoming slang analysis and the slang expressions that students choose to investigate.

- Chapters 1 and 2 of How English Works by Anne Curzan and Michael Adams

- New York Times essay "Slang for the Ages" by Kory Stamper
- Chapter 3 from The Life of Slang by Julie Coleman
- Chapter 1 from Slang: The People's Poetry by Michael Adams
- Academic article "Appropriation of African American Slang by Asian American Youth" by Angela Reyes
- Atlantic essay "It Wasn't 'Verbal Blackface.' AOC Was Code-Switching" by John McWhorter[1]

Example Steps

After reading about slang, students decide on a slang word or phrase to investigate. This becomes their slang expression, which they will explore with the help of dictionaries, social media, a web-based corpus, and the student's own community. Students begin their explorations with the origin and definition(s) of their expression, if possible, with the help of the online Oxford English Dictionary (OED). They additional explore its definition and uses in at least two edited dictionaries (e.g., American Heritage, Merriam-Webster) and at least one user-driven dictionary (e.g., Urban Dictionary), as well as on at least two of their own social media accounts or other online platforms. These steps in the process already send an important message: digital tools we use reinforce linguistic diversity all the time, as well as beliefs about linguistic diversity. We can approach dictionaries as they are, a record of human language use and language expectations at any given time, rather than as a single source for upholding or shaming certain language use.

Students tell ten or more people they know, preferably from a range of ages, about their assignment, asking them each to define the slang expression and use it in an example sentence as well as note where they are from, their age, languages they speak, and dialects they speak if they can name them. Students look for patterns or differences in their respondents' example sentences: how is the expression used, and in what contexts? What is its grammatical environment—how does it usually function syntactically (e.g., subject or object? action? description?) and socially (does it signal familiarity? does it show a conversational turn? is it negative or positive? does it describe one gender or group more than others?). They consider whether there is agreement about the term and what kind (e.g., is it based on generations of social group?).

Through this first part of the process of exploring online uses and survey responses, students thus select a slang expression and begin to identify relevant descriptive details about its definition, formation, history, and use. The next step

---

1. For an audio-visual option, John McWhorter's interview on NPR about the use of "thug" is also useful for highlighting questions about the use and appropriation of slang words (https://www.npr.org/2015/04/30/403362626/the-racially-charged-meaning-behind-the-word-thug).

is for students to explore their slang expression more globally, which corpus tools allow them to do. To introduce any new corpus tool in class, I have students try using it together in groups first, e.g., with one computer to every 2–4 students. In this case, they come to class having begun their slang analysis and perused the overview of the GloWbE corpus described below. In class, groups form and decide on which student's slang expression to begin with first.

Example Online Corpus Tools

The Corpus of Global Web-based English (GloWbE: http://corpus.byu.edu/glowbe/) was developed under the leadership of Mark Davies, emeritus professor of Linguistics at Brigham Young University (BYU) whose work has especially focused on development and use of corpora of Spanish, Portuguese, and English across genres to facilitate analysis of historical, syntactic, and other patterns within and across languages. GloWbe is a digital tool that displays global linguistic diversity and makes exploring it possible, by capturing English on public-facing websites (including blogs) across 20 countries with large populations of English speakers.[2] As a first step before or in class, students can read the overview and its embedded links by clicking on the "overview" tab in the upper-right corner of the screen.

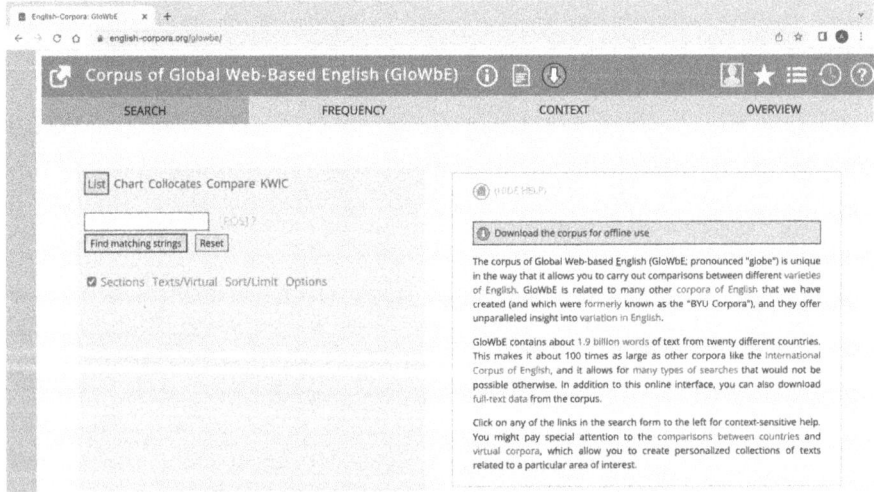

Figure 16.1. GloWbE Corpus Interface, Overview

When students are ready to begin their first query, they can click on the "search" tab in the upper-left corner of the screen. For instance, in the screen

---

2. The web corpus (https://www.english-corpora.org/iweb/), linked to the same page, offers millions of examples used across the internet if students are interested in even more examples. Mark Davies' web page provides additional information about corpus compilation and collaborators: mark-davies.info.

capture of the GloWbE interface in Figure 16.2, I have selected the "chart" tool and entered the slang word *swag* into the query box.

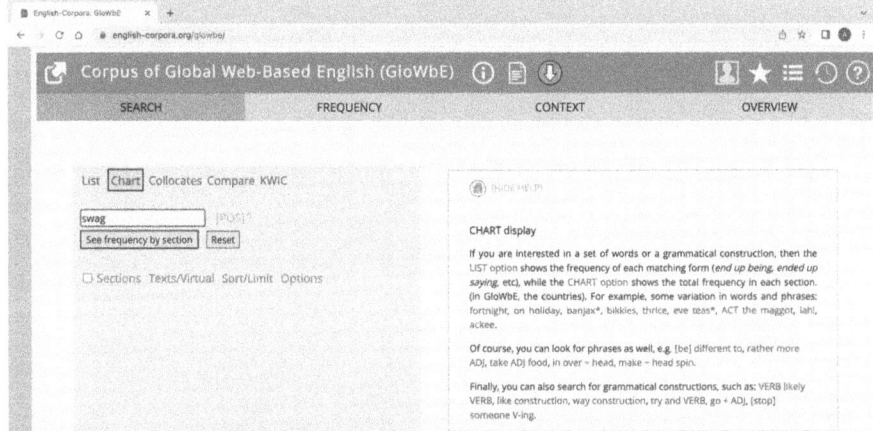

Figure 16.2. GloWbE Corpus Interface, Search Bar

As seen in the screen capture in Figure 16.3, the results show that while *swag* is regularly used in Jamaica (JM) and Nigeria (NG), it is used most frequently on web postings in Ghana (GH). Uses in the United States (US) are outpaced by these three countries as well as Singapore, Australia, and (slightly) Canada.

SECTION	ALL	US	CA	GB	IE	AU	NZ	IN	LK	PK	BD	SG	MY	PH	HK	ZA	NG	GH	KE	TZ	JM
FREQ	2340	632	229	238	53	325	93	31	12	8	8	79	27	83	28	43	105	146	56	22	122
WORDS (M)	1900	386.8	134.8	387.6	101.0	148.2	81.4	96.4	46.6	51.4	39.5	43.0	41.6	43.2	40.5	45.4	42.6	38.8	41.1	35.2	39.6
PER MIL	1.23	1.63	1.70	0.61	0.52	2.19	1.14	0.32	0.26	0.16	0.20	1.84	0.65	1.92	0.69	0.95	2.46	3.77	1.36	0.63	3.08

Figure 16.3. GloWbE Chart Results, Use of Swag

To get a sense of how the slang expression is used, we can look to see the word in context by selecting the "Keyword in Context" (KWIC) tool (rather than the "chart" tool) on the main search page. As shown in the screen capture in Figure 16.4, the KWIC tool includes a range of co-text, or the number of words highlighted on either side, below the search term. Here, I have chosen three words to the left (L) and three words to the right (R).

Clicking on the "Keyword in Context (KWIC)" button will generate a *concordance*, or the list of all instances of a search item in the corpus, under the "context" tab. A concordance includes co-text surrounding the search item, as we can see in the results of the KWIC *swag* search in Figure 16.5.

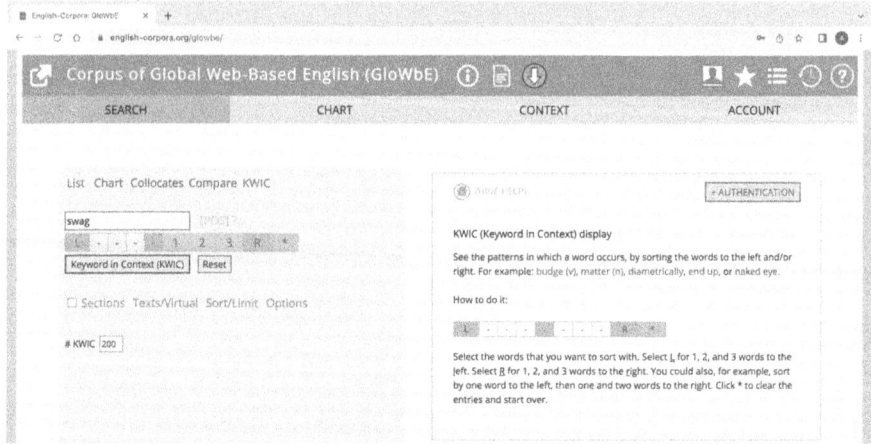

Figure 16.4. GloWbE Search Query, Use of Swag *in Context*

Figure 16.5. GloWbE KWIC Results, Use of Swag

Even this initial concordance shows some patterns across Canadian (CA), Australian (AU), Singaporean (SG), Great Britain (GB), and other uses of *swag*: it is especially used to label a noun, to refer to a style or possession. It is also used as a verb (e.g., *to swag away*), a use my U.S. students find less familiar. To continue to explore syntactic patterns in the use of *swag* (and later, other slang), students can explore *swag* + using the part of speech (POS) tool that appears to the right of the search box in Figure 16.4. Students can look for patterns of use that draw on and challenge their intuitions about language, beginning with such searches of their own and other slang expressions.

Example Observations

This project and its associated tasks invite students to see and think deeply about the social, intersubjective nature of language—the ways that it can, for better and worse, foster and signify group belonging and exclusion and group empowerment and appropriation. The contemporary appropriation of slang from minoritized groups into majority white, heterosexual U.S. culture can often be traced thanks to social media (e.g., *bae* and *spilling tea* to Black vernacular English, *throwing shade* to drag culture), and so student's first step when they are interested in a slang expression is to determine its origin and use. Because their peer discussions and written analysis include context for their slang expression, students must think about how to discuss these details thoughtfully.

This project often highlights the limitations of students' understanding based on their own social lived experiences. Two examples come up regularly. One is that students—and often their parents and instructors—have fallen prey to what lexicographer Kory Stamper calls the "recency illusion," or the belief that because a word is slang, it is new and/ or invented by contemporary youth. Another is some students' assumption that the U.S. is the center of language and/or slang, which corpus analysis of global language use quickly disrupts. For instance, I have had students come to class surprised—and quick to share their new knowledge with their peers—that the word *bling* had much more widespread use and earlier in Jamaica than in the U.S.; in other examples, students have been surprised by several slang expressions used more in Singapore than in the U.S. A third is that students' notice their lexical knowledge more than their syntactic knowledge, but they possess and can consciously cultivate both. When they look through example uses, they can look for how words tend to be used, as a descriptive tool for honing grammatical knowledge. These kinds of discoveries offer an evidence-driven way into discussions about language use, language assumptions, and language appropriation.

SWAE Analysis
Brief Description and Goals

Corpus analysis is well suited to first-year writing goals focused on supporting genre analysis and awareness, because it allows students to explore language patterns as a constitutive part of genres and disciplines and their corresponding audience expectations. A first-year project described below specifically asks students to explore a genre and/or discipline that interests them based on a pattern they have read about in corpus studies of academic writing in English. The process foregrounds students' interests, and it draws explicit attention to diversity and homogeneity in SWAE.

As part of those explorations, the process invites critical questions about accessibility and the constitutive nature of SWAE, or the ways that SWAE language patterns reflect and reify values in different academic discourse communities. For instance, in his article noted below, Ken Hyland shows how different frequencies and uses of first-person pronouns constitute differences between disciplines. He traces first person pronoun use, which he labels *self-mentions*, to the emphasis on interpretive reasoning in humanistic writing versus the emphasis on experimental processes in scientific writing.

Example Reading

Depending on student and instructor interest, individual students or the class can read studies that focus more on writing of genres or across genres or fields. Some possibilities include excerpts from any of the following texts, which I've listed according to the focal genre(s) and level(s) in the studies.

- Stance and engagement features in published academic articles across disciplines (Hyland)
- Dialogue with other sources in published academic writing and first-year and upper-level student writing (Lancaster)
- Genre patterns and variation in the MBA "Thought Essay" written by first-year MBA students (Loudermilk)
- Genre-specific patterns in argumentative essays and rhetorical analyses written by multilingual first-year students (Staples and Reppen)
- Level-specific patterns in argumentative essays by first-year students compared to writing by upper-level students and published academic writers (Aull *How Students Write*)
- Genre-specific patterns in argumentative essays versus explanatory reports written by first-year students (Aull *First-Year*)

In the following texts, students can read specific studies that use the corpus I discuss below, the Michigan Corpus of Upper-level Student Papers (MICUSP):

- Background information about MICUSP (Römer and O'Donnell)
- Description of how to use MICUSP to study disciplinary variation (Römer and Wulff)
- Disciplinary variation in student writing using MICUSP (Hardy and Römer)
- Genre variation in student writing using MICUSP (Hardy and Friginal)

Example Steps

Students begin by reading some of the above studies and the description of how to use MICUSP (Römer and Wulff). They come to class with a discipline, genre, and/or language pattern they read about that they are interested in analyzing.

Students form groups, e.g., with one computer to every 2–4 students, and they begin by discussing these patterns of interest. Together, based on what seems most interesting or manageable, they decide on an initial analysis for exploring MICUS For instance, students are often interested in uses of the first person (or what Hyland discusses as *self-mentions*); student groups interested in these patterns use the search bar to look for first-person pronouns in MICUSP. They then look for patterns in first-person pronouns in GloWbe, the corpus they used in the slang analysis, beginning to talk through rhetorical effects of patterns, such as "emphasizes experiences," "emphasizes processes," etc. Descriptive framing for these discussions, even informal discussion of initial observations, is an important part of this process. Students are often accustomed to saying "proper" or "correct" when describing academic writing, and instead can use more descriptive framing such as "website English" and "academic English" to underscore the linguistic equity and different purposes for different uses.

Even in a 60-minute activity (including searches, analysis, and discussion), students can identify initial, exploratory usage patterns—what disciplines use what first-person pronouns the most, and what tends to appear on either side of the pronouns in example uses. Students' initial observations lead to interesting discussions about disciplinary differences. Writing in mechanical engineering, for instance, includes the highest relative use of the plural first-persons *our* and *we*, followed by physics and philosophy, while writing in English includes the highest relative use of the singular first persons *my* and *I*. I caution students against extrapolating beyond their specific observations (and the number thereof), but in dialogue with Hyland's study, these patterns already speak to possible discipline-specific values, such as the importance of collaborative research processes in physical sciences, and the importance of individual reasoning in humanistic fields like English. Philosophy challenges this neat dichotomy but shows the pattern of using *our* and *we* to consider broad human behaviors and beliefs. Groups and the full class can share these initial writing observations and gain familiarity with MICUSP before using it on their own.

After this group work and further reading of studies noted above, students can conduct their own corpus analysis using MICUSP, analyzing patterns in a genre and/ or discipline of interest to them. Another popular selection for my students is analysis of stance features discussed by Hyland and me, especially, the use of hedges (e.g., *might, perhaps*) and boosters (e.g., *must, definitely*). Hyland shows that published academic writers tend to use a balance of these features; but authors also show that first-year writers tend to use more boosters. Students can analyze patterns in hedge and booster use to see how writers craft their stance in a discipline they might major in. In group discussions or presentations, students can compare their findings and begin to draw inferences about similarities and differences across academic writing expectations.

Students can also apply the findings from a study above to analyze their own writing, by hand or with the help of corpus tools. For a study that is informed by corpus research but is qualitative, students can select a pattern or two of interest discussed in a study listed above. Then, by hand, they can analyze a paper or two of their own to see whether the same patterns appear. For a study that uses corpus analysis, students can begin by compiling a corpus of writing by the class, by saving students' papers in plain text files. Then, individual students or groups can select patterns of interest from a study of academic writing listed above. To analyze these patterns in the class corpus, they can use free concordance software such as AntConc (Anthony), which my students tend to find user-friendly and straightforward. Students and instructors can find steps for using AntConc on their own writing in chapter three of (Aull *First-Year*).

Example Online Corpus Tools

The Michigan Corpus of Upper-level Student Papers (MICUSP) consists of over 800 A-graded papers written by students across seven paper genres, sixteen disciplines, and final year of undergraduate through the first three years of graduate school. As you can see from the left side of the screen capture below, the interface allows you to restrict by student level, nativeness (or what students identified as their "native language" when submitting papers), paper types, disciplines, and overall textual features such as a literature review section or methodology section. (See Römer and O'Donnell for a description of these interface options and the process of designing them.) To the right of these options, we can see visual displays of the disciplines and their relative representation in terms of student paper numbers (in the bar graph) and in terms of paper types (in the pie chart).

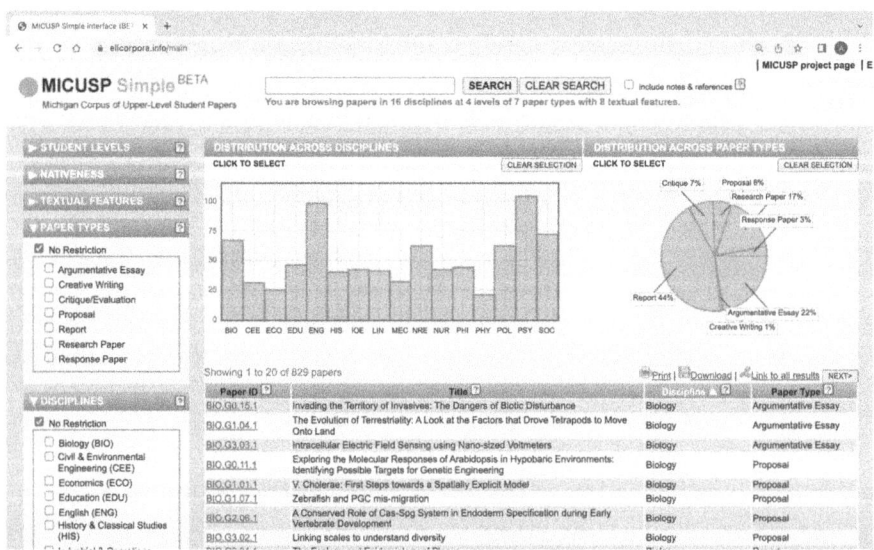

Figure 16.6. MICUSP Interface

Fortunately, once you have typed in a search word or phrase, the interface also allows you to search for uses "per 10,000 words," which allows students to see relative (or normalized) uses across disciplines. The bar graph is interactive, so students can use it to look at uses in a specific discipline. Likewise, the pie chart representing paper types is interactive. Once you enter a search word or phrase and/or restrict by discipline (or student level, etc.), the bar graph and pie chart will update to reflect the new discipline based and genre-based distributions.

Below these two interactive graphics, you can see and click on individual papers, which are tagged according to discipline, level, and number of papers for the student submitting. For instance, in the screen capture in Figure 16.6, BIO. G0.15.1 refers to: a biology paper submitted by a final-year undergraduate student (G0), the fifteenth paper in the corpus at that discipline and level, and the first (and/or only) paper submitted by that student.

Let's consider a brief example query, one I use with students after they have read Hyland's "Stance and Engagement" article. When we search for the plural first person possessive pronoun *our* and select "per 10,000 uses" (above the bar graph), the interface adapts, as shown in the screen capture in Figure 16.7. This query shows that uses of *our* are salient in the discipline of mechanical engineering (as seen in the bar graph) and in the paper genre of reports (as seen in the pie chart). Below this overall glimpse, we see example uses in the concordance.

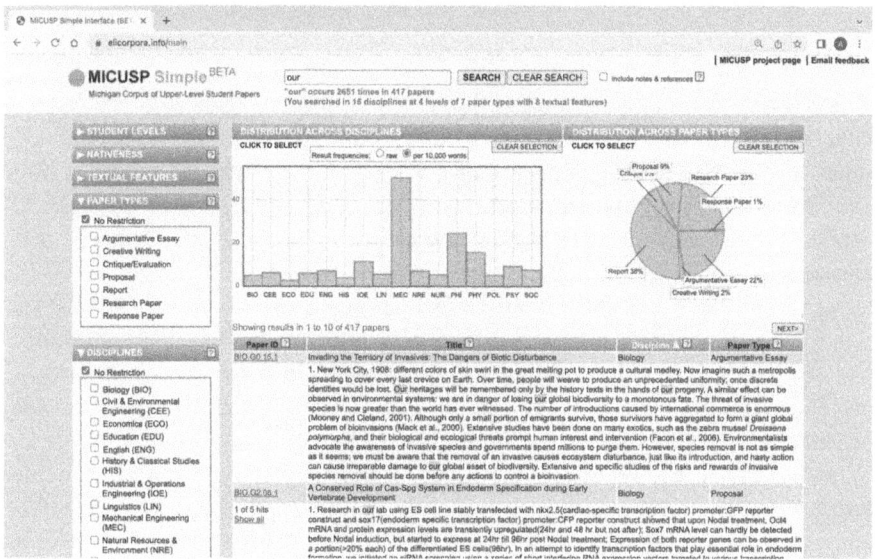

Figure 16.7. MICUSP Search Results, Use of Our

In this case, the start of the concordance shows example uses of *our* in a biology argumentative essay; these uses emphasize collective human needs. Below that example, we can see uses of *our* in a biology report; these uses emphasize the work of a research team. Biology appears first alphabetically, but clicking on any of the discipline bar graphs, or clicking 'next' in the concordance, will bring up the uses from other disciplines. For instance, if we click on the bar representing mechanical engineering (MEC), we can see uses of *our* appear in genres common to this discipline: reports, research papers, and proposals.

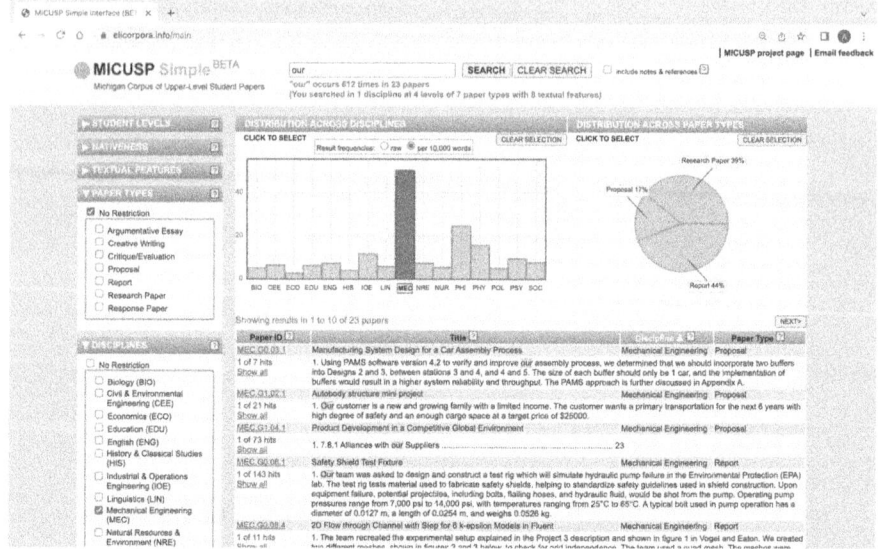

Figure 16.8. MICUSP Search Results, Use of Our *in Mechanical Engineering*

As is true in the concordance in the screen capture in Figure 16.8, mechanical engineering uses of *our* describe experiments and objectives of a research team, often in the subject (noun) phrase of a sentence (e.g., "*Our* experiments have allowed us to create a mathematical model . . ."; "*Our* objective is to use a MEMS accelerometer . . ."). These rhetorical and syntactic uses also appear in the concordance examples in other disciplines such as biology (e.g., "Research in *our* lab using ES cell line . . ."; "*Our* case analysis focused on . . ."), but biology, a natural science, and English, a humanistic field, also include uses of *our* to emphasize broader needs and understanding; e.g., in English, "It is *our* responsibility . . ." and "*Our* aphorisms include . . ."; in biology, "*Our* understanding of flu"; "*Our* understanding of evolutionary convergence . . .").

Finally, should students wish to analyze similar patterns beyond academic writing and/or in published academic writing, they can return to an interface connected to the GloWbe corpus noted in the previous section. The Corpus of Contemporary American English (COCA: https://www.english-corpora.org/coca/) allows students to analyze English use across spoken language, television and movie scripts, and fiction, newspaper, magazine, and academic writing since 1990. (For more than a few queries, students will need to set up a free account.) To continue the above example and compare across these registers, we can go to the corpus interface, select "chart," and enter *our* into the main search box.

Language Policing to Language Curiosity   151

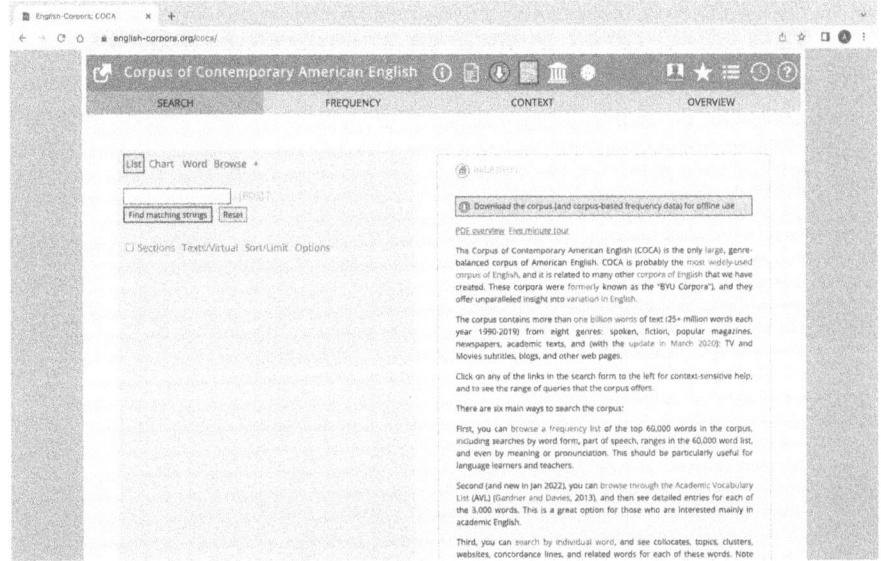

Figure 16.9. COCA Interface

The resulting "chart" patterns displayed in Figure 16.10 show that *our* is especially salient in spoken language (SPOK) and blog writing, followed by website writing (WEB). It is stable over time from 1990 to 2019, and it is used least in newspaper (NEWS) and academic writing (ACAD), two registers considered relatively informational.

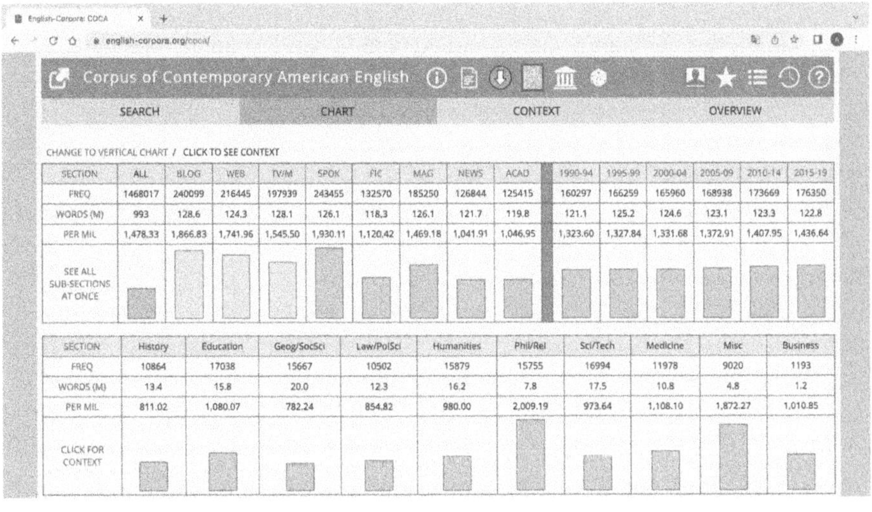

Figure 16.10. COCA Results, Use of Our Across Registers and Academic Disciplines

If we click on the "ACAD" link above the first bar graph, a bar graph representing disciplines will appear below it, as it does in the screen capture displayed in Figure

16.10. Slightly different discipline groups appear in this corpus, though we can see that the overlapping disciplines confirm uses of *our* that also appeared in the upper-level writing in MICUSP: writing in philosophy/religion contains many uses of *our*, and in this case, medicine follows. Uses of *our* in academic writing appear most salient in the "miscellaneous" (MISC) category, which contains academic writing for a general audience, such as in academic essays in *American Scholar*. We can see these uses by clicking on the "context" tab above the chart results.

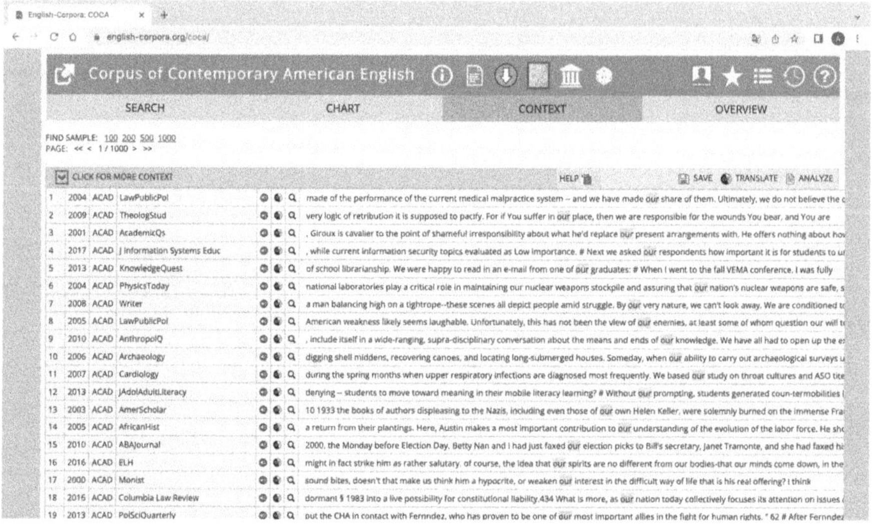

Figure 16.11. COCA Results, Use of Our *in Context*

These examples show that uses of *our* in writing for general academic audiences focus less on research processes and more on personal and collective ideas and behaviors. As in the last example, even this initial search reveals possible disciplinary and genre-based differences in uses of *our*, which students can explore in more depth.

A parallel initial analysis of *my* offers an interestingly different picture. Going back to the main COCA search box, again selecting "chart," and entering *my* will pull up the corresponding results. As displayed in Figure 16.12, this singular possessive pronoun is used especially in television and movie scripts, followed by fiction writing. Like *our*, the use of *my* is stable over time from 1990 to 2019. But in this case, *my* is clearly used the least in the academic writing in the corpus.

If we again click on the "ACAD" link above the first bar graph, another bar graph appears that shows that writing in philosophy/religion again contains the most relative uses vis-à-vis disciplines, as in the case of *our*, but the singular *my* is used about half as often. In another parallel to uses of *our*, *my* appears most in the "miscellaneous" category, which contains more essays written for a general audience. In this category, use of *my*, in individual, personalized narratives and reflections, is more frequent than the use of *our* in shared, collective ones.

Language Policing to Language Curiosity 153

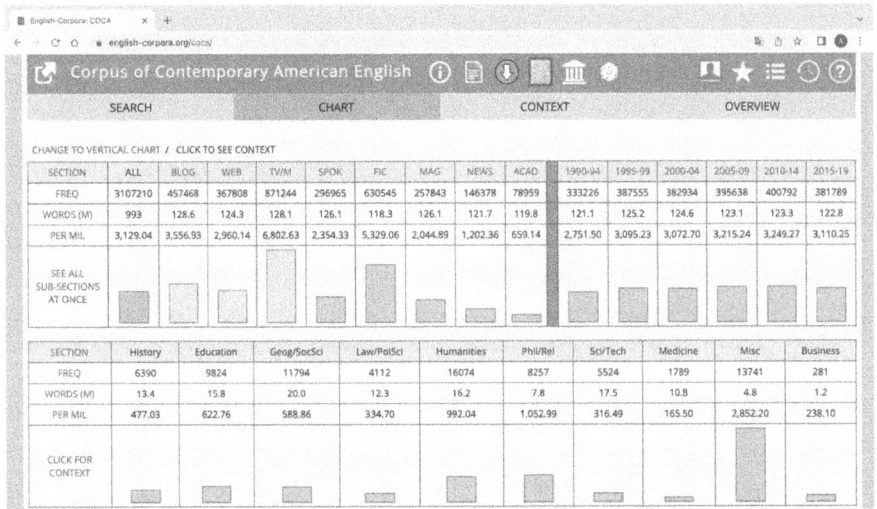

Figure 16.12. COCA Results, Use of My *Across Registers and Academic Disciplines*

Example Observations

In my experience, having students begin with slang analysis before analysis of academic writing facilitates a descriptive approach to language. This sequence helps prime students to see that like slang and other informal language use, academic writing is social. It is informed by communal values and norms; it is learned. It is not impenetrable, and it is not the result of some people being born "better writers" than others. Like other language use, SWAE can include and exclude, according to who uses it and practices it. Even after basic analyses focused on first person pronouns, for instance, we can discuss the reasons and consequences for emphasizing or deemphasizing individuals and collective groups in SWAE, and why that rhetorical choice is more frequent in academic writing for a general audience than for discipline-specific audiences. Students can find exceptions and consider how and why they might challenge or follow these norms.

Analysis of SWAE also helps students explore things they have heard about language use that may not be true. For instance, many students have heard that academic writers, or certain kinds of academic writers such as scientists, do not use first person pronouns to be more objective. Even initial analyses, facilitated by steps outlined above, shows that this is clearly not true. In turn, corpus analysis activities help highlight that even pervasive beliefs about language use and language rules are not necessarily accurate. Such activities lead us to discuss how we might explore language use according to what it does—not what we have heard it should do. In this way, corpus analytics provides evidence that challenges our intuitions and reminds us that without digital tools, our view is limited to a smaller view.

Conclusion

Just as language policing takes years of conscious and unconscious practice, language curiosity will take practice and support for new instructors who are trained for the opposite. Like all embedded, socially constructed value system, language hierarchies run deep, sometimes willfully, and sometimes covertly. When I went north for college after growing up in a small town in Georgia, I was teased so much for the slow pace of my speech that for years, I practiced speaking faster and stopped leaving voice messages. Yet when I first became a teacher, I imposed just the same linguistic hierarchies on students, never thinking how I might be shaming the language(s) most familiar to them. On some level, I felt I had "made it," without knowing really what the "it" was, or its cost. Now, as a teacher, researcher, and writing program administrator (WPA), I am striving for what Staci Perryman-Clark describes, for "my role as a [WPA]" to become "a social justice role that challenges racial and linguistic biases and interrogates institutional structures, so that all students have the same opportunities for success" ("Who" 206). For me, that demands reflection, learning, and unlearning that I am still working to identify and pursue.

Even as it will take ongoing reflection on socially constructed hierarchies that are real and subtle, as well as openness to linguistic training or at least linguistic findings, this paradigm shift to language curiosity is necessary and valuable. It supports student diversity and inclusion, and it supports related goals of our writing courses, including awareness of writing in registers, genres, and disciplines pertinent in student lives. Shifting how we approach language in writing classrooms helps us invite students into what we are valuing—what discursive realities we are constituting—in patterns of SWAE and its alternatives.

Corpus analysis offers a method, a set of actions and activities, for this work. It makes language something we explore, describe, and discover, including discoveries that disrupt things we have heard or internalized in a conventional paradigm that approaches language in terms of rules and intuitions. In these ways, corpus analysis can help us center our pedagogies on linguistic diversity and escape the contradiction in writing classrooms between belief in diversity and homogeneity in practice. It is one way we might empower our students to do a better job than we have in these efforts.

Works Cited

Adams, Michael. *Slang: The People's Poetry*. Oxford UP, 2012.

Anthony, Laurence. "Antconc." 3.2.4 edition, Laurence Anthony, University of Waseda, 2011, http://www.laurenceanthony.net/software/antconc/.

Aull, Laura. *First-year University Writing: A Corpus-based Study with Implications for Pedagogy*. Palgrave Macmillan, 2015.

———. "How Students Write: A Linguistic Analysis." Modern Language Association, 2020.
Bawarshi, Anis. "The Genre Function." *College English*, vol. 62, no. 3, 2000, pp. 335–60.
Beaufort, Anne. *College Writing and Beyond: A New Framework for University Writing Instruction*. Utah State UP, 2007.
Biber, Douglas, and Bethany Gray. "Challenging Stereotypes About Academic Writing: Complexity, Elaboration, Explicitness." *Journal of English for Academic Purposes*, vol. 9, no. 1, 2010, pp. 2- 20.
Bitzer, Lloyd F. "The Rhetorical Situation." *Philosophy and Rhetoric*, vol. 25, 1992, pp. 1–14.
Bizzell, Patricia. "Hybrid Academic Discourses: What, Why, How." *Composition Studies*, vol. 27, no. 2, 1999, pp. 7–22.
Bowker, Lynne, and Jennifer Pearson. *Working with Specialized Language: A Practical Guide to Using Corpora*. Routledge, 2002.
Butler, Paul. *Out of Style: Reanimating Stylistic Study in Composition and Rhetoric*. Utah State UP, 2008.
Canagarajah, A Suresh. "The Place of World Englishes in Composition: Pluralization Continued." *College Composition and Communication*, 2006, pp. 586–619.
Conference on College Composition and Communication. "Students' Right to Their Own Language." *College Composition and Communication*, vol. 25, no. 3, 1974, pp. 1–32.
Conference on College Composition and Commication. "This Ain't Another Statement! This Is a Demand for Black Linguistic Justice!" edited by April Baker-Bell, National Council of Teachers of English, 2020. https://cccc.ncte.org/cccc/demand-for-black-linguistic-justice.
Coleman, Julie. *The Life of Slang*. Oxford UP, 2012.
Connors, Robert J. "The Erasure of the Sentence." *College Composition and Communication*, vol. 52, no.1, 2000, pp. 96–128, http://www.jstor.org/stable/358546.
Crossley, Scott A., Kris Kyle, Danielle McNamara, and Laura Allen. "The Importance of Grammar and Mechanics in Writing Assessment and Instruction: Evidence from Data Mining." *Educational Data Mining 2014*, 2014.
Curzan, Anne. "Says Who? Teaching and Questioning the Rules of Grammar." *PMLA*, vol. 124, no. 3, 2009, pp. 870–79.
Curzan, Anne, and Michael Adams. *How English Works: A Linguistic Instruction*. Pearson, 2014.
Davila, Bethany. "The Inevitability of 'Standard' English: Discursive Constructions of Standard Language Ideologies." *Written Communication*, vol. 33, no. 2, 2016, pp. 127–48.
Devitt, Amy J. "Re-Fusing Form in Genre Study." *Genres in the Internet: Issues in the Theory of Genre*, vol. 188, 2009, pp. 27–47.
———. *Writing Genres*. Southern Illinois UP, 2004.
Downs, Douglas, and Elizabeth Wardle. "Teaching About Writing, Righting Misconceptions:(Re)Envisioning 'First-Year Composition' as 'Introduction to Writing Studies.'" *College Composition and Communication*, vol. 58, no. 4, 2007, pp. 552–84.

Driscoll, Dana Lynn, and Roger Powell. "States, Traits, and Dispositions: The Impact of Emotion on Writing Development and Writing Transfer across College Courses and Beyond." *Composition Forum*, vol. 34, 2016.

Duncan, Mike, and Star Medzerian Vanguri. "Introduction to the Centrality of Style." *The Centrality of Style*, The WAC Clearinghouse/Parlor Press, 2013, pp. xi-xiv, https://doi.org/10.37514/PER-B.2013.0476.

Freedman, Sarah W. "How Characteristics of Student Essays Influence Teachers' Evaluations." *Journal of Educational Psychology*, vol. 71, no. 3, 1979, pp. 328-38.

Gilyard, Keith. "Literacy, Identity, Imagination, Flight." *College Composition and Communication*, vol. 52, no. 2, 2000, pp. 260-72.

Gonzales, Laura. *Sites of Translation: What Multilinguals Can Teach Us About Digital Writing and Rhetoric*. U of Michigan P, 2018.

Hardy, Jack A., and Eric Friginal. "Genre Variation in Student Writing: A Multi-Dimensional Analysis." *Journal of English for Academic Purposes*, vol. 22, 2016, pp. 119-31.

Hardy, Jack A., and Ute Römer. "Revealing Disciplinary Variation in Student Writing: A Multi Dimensional Analysis of the Michigan Corpus of Upper-Level Student Papers (Micusp)." *Corpora*, vol. 8, no. 2, 2013, pp. 183-207.

Hart-Davidson, Bill. "Genres Are Enacted by Writers and Readers." *Naming What We Know: Threshold Concepts of Writing Studies*, edited by Linda Adler-Kassner and Elizabeth Wardle, Utah State UP, 2015, pp. 39-40.

Hasty, J. Daniel, et al. "Valuing a Variety of Voices: Using Digital Badges to Support Linguistic Diversity in First-Year Composition." *American Speech: A Quarterly of Linguistic Usage*, vol. 95, no. 2, 2020, pp. 243-52.

Horner, Bruce, Min-Zhan Lu, Jacqueline Jones Royster, and John Trimbur. "Language Difference in Writing: Toward a Translingual Approach." *College English*, vol. 73, no. 3, 2011, pp. 303-21.

Hyland, Ken. "Stance and Engagement: A Model of Interaction in Academic Discourse." *Discourse Studies*, vol. 7, no. 2, 2005, pp. 173-92, https://doi.org/10.1177/1461445605050365.

Inoue, Asao B. *Antiracist Writing Assessment Ecologies: Teaching and Assessing Writing for a Socially Just Future*. The WAC Clearinghouse/Parlor Press, 2015, https://doi.org/10.37514/PER-B.2015.0698.

Johns, Ann M. *Genre in the Classroom: Multiple Perspectives*. L. Erlbaum, 2002.

Lancaster, Zak. "Do Academics Really Write This Way? A Corpus Investigation of Moves and Templates in 'They Say/I Say.'" *College Composition and Communication*, vol. 67, no. 3, 2016, pp. 437-64.

Lee, Jerry Won. "Beyond Translingual Writing." *College English*, vol. 79, no. 2, 2016, pp. 174-95.

Loudermilk, Brandon Conner. "Occluded Academic Genres: An Analysis of the Mba Thought Essay." *Journal of English for Academic Purposes*, vol. 6, no. 3, 2007, pp. 190-205,

Lovejoy, Kim Brian, Steve Fox, and Katherine A Wills. "From Language Experience to Classroom Practice: Affirming Linguistic Diversity in Writing Pedagogy." *Pedagogy*, vol. 9, no. 2, 2009, pp. 261-87.

MacDonald, Michael T., and William DeGenaro. "Negotiating a Transcultural Ethos from the Ground up in a Basic Writing Program." *Journal of Basic Writing*, vol. 36, no. 1, 2017, pp. 25–55.

MacDonald, Susan Peck. "The Erasure of Language." *College Composition and Communication*, vol. 58, no. 4, 2007, pp. 585–625.

Martín, Cristina Sánchez, Lavinia Hirsu, Laura Gonzales, and Sara P. Alvarez. "Pedagogies of Digital Composing through a Translingual Approach." *Computers and Composition*, vol. 52, 2019, pp. 142–57.

Matsuda, Paul Kei. "Let's Face It: Language Issues and the Writing Program Administrator." *Writing Program Administration*, vol. 36, no. 1, 2012, pp. 141–64.

McWhorter, John. "It Wasn't 'Verbal Blackface.'Aoc Was Code-Switching." *The Atlantic*, vol. 9, 2019.

———. *Word on the Street: Debunking the Myth of a Pure Standard English*. Basic Books, 2001.

Miller, Carolyn R. "Genre as Social Action (1984), Revisited 30 Years Later (2014)." *Letras and Letras*, vol. 31, no. 3, 2015, pp. 56–72.

Nesi, Hilary and Sheena Gardner. *Genres Across the Disciplines: Student Writing in Higher Education*. Cambridge UP, 2012.

Perryman-Clark, Staci M. "African American Language, Rhetoric, and Students' Writing: New Directions for Srtol." *College Composition and Communication*, vol. 64, no. 3, 2013, pp. 469–95.

———. "Who We Are (n't) Assessing: Racializing Language and Writing Assessment in Writing Program Administration." *College English*, vol. 79, no. 2, 2016, pp. 206–11.

Reyes, Angela. "Appropriation of African American Slang by Asian American Youth 1." *Journal of Sociolinguistics*, vol. 9, no. 4, 2005, pp. 509–32.

Römer, Ute, and Matthew Brook O'Donnell. "From Student Hard Drive to Web Corpus (Part 1): The Design, Compilation and Genre Classification of the Michigan Corpus of Upper-Level Student Papers (Micusp)." *Corpora*, vol. 6, no. 2, 2011, pp. 159–77.

Römer, Ute, and Stefanie Wulff. "Applying Corpus Methods to Written Academic Texts: Explorations of Micusp." *Journal of Writing Research*, vol. 2, no. 2, 2010, pp. 99–127.

Rounsaville, Angela, Rachel Goldberg, and Anis Bawarshi. "From Incomes to Outcomes: Fyw Students' Prior Genre Knowledge, Meta Cognition, and the Question of Transfer." *WPA: Writing Program Administration*, vol. 1, no. 32, 2008, pp. 97–112.

Russell, David. "Writing and Genre in Higher Education and Workplaces: A Review of Studies That Use Cultural—Historical Activity Theory." *Mind, Culture, and Activity*, vol. 4, no. 4, 1997, pp. 224–37.

Severino, Carol. "Teaching and Writing: 'Up Against the Mall.'" *College English*, vol. 59, no. 1, 1997, pp. 74–82.

Shapiro, S. (2022). *Cultivating critical language awareness in the writing classroom*. Routledge.

Smagorinsky, Peter, Elizabeth Anne Daigle, Cindy O'Donnell-Allen, and Susan Bynum. "Bullshit in Academic Writing: A Protocol Analysis of a High School

Senior's Process of Interpreting Much Ado About Nothing." *Research in the Teaching of English*, vol. 44, no. 4, 2010, pp. 368–405.

Smitherman, Geneva. "Ebonics, King, and Oakland: Some Folk Don't Believe Fat Meat Is Greasy." *Journal of English Linguistics*, vol. 26, no. 2, 1998, pp. 97–107.

———. "'Students' Right to Their Own Language': A Retrospective." *The English Journal*, vol. 84, no. 1, 1995, pp. 21–27.

Stamper, Kory. "Slang for the Ages." *New York Times*, Opinion, 3 Oct. 2014.

Staples, Shelley, Jesse Egbert, Douglas Biber, and Bethany Gray. "Academic Writing Development at the University Level: Phrasal and Clausal Complexity across Level of Study, Discipline, and Genre." *Written Communication*, vol. 33, no. 2, 2016, pp. 149–83, https://doi.org/10.1177/0741088316631527.

Staples, Shelley, and Randi Reppen. "Understanding First-Year L2 Writing: A Lexico-Grammatical Analysis across L1s, Genres, and Language Ratings." *Journal of Second Language Writing*, vol. 32, 2016, pp. 17–35.

Sullivan, Patrick. "The Unessay: Making Room for Creativity in the Composition Classroom." *College composition and communication*, vol. 67, no. 1, 2015, p. 6.

Swales, John. *Genre Analysis: English in Academic and Research Settings*. Cambridge UP, 1990. Cambridge Applied Linguistics Series.

Appendix: Additional Corpora

The Corpus of Contemporary American English (COCA), at https://www.english-corpora.org/coca/ also links to the following:

- The Corpus of Historical American English (COHA, http://corpus/byu.edu/coha/) allows us to track changes in American English over the 19th and 20th centuries.
- The Time Magazine Corpus (http://corpus.byu.edu/time/) can provide interesting data about changes in written, edited American English in Time since the 1920s.
- Note: There are several videos about using COCA on YouTube; I recommend the one (and the other resources) on David West Brown's page thegrammarlab.com: https://www.youtube.com/watch?v=sCLgRTlxGoY

The Google Books Ngram Viewer, at https://books.google.com/ngrams/, allows us to explore language use in books in several languages since the beginning of the 19th century. If you hover over the right end of the query box, you will also see links to additional information and advanced search options (also available at https://books.google.com/ngrams/info).

Chapter 17. The Pleasurable Difficulty of Programming

Benjamin Miller
UNIVERSITY OF PITTSBURGH

Land Acknowledgment. I write from the city of Pittsburgh, in the ancestral territories of the Osage Nation and the Shawnee Tribe; much of my climb up the learning curve I will describe below took place in New York, home of the Wappinger and Munsee Lenape peoples ("NativeLand.Ca"). As I have striven in my research to situate graduate education in composition/rhetoric amid a flux of topics, methods, and mentors, so too do I situate that disciplinary flux itself within the long history of occupation, exclusion, preservation, and celebration of these peoples and their traditions. I honor and thank those whose sacrifices made possible my access to the resources I use every day, as well as those who continue to educate me about these histories and their ongoing effects.

Why Programming? Why Now?

In *Coding Literacy*, Annette Vee traces the ways that computer programming has suffused modern life, such that even people who don't program themselves still need a "computational mentality": the ability to anticipate and respond to the ways computer programs shape our lives and interactions (196–97). Alongside everyday software applications like email and online shopping are a growing number of tools for academic work, from library search portals to multimedia composing platforms to suites for data analytics and visualization. In most cases, the tools are available to non-programmers and programmers alike, because the software provides user-friendly graphical interfaces: programming, that is, that seems to obviate the need to look too deeply into the programming. "At first glance," Vee writes, "thousands of apps, menus, and interfaces promise to deliver the power of programming to those who do not know how to write code" (22). Yet she cautions that the ability to read and write code, with its requisite habit of thinking "in hyper-explicit terms" (ibid), is no less important now. Increasingly, she writes, "to navigate many professions and the demands of life in the twenty-first century, we need to have computational skills, or at least know someone who does" (197).

The history of computers and writing (C&W) offers plenty of examples of "writing teachers writing software" (to borrow the title of Paul LeBlanc's 1993 book). Even by 1984, efforts in process-oriented computer assisted instruction could fill out a thirteen-chapter collection (Wresch), and a much larger bibliography by the time of Mike Palmquist's 2003 review. Since then, large-scale peer review platforms like Eli Review (Hart-Davidson et al.) and MyReviewers/USF Writes (Melançon), along with text-markup tools like <emma> (Desmet et al.) and Docuscope (Kaufer et al.), both support writing pedagogy and generate datasets for further analysis. More bespoke data visualization efforts in the field, such as those in a recent special issue of *Kairos*, use programming frameworks like d3.js (Lindgren and Ridolfo), amcharts (Turner and Gonzales), and R (Dighton), among others.

All the same, as Tim Lockridge recently noted, while "this type of work [i.e., building a digital tool to solve a problem] was once the norm in computers and writing [. . . it] seems less so today" ("The Problem"). There are several good reasons for this, as the rest of the present collection makes clear. First, many of the questions and problems facing C&W are better addressed by interpersonal means, rather than algorithmic ones; indeed, some problems are even *caused* by algorithms, which tend to embed cultural assumptions as biases or blindspots (Noble; Klein and D'Ignazio). If you're analyzing the uses of digital multimedia by musicians (Craig), or the impact of telepresence on a writing center conference (Feibush), then individual, embodied human perspectives are essential. Second, many of the digital tools by which we can preserve or present, say, interviews, already provide a great deal of flexibility and power to their users, even without having to touch a line of code. There's no need to reinvent the reel to take advantage of digital video editing software, for example, on top of which, the level of programming skill required to make such software lends itself to dedicated specialists: engineers, rather than writing scholars. Even questions and problems for which an algorithmic approach makes sense, such as statistical analyses of large bodies of text, are increasingly addressable without having to produce the code that powers the algorithms. Web-based corpus analytics suites such as Voyant Tools, or built-in search-and-filter functions in scholarly databases like COCA (the Corpus of Contemporary American English), have lowered the barriers to these kinds of computational research methods in ways that are surely worth celebrating.

All the same, I find myself drawn to the open-endedness of programming. As a discourse, it has much in common with writing more generally: rather than a proscribed set of options to select from in a menu, programming languages offer the materials by which to shape new approaches that fit the data and questions we bring to it. In that sense, codework is rhetorical, addressing the present situation by drawing flexibly on insights from the past. Like other forms of writing, writing with code can be both frustrating and tremendously rewarding, sometimes even in the same working session. And as with writing, the process of working through those frustrations is itself epistemically generative, forming a feedback loop that can shift one's sense of what's important and how the pieces fit together. So, despite the steep initial learning curve—and, yes, the ongoing challenges of maintaining the ever-expanding set of files and executable scripts that form my research codebase—I have continued to return to programming as a way of centering my attention on a research project, getting a handle on my data, and refining my understanding of what it must teach.

In this chapter, I write to explain the draw (as well as some drawbacks) of this kind of digital composing as a research method, and to demystify the process for those curious about but unfamiliar with code. Toward that end, the heart of the chapter is an extended example, or re-enactment, of a recent challenge in my research, and the programming workflow I used to solve it. Inspired in part by Dana Kantrowitz's "The Making of a Poem, Live and Uncensored" in *The Subject is Writing*, I trace a series of aims, misses, and rescues, presenting not only a reconstruction of what I was thinking, but also (some of) the code produced along the way. In doing so, I will highlight key affordances of functional programming that make it not only useful from the perspective of knowledge production, but also affectively rewarding.

A Note About the Code in this Chapter

The code I share is not "live and uncensored"; it's only a small part of a much larger codebase, curated retrospectively. Even so, I realize it's still a lot of technical language and syntax to throw at you—and that, for some readers, *any* amount of code will feel alien, or alienating. What's more, my example comes from a statistically oriented programming language, R, which may not be the first language you want to try, even if you are convinced of the value of programming for writing research. Nevertheless, I believe it is important to show the code itself, for several reasons.

First, I want to make the sight of code *less* alien. If we allow graphic user interfaces (GUIs) to hide all the conditional statements and assumptions that the code makes explicit, we cede the ability to intercede in those operational decisions. Even if you have no interest in programming yourself, developing what Vee calls a "coding literacy" will help you communicate with those who do, with a better sense of what the code makes easy or hard. Increased circulation of coding literacy has ethical implications: "If we want a more inclusive and equal society," Vee argues, "the writing of code should not be left to a handful of elite or isolated groups" (224). Diversifying and expanding the group of people able to *read* code is an important first step toward that more inclusive society.

Second, setting several examples alongside each other can help make visible recurring patterns in the code, especially those that cross programming languages. One or two examples could show you what programming looks like in the abstract, but to really get a sense of how programming can work in the context of writing research and problem-solving, I need to show you more than that. One key concept I want to highlight is the high frequency of *control flows*: functions with inputs and outputs, iterative loops that run a series of inputs through the same chunk of code, if/then/else statements that divert the flow from one code chunk to another. Second, I also want to call attention to the recursive nature of programming: the ways *new code integrates and recontextualizes old code*, sometimes necessitating changes to the old code (a.k.a. refactoring) to address false or incomplete assumptions made apparent by the new use-case. A third key concept of programming as method is *task decomposition*, which entails breaking large objectives into smaller pieces. Seeing the iterative, interactive process of identifying, constructing, and combining those smaller pieces is essential to understanding what's involved.

In addition, I want to step through an extended sequence from problem to program in order to recognize that plans for coding, like plans for writing, must often shift as they are implemented. Learning to code can be difficult, and setbacks are assuredly frustrating. But they are also a persistent feature of composing, and I don't want to paper over that fact, or leave it for readers to discover and become discouraged by. I come from a privileged background, in which I was encouraged to believe that I could do anything if I put my mind to it, in which the language at my well-funded public schools never felt foreign (both my parents went to college, and my father has a Ph.D.), and thus early successes seemed in easy reach. I only took one computer science course, and not until college, but it was a lecture-and-recitation at Harvard that assumed most of us would explore documentation and find most examples on our own. This again reinforced the message that success was a given—but also implied that it was a matter of individual persistence. Even with my already-internalized sense that challenges are only temporary, only puzzles to play with, I found programming difficult; I can see how, without that sense of arbitrary self-efficacy, it would be easy to respond to such difficulty by saying, "programming just isn't for me."

So, it's important to me to counteract the idea that good programmers just do it right, the first time, on their own. On the contrary, when I really began learning how to program for analysis while writing my dissertation, I had the advantage of peer mentors from across the digital humanities whom I could turn to for example code and turn back to with questions. I had coursework and a fellowship in Interactive Technology and Pedagogy that helped me build that network of peer mentors. Because I recognize that not everyone reading this will have the same local support networks, or the same lifelong drumbeat of positive reinforcement, I hope the code I share here—including the code I wrote that failed, and the kinds of steps I took to try and fix it—will offer at least the starting place my friends[1] and *their* code were able to offer me, both as a graduate student at CUNY and as early faculty at University of Pittsburgh. At the end of this chapter, I will point to additional open resources for those interested in taking up programming as a digital research method.

My Research Program

The context for the work I'm discussing in this chapter is a book-length study of doctoral dissertations in rhetoric, composition, and writing studies—several thousand of them, submitted over a fifteen year span—as a way of advancing what Derek Mueller calls a *network sense* of the field: "incomplete but nevertheless vital glimpses of an interconnected disciplinary domain focused on relationships that

---

1. Thanks to Micki Kaufman, Evan Misshula, Matt Lavin, and Scott Weingart.

define and cohere widespread scholarly activity" (3). Dissertations are well-suited to such questions of disciplinarity: they are widely distributed, sustained, and required to remain recognizable as work "within" the field, even as they advance new claims.

My book is primarily a descriptive study, aiming to intervene in scholarly debates about what the field *should* be doing by stepping back to first consider what we *have* been doing. One way to understand the goal of describing the field's practices (without predicting future behaviors or pre/proscribing what people ought to do) is that I'm engaged in a mapmaking project: I'm looking to chart the disciplinary landscape, to identify the existing balance of subject areas and methods, and thereby help newcomers navigate the potentially overwhelming range of possibilities.[2]

Digital tools offer two key advantages in this pursuit. First, they can read a lot faster than I can; and second, they make analysis more replicable. As Mueller points out, the size of our disciplinary domain has grown beyond what even a diligent reader could attend to, even reading all day, every day. Computers, though, can abstract data into metadata, consolidating great quantities of information into tables and graphs, which in turn amplify signals that human readers can interpret. Susan Lang and Craig Baehr clarify that such computer-assisted analysis doesn't change the responsibility or focus of human interpretation so much as the scale of what's being considered. Even so, "data and text mining extend [traditional humanities research activities] beyond what it is possible for us to do as individuals without the assistance of computer technology, as large amounts of numeric or textual data can be examined for various types of relationships, including classes, clusters, associations, and patterns" (Lang and Baehr 178). One of the traditional activities they specifically call out is reflection, reminding us that these patterns can't be taken as neutral or inevitable. Still, by externalizing part of the process of discovery into code, computers make it easier for subsequent researchers—or even ourselves—to repeat the process in a new context, to thoughtfully examine what changes, what's expected but missing, what other explanations might underlie the patterns we see.

Programming My Research

As I suggested above, several software tools—including free tools—now exist to make it easier to classify, cluster, or otherwise detect associations and patterns in textual data. Laurence Anthony's concordance software, AntConc, can identify words that stand out more in one group of documents than another; it can also

---

2. I want to be clear, though, that I'm not trying to make a once-and-only map of the field. For one thing, maps always, of necessity, leave things out: a map that includes everything is just the territory itself, simultaneously perfect and pointless. I am, rather, trying to capture one set of phenomena; different methods, and different vantages, offer different senses of the network, and each will be useful in their own ways. For another thing, fields do and should change over time. But if we are interested in how things change over time, we need to take stock periodically, to establish points of comparison.

show keywords or phrases of interest surrounded by the preceding and following parts of each sentence where they occur. Voyant-Tools, a full-service text-analytics suite that runs in a web browser, offers these and many other operations besides: it can show the frequency of words rising and falling across the documents in a textual corpus; it can visualize the corpus as a word cloud, or as a set of two-word phrases that appear frequently together (bigram collocates), and much, much more. That these and similar tools are available, and free to use, marks an incredible advance in access to digital research methods, and I highly recommend them, especially in the early stages of becoming familiar with a body of texts.

At the same time, there are limits to what they provide. In particular, the outputs are essentially endpoints: the tool produces a graph or a table, and that is the graph or table it produces. Further transformations are not generally possible within the website or dialog box from which you operate the software. To be fair, there are usually options that you can vary, and you can sometimes filter an output table by one search term at a time, e.g., to narrow a list of all collocated terms to one particular term of your choice; but if you wanted to, say, identify a subset of documents based on the presence or absence of those collocates, and to proceed with a follow-up analysis of that subset, that's usually a move the tool won't support. You would want to program your own custom function.

Because I'm interested in what subject matter people are writing about, I've been drawn to *topic modeling*, a machine-learning method for identifying groups of words that tend to co-occur within sets of documents in a large corpus (Blei et al.; Weingart). Given several such groups to find, the algorithm calculates two sets of probabilities, one matching words to groups—the "topics"—and one matching topics to documents. The software generating the topics will generally also tell you how much of the corpus is associated with each topic. In the case that I describe below that software is MALLET,[3] an open-source command-line tool[4] most often used for topic modeling using the Latent Dirichlet Allocation method (but which is also generalizable to other applications, and other implementations, for those with a coding knowledge of the Java programming language).

By default, topics in MALLET (and, often, elsewhere) come labeled with the words associated with them at the highest probabilities, leading to labels such as these:

44. online web site media internet sites social users

---

3. MALLET is an acronym for MAchine Learning for LanguagE Toolkit; see http://mallet.cs.umass.edu/about.php. VoyantTools can also produce topic models, using a JavaScript implementation of the same algorithm (Latent Dirichlet Allocation); see https://voyant-tools.org/docs/#!/guide/topics.

4. The "command line" refers to the text-only interface accessed via Terminal on Mac computers, or PowerShell on Windows, and as the primary mode of engaging with Linux systems. For more information on the command line, see https://learnpythonthehardway.org/book/appendix-a-cli/ex1.html.

information blog community people post virtual communication blogs website content page websites

45. technology digital computer computers technologies online media university web writing electronic technological composition software design
access information internet hypertext multimodal

From just the words alone, we can infer that documents with high levels of these two topics discuss matters of likely interest to the computers and writing community: online communication and community, electronic writing, multimodal design, and so on. But suppose you wanted to go beyond the words themselves, to look at abstracts or the full text as a way of understanding the topics? Andrew Goldstone has built a beautiful interactive browser that allows navigation among terms, topics, and documents (Goldstone), but to make it work with your own data, you'll need to be able to download and run his custom scripts in the R programming language—and potentially to modify them, too.

To help explain what that would entail, in the pages that follow I present an example of my own workflow in R. It begins with a question about how best to interpret the topic model, and a challenge in the way MALLET represents the model data. I then write a multi-step plan, in English, for how to surmount that challenge. As I move to implement the plan in code, it reveals new problems, requiring a revision of the plan. The final working implementation strings together several smaller pieces of code into a composite script. Interspersed throughout the examples—which will appear in a fixed-width font when they are written for the computer to execute—I will point out important patterns that transcend programming languages, as well as define terms or explain bits of R-specific syntax that are essential to reading comprehension of the code.

I write, revise, and execute my code using a piece of software called RStudio, an integrated development environment (IDE). What it integrates, specifically, are several elements of a programming workspace that will be common across languages: in that sense, my descriptions of R would be equally applicable to working in Python (through an IDE like Spyder or IDLE) or Ruby (through an IDE like Aptana). These include:

- A *text editor*, where you can write and store programs that can be executed repeatedly at a later time. These files can then also refer to each other, e.g., to load or execute a function you have written previously. Ideally, the text editor includes features to improve the legibility of the code, such as syntax highlighting[5] or bracket folding.[6]

---

5. That is, formatting chunks of text in different colors or weights to signal the role each chunk plays in the program.

6. That is, allowing the user to collapse or expand discrete sections of code that act as a single unit, which are often demarcated with parentheses or brackets.

- A *console*, in which commands entered take effect immediately and any outputs or errors are displayed.
- A list of current *variables* and what they store, sometimes called the *environment*. In RStudio, this list also includes any user-defined *functions* that are currently loaded.
- A *package manager*, indexing the external libraries that are available on the system and enabling quick installation, loading, or unloading of those libraries.
- Searchable *documentation* for functions (both those included in the base distribution and in distributed packages), clarifying the expected inputs and outputs. These often provide examples, though these are not always as illuminating as one might hope; in such cases, external sources like Stack Overflow (https://stackoverflow.com) become an essential part of my workflow.

RStudio also includes a history of commands executed by the console, and a window for displaying plots and charts. These elements work together: in most IDEs, you should be able to write code in the text editor and execute it in the console, either all at once or only selected lines; the outputs can then be stored in variables, if your code says they should, so you can do what you'd like with them next. This is essential for finding and fixing bugs in complex programs because it allows you to check interim values and confirm that your code is doing what you think it's doing. (For me, at least, this is not always the case, especially at first.)

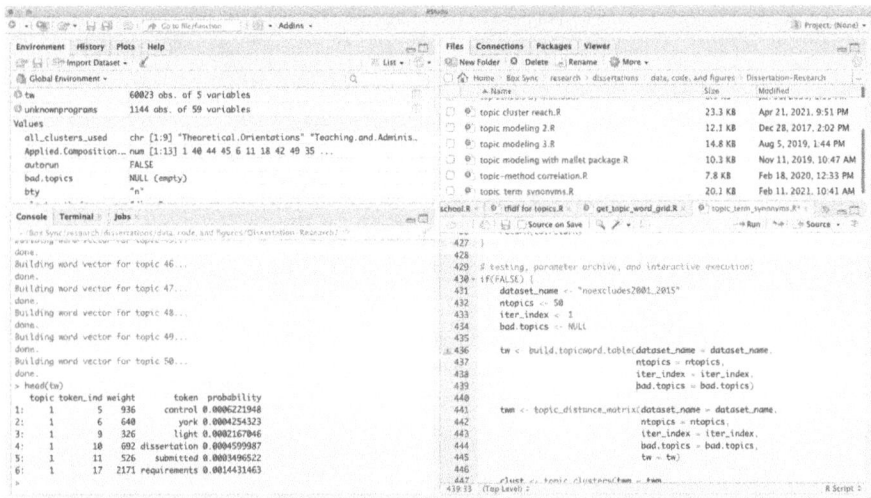

Figure 17.1. The RStudio Integrated Development Environment (IDE). Clockwise from bottom right, the four quadrants show the text editor; the console; the environment of defined functions and variables; and the package manager. Documentation can be accessed through the "Help" tab in the upper left quadrant. (Note that these locations can also be customized.)

Setting the Stage: A Data Challenge and a Plan

For my research purposes, to better grasp the distribution of subject matter across RCWS dissertations, I was especially interested in finding clusters of related topics, like Topics 44 and 45 above. Following Rolf Fredheim and Ben Schmidt, I am convinced that trees showing such relations among topics help to mitigate the challenges in choosing the number of topics, as the LDA algorithm requires. Clustering topics also gives statistical heft to the intuition that areas of inquiry overlap and diverge in complex ways: when we say, for example, that computers and writing is like technical communication in some ways or like cultural studies in others, clustering can add to the evidence we have for such affinities and make them easier to compare.

To figure out what "relations among topics" means, though, takes a bit of digging around under the surface of topics' labels—and, in general, programming for data analysis often begins with determining the shape of the data, and whether reshaping it will make the data more amenable to computation. (It often does; see Lang et al. section 5.2.) Underlying MALLET's assessment of "top words" in a topic is a table of links between words and topics, stored as a plaintext (*.txt) file that looks like this:

```
0 em 11:13057 49:6232 33:736 15:654 4:190 36:123 40:119 37:103
44:67 48:44 42:40 26:38 18:33 16:25 13:24 3:4
1 vernacular 4:2080 19:1625 13:1611 20:1502 8:737 45:274 49:148
11:116 43:48 16:34 25:20 33:7 28:7 31:3
2 rhetorics 32:7604 1:3383 31:2085 8:1577 22:1480 4:1332 19:798
37:725 9:631 3:543 45:460 42:96 49:43 44:31
3 transgression 37:260 47:246 20:208 12:195 1:117 9:103 6:97
38:51 24:48 28:35 15:34 14:25 48:24 42:19
4 control 5:8000 20:6867 37:4924 45:4198 12:4089 17:3373
48:2853 30:2802 44:2679 41:2649 18:2496 1:2208 28:1720 3:1423
43:1028 0:936 27:871 47:824 26:805 15:638 6:572 31:542 11:449
22:438 46:398 16:378 21:345 42:342 19:258 23:250 7:245 49:211
29:125 38:117 24:110 39:99 4:96 32:41 13:41
```

Each line begins with an integer as an index, starting from zero and going up to the number of tokens in the corpus—in this case, over 1.6 million.[7] This is followed by a space and then the token itself, followed by a space-delimited list of key-value pairs; that is, each colon-linked pair includes a topic number and an observation count showing the model's current estimate of how many times that token appeared in the context of the given topic, i.e., accompanied by other tokens also associated with that topic.

---

7. I don't recommend opening a file of that size with Microsoft Word! To get the preview, essential for determining the file's structure—and thus for any follow-up analy—ses of that data—I used the Terminal command **head**, which displays only the first few lines of a given file.

MALLET's format here presents several obstacles for finding the proximity (or, equivalently, the distance) among topics. First, these topic-observation pairs are given not in order of topics, but in descending order of observation count for each token; there's no immediate way to read all the values for a topic of interest. Second, because many tokens are never observed in the context of many topics, the number of observations in each row varies significantly. So, we can't simply transpose the rows and columns of the table to get a readout of words observed for each topic—even though something similar must be happening somewhere under MALLET's hood to produce those labels of top words per topic.[8]

Just because the operation isn't a simple one, though, doesn't mean we can't perform it; we just have to do a little extra work. Now that we have a sense of what the data looks like, we can plan to transform the data into a shape that will make it easier to measure distances. To build a table indexed by topic, not token, we need to . . .

1. Read in the data, ideally in a format that's easy to index.
2. Find a given topic, if it exists, as the key in a key:value pair somewhere in the row for a token. Store the value (the observed count of that token) for that topic.
3. Repeat step 2 for each token, making a cumulative list of tokens and counts for our given topic.
4. Repeat step 3 for each topic.

Once we have that table of topics, existing functions should be able to measure the distances.

Coding's Core: Defining Functions, Explaining Syntax

To begin step 1, reading the data file into R, I begin like this:

```
get.wordtopic.grid <- function(dataset_name =
"noexcludes2001_2015",
ntopics = 50,
iter_index = 1
){
# Things will happen here
}
```

I'm going to pause there for a moment to explain the syntax, for any readers new to code or to R specifically. In R, most alphanumeric strings[9] are treated by

---

8. Perhaps if I were fluent in Java, I could locate and save such an internal MALLET state. Alas! But all the more reason to become proficient in more programming languages.

9. How a "string" is delineated can vary from language to language. In R, as shown here, only a space ends a variable name, allowing periods and underscores to be included; in Java-Script, by contrast, the period is reserved for another function, and would not be allowed.

default as variables—labels, essentially, for some other object in memory. Here, for example, `get.wordtopic.grid` is a variable, as are `dataset_name`, `ntopics`, and `iter_index`. A string that's meant to be a text value, rather than a variable, is framed in quotation marks, as in my name for the dataset I'm analyzing here, "noexcludes2001_2015". To define the contents of a variable, you can *assign* something to it, either with a single equals sign (as on the right, where the number of topics, `ntopics`, is defined as 50) or with a kind of arrow made of a less-than sign and a hyphen (`<-`), which stores whatever comes to the right of it inside the variable to the left.

In this case, what's "to the right of" the arrow is much longer than a single value, because it begins with `function`. This signal word tells R to include, under the label `get.wordtopic.grid`, everything inside the parentheses and curly braces that follow. I'll have more to say about functions in a moment.

The final piece of syntax you'll need to read R code is the *comment*, shown here in gray. Essentially, any text from the # symbol through the end of the line where it appears is ignored by the computer. Instead, such "commented out" lines are aimed at a human audience, whether the programmer themselves or any other readers coming into the code, to try to make it easier to understand. (Note that other programming languages will use other symbols to signal the start of comments, and in some cases also to signal explicitly where they end.) Comments are most often used to label chunks of code, explaining what they're meant to do; they can also be written in advance of the code itself, as a way of making plans and marking placeholders.

Running the code snippet above will, as Auden said of poetry, make nothing happen—and not only because I've used a comment to simplify it. The code, as I mentioned above, defines a *function*, which means it can take a series of inputs, or *parameters* (the variables inside the parentheses), and act on them, eventually returning an output. Defining the function, however, does not execute the function; rather, it waits for something else—another script, or the user at the console—to pass it inputs. In that sense, as Auden also said of poetry, a function is "a way of happening, a mouth" through which information can later stream.

When I first started to use programming as a research method, while writing my own dissertation, I initially thought of scripts as files that would immediately execute a series of commands whenever I opened them, and that running entire files would be the primary way I would engage in analysis. If anyone reading this is sympathetic to that view, I hear you—and yet. I quickly came to realize that I needed, often, to batch those batches together, in various configurations. I came to realize that if I wanted to run the same analysis on two different subsets of data, or to try an analysis with two different assumptions about (say) how much of a document had to involve a particular topic for the document to count as being "about" that topic, I wanted to be able to save those different configurations without having to save multiple versions of essentially the same file, different only in one or two lines. I realized, in other words, that instead of files that always *run* functions, I wanted files that would *load* functions, so I could then call the functions interactively, at the console. Many of my files now consist solely of a set of custom function definitions, followed by a section which will never run on its own, where I save function calls in the various configurations I want to return to.[10]

Loading Data and the Importance of Parameters

Armed with that reading framework, I can now share a fuller version of the code snippet above, incorporating some more content inside the curly braces.[11] Inline comments beginning with a single # are standard descriptive comments; to gloss specific R commands for this chapter, I'll use ##.

```
get.wordtopic.grid <-
  function(dataset_name = "noexcludes2001_2015",
           ntopics = 50,
           iter_index = 1
  ){
    # Build the filename to load, based on parameters of
    # the model (which dataset, the number of topics, the
    # particular iteration of the model-building
    # algorithm) and MALLET's naming convention.
    
    filename <- paste0(dataset_name, "k", ntopics,
              "_iter", iter_index, "_wordtopics.txt")
    
    ## NB: the paste0() function, built into R,
    ## combines its parameters into a single string,
    ## with no spaces.
    
    # Next, store and format the file - but only if it
    # exists. Otherwise, return an error message
    # clarifying what went wrong.
    
    if(file.exists(filename)) {
```

---

10. Careful functional programming also solves a problem of variable isolation or contamination, what is sometimes referred to as a "clean" or "unclean" workspace. In many languages, including R, values assigned to variables within the scope of a function do not propagate outside of that function: in fact, variables declared only within that function do not even exist except while the function is being executed. This is important because it prevents values from being overwritten when, as sometimes (okay, often) happens, the same variable name is used in more than one file. Should some, but not all, shared variables be changed in the global environment assumed by freestanding batch-style code execution, the scripts would run with a mixed set of assumptions, leading to errors or nonsensical results that may be difficult to retrace.

11. Note that I'm ignoring, for the sake of streamlining the code, considerations like data files located elsewhere on the disk, but those locations could be included as well, if needed.

```
    wt <- read.table(filename, header=FALSE,
            fill=TRUE, col.names=c("index", "token",
            paste0("TopicRanked", 1:ntopics))

    ## NB: read.table() is also a built in R function,
    ## with parameters for the source file, how to name
    ## columns, etc. Here, paste0() is used to generate
    ## column names in a sequence from 1 to the value
    ## of the ntopics variable.

    require(data.table)
    wt <- data.table(wt)

    ## require() loads a library of external functions;
    ## here, I use the data.table() function in that
    ## library to improve the formatting and indexing
    ## of the word-topic table.

} else {

    stop("'get.wordtopic.grid R': could not load
        word-topic pairs from file ", filename)

    ## stop() is a built-in R function to exit early
    ## and return an error message.
}

return(wt)

    ## Exit the function, with the value of the wt
    ## variable as the output.
}
```

More than the specific tasks performed by this short function, I want to draw your attention to the ways the function's parameters—the list of inputs—are incorporated into the function body. Almost immediately, they are combined into a new variable, filename, which in turn is used to check conditions (if(file.exists(filename))) and, depending on the outcome of that check, to generate either a new data object or an error message. There is little in the function that can work without drawing on one or more of the parameters named. Significantly, parameters are *inherently changeable*: the values after the equals signs at the start of the function will be used by default, if nothing else is specified in the function call, but they can be overridden easily at call time. Depending on how the function is written, no defaults need to be provided at all—in which case, some value for that parameter must be named outright every time the function is called. In this way, parameters encourage researchers to be explicit about what conditions they're assuming; they also encourage systematic variation of those inputs, which helps me interrogate my assumptions, and what they reveal or mask.

In the present example, by splitting out the `dataset_name` as a changeable parameter, I signal that I expect to use different corpora and subcorpora as I continue with this project. By allowing the number of topics to vary, in `ntopics`, I remind myself that the topic model will look different if I split the corpus into 100, or 150, or 10 topics, instead of the 50 I'm working with primarily. And the final parameter, `iter_index`, reminds me that the LDA algorithm is non-deterministic, and that even repeated runs of that algorithm with the same dataset and number of topics will vary, at least a little, in its assignments of tokens to topics. (We can expect that the major divisions of the corpus will remain—one reason I want to study topic *clusters*—but this expectation needs to be interrogated.)

Task Decomposition: Lines, Loops, and Mid-Process Feedback

The `get.wordtopic.grid()` function above, when called, will do more than load the plaintext output by MALLET into R; it will also convert the space-delimited values into an actual table, aligning and adding column labels as it goes, making the data much easier to read and index. The first few lines now look like Table 17.1, with the columns continuing off to the right up through TopicRanked50:[12]

Table 17.1. Data loaded into R and reformatted

index	token	TopicRanked1	TopicRanked2	TopicRanked3	TopicRanked4	...
0	em	11:13057	49:6232	33:736	15:654	...
1	vernacular	4:2080	19:1625	13:1611	20:1502	...
2	rhetorics	32:7604	1:3383	31:2085	8:1577	...
3	transgression	37:260	47:246	20:208	12:195	...
4	control	5:8000	20:6867	37:4924	45:4198	...
5	york	12:20054	18:12124	13:9297	1:6256	...

RStudio makes it possible to view the results in the console or in a more tabular data inspector. But if we want to do more than look at the results—which was the whole point of programming, rather than using pre-built tools—then we need also to bind the results to a variable that we can then pass along to other functions. Thus, when calling the function, we instruct R to hold onto the output: `wt <- get.wordtopic.grid()`. (Leaving the parentheses empty uses the default values for dataset, number of topics, and model iteration.) After entering this call in the console, the variable `wt` will now hold all million-plus lines and 52 columns.

---

12. In truth, for this particular iteration of the model, the columns TopicRanked50 and TopicRanked49 are blank—but most have a value even as far out as TopicRanked48.

In the plan outlined above, we have now reached step 2, in which we'll build a function to find and store values from one small unit, so we can then call that function repeatedly for the whole big list of units:

1. Read in the data, ideally in a format that's easy to index. [Done!]
2. Find a given topic, if it exists, as the key in a key:value pair somewhere in the row for a token. Store the value (the observed count of that token) for that topic.
3. Repeat step 2 for each token, making a cumulative list of tokens and counts for our given topic.
4. Repeat step 3 for each topic.

Because we'll need to search every topic and row, I don't want default values for these parameters. And by requiring that a word-topic table be passed in as a parameter, I insist that it already exist before this new function is called: otherwise, we would have to build it anew each time, at a tremendous cost of time.

```
find.topic.in.one.row <-
   function(topic,            # what we're looking for
            rowindex,         # which row to look in
            wt                # a word-topic table
){
   # Build the search string from a topic number,
   # converting from 0-indexed to 1-indexed

   my_expr <- paste0("^", topic-1, ":")

   # Use it to find a column. It should match exactly
   # one, or none.

   colindex <- grep(my_expr, wt[index == rowindex])

      ## grep() is a built-in search function.

   # If nothing's found, the length of colindex will
   # be 0, which an "if" statement will interpret as
   # False; if the length is greater than 0, "if" will
   # interpret it as True.

   if(length(colindex)) {
      value <- just.value(wt[rowindex, ..colindex])

         ## just.value() is a function I've defined
         ## elsewhere to extract the second half of a
         ## key:value pair, a task that recurs fairly
         ## often.

   } else {
      value <- NULL
```

        }

        return(value)
}

One key advantage of the process of *decomposing* the overall data-transformation task into a small chunk we can repeat—into a series of functions, rather than one big function—is that it allows us to confirm each small chunk works as expected . . . or doesn't. When I run find.topic.in.one.row() on a known token ("vernacular," with row index 1 in the word-topic table shown earlier), and I search for its top-shown topic (topic 4), the value returned is not 2080, as expected, but NULL. A little digging in the help page for the search function, grep(), reveals why: it assumes that the search space will have a particular, consistent format, and it turns out that R tables use that format only for columns, not rows. The search is quietly failing. Had we not put specific known values in to test with, we could have looped through tens of thousands of rows and gotten no results—or worse, misleading results—before realizing something was wrong.

I have argued before (Miller) that writing is like finding one's way through a maze,[13] and in my experience writing code is similar. The setback of an unexpected data-type mismatch is a frequently recurring obstruction in the maze. One solution is to try to find another tool, i.e., another function, that *does* work with the datatype we're looking at; in this case we'll need to delve into a side labyrinth of linked help pages, maybe even searching the web to discover a whole new library that deals with tables in a new way. Another solution is to re-examine our initial plan and see if there's a way to just get *around* the barrier without too much cost.

In this case, because the search tool already works with columns, we can update our plan to search by columns instead of by rows:

1. Read in the data, ideally in a format that's easy to index [still done!]
2. Find a given topic, if it exists, as the key in a key:value pair everywhere it appears in the column for a particular topic-rank
3. For each match in step 2, note the token, and store the observed count of that token for that topic
4. Repeat steps 2 and 3 for each column / topic-rank, making a cumulative list of tokens and counts for our given topic
5. Repeat steps 2, 3, and 4 for each topic

The row vs. column question is a recurrent problem-class for data analysis: the sooner we learn to recognize it as a pattern, the sooner we'll notice when it happens, and the more confident we can be that we have a solution . . . and what

---

13. More specifically, a Zelda-like dungeon filled with traps, puzzles, and enemies—but with treasures and increased life-force as a reward for making it through.

kinds of new wrinkles those solutions introduce. In this case, one wrinkle is that we've gone from a unique result for each step in the loop to a list of matches, because the same topic can be top-ranked for more than one word. I therefore need to return a table at each point, which will need to be merged later.

```
find.topic.in.one.col <-
    function(topic,          # what we're looking for
             rank.col,        # which column to look in
             wt               # a word-topic table
    ){
    
    # load required library
    require(data.table)
    
    # Build the column name from a topic rank
    colname <- paste0("TopicRanked", rank.col)
    
    # Build the search string from a topic number,
    # converting 0-index to 1-index)
    my_expr <- paste0("^", topic-1, ":")
    
    # Search the column, allowing for more than one
    # possible result
    index <- grep(my_expr, wt[[colname]])
    
    # Use the search results to extract tokens
    tokens <- wt[index, token]
    
    # ... and key:value pairs
    key.value.pairs <- wt[index, ..colname]
    
    # Extract values from the key:value pairs
    values <- sapply(key.value.pairs[[1]], just.value)
    
        ## The need to apply a function across all members
        ## of a list is common enough that R has a set of
        ## built-in functions, including sapply(), to make
        ## it easy.
    
    # and return as a table
    result <- data.table(token_ind = as.integer(index),
                         token = as.character(tokens),
                         weight = as.integer(values))
    return(result)
}
```

Again, we'd better test to make sure that works! Trying as above to find "vernacular," we can run find.topic.in.one.col(topic = 5, rank.col = 1, wt = wt), which returns this table (of which only the first 5 and last 5 rows are shown):

```
       token_ind token      weight
1:             2 vernacular 2080
2:           267 chinatown  35
3:           462 american   33101
4:           474 americans  11094
5:           568 races      1494
---
24871:   1615776 asunky     1
24872:   1615781 lesssss    1
24873:   1615782 unprobable 1
24874:   1615783 sollubles  1
24875:   1615784 hypnotical 1
```

There's our expected result at the top of the list. We're safe, then, to move on to step 4: repeat the process across all columns, building up a combined list of tokens and weights for a single topic.

Insights and Upgrades Along the Way

Eagle-eyed readers will have noticed that the top topic for "vernacular' had been listed as 4, but our search was for topic 5. This is because the fifty topics in MALLET's output are numbered 0–49 but trying later to write a query with a topic of 0 would return an error, so we need to increment them all by one. Care to guess whether I anticipated that error in advance, or had to stub my toe on the error to discover it? There's a reason I try to move slowly, confirming my footing at each step.

Other things we can discover by moving slowly and inspecting our interim results include those strange words down at the bottom of the frequency list: "asunky," "lesssss," "unprobable." Each of these tokens was observed only once, even though we're limiting our search here to the topic with the *highest* value in each row. With the table at well over a million rows, we can obtain a significant speed boost by setting a lower bound on how many observations we want to consider: another function, taking as parameters the word-topic table and a threshold frequency for each word. (After some experimentation, I found that a threshold of 2 reduces the table from 1,616,842 words to 544,036; a threshold of 5 drops it down to a still sizable 254,092. And five mentions of a term in a few thousand documents still signals a very low-frequency word.)

Now, Where Were We?

I jest, but for a serious reason. Programming—and especially debugging—frequently asks me to scale-shift, sometimes zooming way in to the level of single punctuation marks for debugging, sometimes zooming out to remember why I wanted this function in the first place; a lot of the time is spent in between. This is also true of other forms of writing, to be fair, but it sometimes seems an especially prominent feature of programming, which rewards coders for breaking down large-scale challenges—like measuring the similarity of topics—into ever smaller, modular pieces that can be carefully inspected and quality-controlled before being assembled into ever larger, more complex machines. I forgive you, and hope you'll forgive me, if you'd momentarily forgotten that we're building a table directly relating topics to the observed frequencies of tokens in the context of those topics. Or that the purpose of building such a table was so that we can measure the distance from one topic-word vector to another, and thus to identify clusters of topics. The topic-clusters themselves are in service of the larger goal of mapping the range of research activity in graduate dissertations, as representative of the field. But, to scale back down again, the example of the dissertation topic-clusters is, in this chapter, just one example of the kind of custom analytical work made possible by programming, work not supported by more plug-and-play digital research tools.

Wrapping Up by Wrapping Functions in Other Functions

From above, we have a function that finds the tokens associated with a topic when it appears at a particular rank. Two more functions will suffice to get us from there to the fully searchable table: one, keeping the same topic, that iterates across all ranks; then another to iterate *that* function across all topics. I'll simplify a little to show the essentials:

```
find.topic.in.all.cols <-
    function(topic,             # what we're looking for
             ntopics,            # how many loops to make
             wt,                 # a word-topic table
             threshold = 5       # minimum weight per token
    ){

    require(data.table)

    # start with an empty container,
    # with specified data types

    topic_word_vec <- data.table(token_ind = numeric(),
                                 token = character(),
                                 weight = numeric())

    # then, to fill it, loop through the columns,
    # from 1 through the total number of topics,
    # because that will also be the largest possible
    # topic rank.

    for (column in seq_len(ntopics)) {

        # each time through the loop, attach one more row
        # to the existing list...
```

```
        topic_word_vec <-
            rbindlist(list(topic_word_vec,

            # ... by calling the function defined earlier.
            find.topic.in.one.col(topic, column, wt)
        ))
    }
    # (here we could trim, sort, label, do some norming,
    # etc)

    return(topic_word_vec)
}
```

The final function to build the topic-word table (which I creatively call build.topicword.table()), works very similarly to the one above: start with an empty table with labeled columns, loop through all the topics, and at each step call the previous function. But this time, the previous function is find.topic.in.all.cols(), which in turn calls find.topic.in.one.col(), which in turn relies on get.wordtopic.grid(), so that by the time we've assembled the whole thing, we no longer need to explicitly run those earlier scripts. Instead, they will be called only from build.topicword.table(), which therefore consolidates all the parameters for the nested function calls, and returns a single clean output: a topic-word table I call tw.

To finally measure distances, a fourth function cleans up tw by ensuring all the words are in the same order for each topic, even if some words have zero observations in the context of some (many) topics; then it isolates just the quantitative values (i.e., it strips out the tokens themselves and their indices within the original MALLET table), and norms them by the number of observations for each topic. This allows the resulting numerical matrix to be passed along to a fifth function that calculates distances between its constituent vectors—which can, finally, produce the topic clusters we were initially after. But only through still another function, with its own parameters and choices to make.

The Takeaway for Digital Research in Writing

As I said earlier, I realize that was a lot of code to throw at you. But my point isn't to show off my sweet, sweet programming skills—in fact, I'm sure I'm exposing some major inefficiencies or infelicities that a professional software engineer would be able to diagnose and fix immediately. Nor are the details of my control flows (if/else statements, for loops, and the like) or the specific R syntax, or calls to pre-made functions from base or imported packages, something I'm trying to teach. However, in the service of explaining my digital research methods, I do think it's important to illustrate 1) the frequent *presence* of control flows and 2) the significance of *each new function calling previous ones.*

In other words, 1) an essential aspect of programming as methodology is preparing to handle and respond to changing contingencies: not to assume that the data you're looking at now, and the circumstances in which you're looking at it, are the only situation for which the code should work. For instance, beginning programmers may be tempted to reference columns of a data table by column number, rather than by a column name—or by assuming the columns will always be named a certain way, rather than looping through an inferred set of names. (I know I was.) However, these assumptions are prone to breakage, e.g., if something inserts or removes a column, such as a row index that may become shifted by saving to Excel. Depending on the outcome, this may result in particularly insidious silent changes, where the function compiles and runs with no explicit errors—but with all the conclusions you would draw from its output based on a mismatch compared to its inputs. True, there's a risk of over-preparing for conditions that never actually arise, but learning to make my code less brittle has been key to my growth as a researcher-who-programs, from when I first started in graduate school and continuing today.

I also wanted these examples to highlight 2) the iterative and cross-referential nature of the process. In contrast to the output-as-endpoint default behavior of most ready-to-use digital analytical tools, functional programming suggests that any output can become an input. The diction surrounding functions emphasizes their relationality: you *call* functions, *pass* them information, and they *return* something back to you. At the same time, the sense of completion implied by that return is only ever temporary: what is returned can be passed again. While the examples above were constructed to show a nested set of calls—outputs passed, as it were, straight up the ladder of scale, such that we could eventually invoke all of them with a single call—the modular nature of the functions also means they can stand in relation to more than one partner.

Take, for example, the table `tw` returned by `build.topicword.table()`. While I built it initially to find that distance matrix, and thus clusters of dis/similar topics, I was also able to repurpose it for the sake of changing how topics are labeled. As I noted earlier, by default MALLET labels topics with the twenty words most frequently found in the context of those topics. But because some topics are related, some words will show up high on the list of several topics. To better differentiate the topics from one another, I adapted a technique more often used in differentiating subcorpora of documents: Term Frequency * Inverse Document Frequency, or TFIDF. This technique reduces the observed occurrence of terms within each single document in proportion to the observed occurrence of those terms across the whole set of documents, essentially muting the terms that have high frequencies purely by virtue of being common words in general. My adaptation, TFITF, substitutes Topic for Document, and for the same reason: to highlight the terms that are more specific to individual topics than to the corpus. As it turns out, the token frequencies needed for the calculation, both within individual topics and across the dataset, are trivial to derive from the topic-word table tw. Analytical scripts, once programmed, beget further analytical scripts.

Conclusions: Learning to Program, and Learning to Like It

Like all literacies, coding is social. As Vee argues, "Ultimately, all programming is collaborative—although it is often asynchronously so. Even if they aren't working alongside other programmers physically or online, programmers work with languages, machines, and programming environments designed by others. They work with libraries of procedures or codebases or frameworks programmed by teams of other programmers" (128). This should, I hope, read as inspiring for any of you who may be new to programming and intimidated by the idea of picking it up: not only are you not expected to go it alone, the very software you'll be using to practice is infused with the traces of prior learners, not only in the languages and the libraries but also in the copious documentation left by their designers. Digital humanists share and discuss their code online, including through sites like The Programming Historian (https://programminghistorian.org), which hosts "novice-friendly, peer-reviewed tutorials that help humanists learn a wide range of digital tools, techniques, and workflows to facilitate research and teaching." Popular languages like R, Python, and JavaScript have large and active online communities, with forums like Stack Overflow (https://stackoverflow.com), where questioners can find answers and explanations—usually without a delay, because chances are good that someone else has had that question before, and the answers are already online – and even vague or halting questions are often met not with dismissal, but with probing queries that help to clarify the nature of the problem. The barriers for entry into digital research methods are lowered not only by software to use as-is, but also by resources (including *human* resources) to help you customize how one bit of software feeds into another.

Even if you find that it's easier to collaborate with a programmer than to write code yourself, trying your hand at programming can facilitate that collaboration. Knowing the kinds of data structures out there, or the way the computer already structures the data you want to analyze or circulate, will help you describe your project and ask your own probing queries about what the programmer can do for you; and knowing something about functions, loops, and changeable parameters vs. fixed values will help you parse or push back on the jargon you may get back in response. Programming ourselves can also help us appreciate the limitations of what code can do, and what modifications are likely to be easy or heavy lifts.

I want to be clear that I'm not advocating we ignore all the excellent digital tools already out there, from some false sense that only code we ourselves have written can be trusted. (On the contrary, some things, like security protocols, are probably better left to the experts.) The choice between existing tools and custom scripts is a false binary: as I hope I demonstrated above with my transformation of output from MALLET, itself one of those ready-to-use tools, they often work especially well in concert. And for many research questions, an existing analysis may be just what you need. What I am saying, though, is that I have found real value in being able to think through my inquiry by thinking through code, in at least two ways.

Programming is epistemic. Just as organizing thoughts to teach someone (whether in person or in writing) can help us bring to consciousness and further develop what we think, so too can organizing our questions to explain them to a computer. Except now we also have to (get to) explain the structure of our data, too—and that helps us better grasp what we have, which, in turn, helps us formulate both new questions and new conclusions. Writing a custom function means being aware enough of my specific research goals and the shape of my data to speed re-entry and replication, yet flexible enough in my assumptions to respond to changes in the data source or the possibility of the function's reuse in another context.

Programming is rewarding. More affectively, I find that programming as a research method affords more frequent opportunities for positive reinforcement than most other forms of writing I do. It's still challenging, with a lot of wrong turns, searching for help, and plenty of debugging—but it's "pleasantly frustrating" (36), to borrow James Gee's description of the appeal of challenging video games: it keeps me coming back for more, with challenges that "feel hard, but doable" (ibid). When an incremental piece of a larger analysis returns the expected result, or when a series of functions finally hand off to one another without error after a while in the weeds of debugging, the feeling of getting it right is just incredibly satisfying. Composing in prose can offer a similar feeling of rightness, in the pleasure of a balanced phrase, say, or a final paragraph that satisfies, finally, the itch of the opening. But the all-at-once-ness of writing, as Ann Berthoff put it (86), means that so much remains in flux throughout the composing process that it can be hard, before the ending, to know what's really worked. Programming is more modular, with more frequent feedback already built in.

In fact, in some ways this pleasurable difficulty is also a liability: it's easy to feel that there's more tinkering to do, a more efficient approach, a follow-up question to ask, one more level to play, and each new attempt introduces new problems to solve. It's important to keep aware of time. But as Gee also argues, this sensation of earned reward is an excellent motivator for learning, and with programming, as with any literate skill, there is always more to learn.

Works Cited

Auden, W. H. "In Memory of W.B. Yeats." *Another Time*, W. H. Auden, Random House, 1940, https://poets.org/poem/memory-w-b-yeats/.

Berthoff, Ann E. *The Sense of Learning*. Boynton/Cook, 1990.

Blei, David M., Andrew Y. Ng, and Michael I. Jordan. "Latent Dirichlet Allocation." *The Journal of Machine Learning Research*, vol. 3, 2003, pp. 993–1022.

Corpus of Contemporary American English (COCA), https://www.english-corpora.org/coca/. Accessed 18 July 2020.

Craig, Todd. "'Makin' Somethin' Outta Little-to-Nufin': Racism, Revision and Rotating Records—The Hip-Hop DJ in Composition Praxis." *Changing English*, vol. 22, no. 4, 2015, pp. 349–64.

Desmet, Christy, Ron Balthazor, Robert Cummings, Nelson Hilton, Angela Mitchell, and Alexis Hart. "<emma>: Re-Forming Composition with XML." *Literary and Linguistic Computing*, vol. 20, no. 1, 2005, pp. 25–46, https://doi.org/10.1093/llc/fqi023.

Dighton, Desiree. "Arranging a Rhetorical Feminist Methodology: The Visualization of Anti-Gentrification Rhetoric on Twitter." *Kairos: A Journal of Rhetoric, Technology, and Pedagogy*, vol. 25, no. 1, 2020, http://kairos.technorhetoric.net/25.1/topoi/dighton/attuning-to-silences.html.

Feibush, Laura. "Gestural Listening and the Writing Center's Virtual Boundaries." *Praxis*, vol. 15, no. 2, 2018, http://www.praxisuwc.com/feibush-152.

Fredheim, Rolf. "Visualising Structure in Topic Models." *Quantifying Memory*, 2013, http://quantifyingmemory.blogspot.com/2013/11/visualising-structure-in-topic-models.html.

Gee, James Paul. "Good Video Games and Good Learning." *Phi Kappa Phi Forum*, vol. 85, no. 2, 2005, pp. 33–37.

Goldstone, Andrew. *dfr-browser: Take a MALLET to Disciplinary History*, http://agoldst.github.io/dfr-browser/. Accessed 26 June 2014.

Hart-Davidson, Bill, Jeff Grabill, Mike McLeod, and Melissa Graham Meeks. "About Eli Review." *Eli Review*, https://elireview.com/about/. Accessed 29 Jan. 2021.

Kantrowitz, Dana. "The Making of a Poem, Live and Uncensored." *Acts of Revision: A Guide for Writers*, edited by Wendy Bishop, Boynton/Cook Heinemann, 2004, pp. 134–43.

Kaufer, David, et al. *DocuScope Project*, http://www.cmu.edu/dietrich/english/research-and-publications/docuscope.html. Accessed 29 Jan. 2021.

Klein, Lauren F., and Catherine D'Ignazio. *Data Feminism*. e-book ed., MIT Press, 2020, http://ebookcentral.proquest.com/lib/pitt-ebooks/detail.action?docID=6120950.

Lang, Susan, Laura Aull, and William Marcellino. *A Taxonomy for Writing Analytics*. 2019, pp. 13–37.

Lang, Susan, and Craig Baehr. "Data Mining: A Hybrid Methodology for Complex and Dynamic Research." *College Composition and Communication*, vol. 64, no. 1, 2012, pp. 172–94.

LeBlanc, Paul J. *Writing Teachers Writing Software: Creating Our Place in the Electronic Age. Advances in Computers and Composition on Studies Series*. e-book ed., National Council of Teachers of English, 1993, https://eric.ed.gov/?id=ED357369.

Lindgren, Chris, and Jim Ridolfo. "Rhetmap.Org: Composing Data for Future Re-Use and Visualization." *PraxisWiki*, 25 June 2020, http://praxis.technorhetoric.net/tiki-index.php?page=PraxisWiki%3A_%3Arhetmap.

Lockridge, Tim. "Building Rhetorlist: A Call for Small, Meaningful Projects in Rhetoric and Composition." *Kairos: A Journal of Rhetoric, Technology, and Pedagogy*, vol. 24, no. 2, 2020, http://kairos.technorhetoric.net/24.2/disputatio/lockridge/index.html.

Melançon, Lisa. *USF Writes*. 2020, http://myreviewers.usf.edu/research.

Mueller, Derek. *Network Sense: Methods for Visualizing a Discipline*. The WAC Clearinghouse/UP of Colorado, 2017, https://doi.org/10.37514/WRI-B.2017.0124.

Miller, Benjamin. "Metaphor, writer's block, and the legend of zelda: A link to the writing process." *Rhetoric/Composition/Play through Video Games*, edited by Richard Colby, Mathew S. S. Johnson, and Rebekah Shulz Colby, Palgrave Macmillan, 2013. pp. 99–111.

"NativeLand.Ca." *Native-Land.ca—Our Home on Native Land*, https://native-land.ca. Accessed 25 Jan. 2021.

Noble, Safiya Umoja. *Algorithms of Oppression: Race, Gender and Power in the Digital Age*. New York UP, 2018.

Palmquist, Mike. "A Brief History of Computer Support for Writing Centers and Writing-Across-the-Curriculum Programs." *Computers and Composition*, vol. 20, no. 4, 2003, pp. 395–413.

RStudio Team. *RStudio: Integrated Development Environment for R*. RStudio Inc., 2019, http://www.rstudio.com.

Schmidt, Benjamin M. "Words Alone: Dismantling Topic Models in the Humanities." *Journal of Digital Humanities*, vol. 2, no. 1, 2012, pp. 49–65.

Turner, Heather Noel, and Laura Gonzales. "Visualizing Translation." *Kairos: A Journal of Rhetoric, Technology, and Pedagogy*, vol. 25, no. 1, 2020, http://kairos.technorhetoric.net/25.1/topoi/turner-gonzales/casestudy.html.

Vee, Annette. *Coding Literacy: How Computer Programming Is Changing Writing*. The MIT Press, 2017.

Voyant Tools. http://voyant-tools.org. Accessed 6 June 2017.

Weingart, Scott B. "Topic Modeling for Humanists: A Guided Tour." *The Scottbot Irregular*, 25 July 2012, http://www.scottbot.net/HIAL/?p=19113.

Wresch, William. *The Computer in Composition Instruction: A Writer's Tool*. National Council of Teachers of English, 1984.

Chapter 18. Multimodal Methods for Mapping Multimodal Composing Processes

Christina Rowell
KENT STATE UNIVERSITY

Ever since I was small, I was told I was a visual, hands-on learner. I have always been the student with every color pen, multiple sets of post-it notes or flashcards, and a whiteboard with notes and diagrams scrawled all over it. So, it is really no surprise that I found my way into researching multimodal composing processes. During my doctoral program, as part of my dissertation research, I began studying the fashion program at a mid-sized, Midwestern state university with the specific goal of understanding multimodal composing processes. I had a desire to explore how non-alphabetic compositions go from inspiration to final product, and my interest was driven by my hyper-awareness of the materiality and multimodality of my own composing processes.[1] I wondered how my own use of different tools, techniques, and materials mirrored those of the fashion design students or how multimodal composing processes overlapped and intersected with other composing processes.

Early on, I began to realize how difficult it would be to capture what I call the complex ecology of composing through the methods that I had been implementing—namely surveys, interviews, and collection of completed projects. There remained a gap between the goals of my research and my methods. I was falling victim to trying to understand multimodality from a frozen, static form, which erases the dynamic nature of the processes that create those forms. So, I searched for methods that would help me capture that dynamic whole (Shipka, "Toward" 28) of multimodal composing processes and account for "the material and social considerations that are always in flux with composing" (Johnson 14). I soon realized that to attend to multimodality in the processes themselves, I must collect data that records as many of those modalities as possible to accurately analyze and represent those processes.

To provide the breadth and depth necessary to capture the complexity of multimodal composing processes and digital writing, this chapter narrows in on

---

1. Though my research has focused primarily on multimodal composing processes, I believe the work I have done and the methods I have employed can also be applied to digital writing research because, as Shepherd contends, "Digital writing and multimodality are deeply intertwined. It is difficult to think of examples of modern . . . digital writing spaces that do not use multiple modes to convey information to readers simultaneously" (103).

ways to attend to the multi-sensory experience of composing by focusing on the implementation and evolution of multimodal methods, i.e., methods that collect multiple streams of data simultaneously and allow researchers to attend to the multi-sensory experience of composing. This chapter narrativizes the evolution of multimodal process interviews, which were born out of in-the-moment, collaborative experiences with my participants and inspired by feminist interviews and multimodal think-aloud protocols.

On Multimodal Composing Processes

Using a definition of literate activity that includes "many streams of activity: reading, talking, observing, acting, making, thinking and feeling as well as transcribing words" (Prior "Writing Disciplinarity" xi), Paul Prior calls to the forefront the need to examine composing processes and literate activity as networked actions. Along this same vein, Pamela Takayoshi asserts that "studies of composing processes easily might have been bounded at one time by a focus on a single individual with a pen and a paper, but contemporary forms of writing are not so easily bounded, as writers engage in virtually every form of writing . . . are entangled in sometimes vast networks of other writers, other texts, and other composing processes" (14). Takayoshi's argument harkens to the notion that composing processes function at networks of actions where each participant, human and non-human alike, impact and shape the processes. Hannah Rule suggests that "situating processes" pushes back against conventional views on process as simply those moments of inscription (6). Lucy Johnson makes a similar contention when arguing that composing is always material and multimodal and calls researchers "to expand our conceptions of available resources—understanding the ways in which bodies, places, and actions can all be cultivated as resources for contending with an enacting multimodality as process" (22). Taking these contentions into account, as digital writing researchers, we should recognize not only the act of inscription but also the impact of thoughts, emotions, motivations, cultural perceptions along with interactions between human and non-human participants.

Prior and Jody Shipka argue that studying writing processes in this way is directly centered on our Environment-Selecting and -Structuring Practices (ESSPs) and is the act of selecting, structuring, (re)structuring, shifting, shaping, and transforming the material and social world around us. We use these external aids to help direct our consciousness and enhance our focus on the task at hand. This can be choosing types of tools for composing, repurposing a software program or app for your own purpose, or selecting a certain place to work, to name a few. ESSPs become central to their understanding of composing as they "highlight people's situated agency, their tuning to and of environments, their making of artifacts of all kinds" (228). Participants' discussions of ESSP's demonstrate the affordances of incorporating different tools, objects, materials, and environments into our composing processes. Moreover, this notion of ESSPs expands the scope of composing process research by examining the impact that human and nonhuman actors have on our composing processes and how we might perform activities that funnel into our composing processes and shape the final composition. Therefore, focusing on ESSPs highlights the many objects, tools, and actors that mediate writing and composing, thus further constructing the network of composing. ESSPs were of particular interest because of my awareness of my own habits and tools that weave their way into my composing processes. Further, I believe that recognizing ESSPs connects with my belief that we must recognize the impact and agency of nonhumans within the network of composing. Thus, my research has built upon the work of Prior and Shipka in that the multimodal compositions my participants created were not solely a product of one dimension of composing, they were a sum of many tools, materials, experiences, environments, people, and circumstances.

Similarly, Shipka contends that composing process research should focus on the process of making and the becoming of a text rather than attempting to discover the "whole truth" of composing processes or even the possibility of the "truth" of a single individual's composing processes ("Toward" 38). Shipka also argues that this is beneficial to the field because "attending closely to processes of making . . . helps illuminate the highly distributed, embodied, translingual, and multimodal aspects of all communicative practices" ("Transmodality" 253). This viewpoint shifts the study of composing processes because it asks for researchers to account for more in the world, to see more, to reconstruct the notion of composing, to move beyond the traditional notion of what it means to be "in process." Using this argument, she sees the act of folding laundry to unlock the mind as part of the composing process; she sees a student's visit to Walmart as an act of brainstorming and research for a project. These moments all play a role in the ecology of composing. Using a framework for examining composing processes, and subsequently, digital writing, that sees these processes as complex ecologies of humans, nonhumans, objects, materials, tools, and environments, I contend that scholars in writing studies must find ways to attend to these many factors when research digital writing and multimodal composing processes.

On Researching Multimodal Composing Processes

The foundation for most of my research on multimodal composing processes began with my interests in the "becoming" of texts but also theories of mediated action and distributed notions of agency. Using a framework for understanding composing processes inspired by the work of Laurie Gries, Alex Reid, Nathaniel Rivers, and Jane Bennett, my larger project aimed at exploring composing processes as complex ecologies or networks of humans, nonhumans, objects, materials, tools, and environment. Thus, each of my participant's multimodal composing processes was viewed as an assemblage (Bennett) or compositional network (Reid) because of this framework for composing processes. Moreover, viewing composing processes as assemblages or compositional networks further encourages researchers to see how composite objects like multimodal compositions are formed by the collaborative relationship between human and nonhuman actors.

Because of the relationship between humans and nonhumans and their respective agency, I believe that it is necessary to value the voice of my participants as well as bring attention to the ways that nonhumans participate within any composing processes. In recognizing the agency and voice of all participants within composing processes, my research is influenced by a sociocultural lens that dictates that all activity within a system is mediated by other actors within the system. Thus, no individual's actions can occur without a relationship or reaction with other participants within the ecology of composing.

Exploring Multimodal Methods

The methods discussed in this chapter were born out of a larger study on the multimodal composing processes of fashion design students. The study and definition of multimodal compositions has been an everchanging landscape even though composing processes and multimodality have been intertwined long before multimodal took a conceptual foothold in writing studies. As Jason Palmeri argues, composing has always already been multimodal as process researchers have viewed writing processes "as a deeply multimodal thinking process that shares affinities with other forms of composing (visual, musical, spatial, gestural)" (25). Multimodal compositions are so complex as texts because they are structured by the modes they employ, the affordances of those modes, and the context in which they are being composed. Further, they often involve tools, techniques, materials, and skills that are typically outside of Writing Studies expertise. These factors often make multimodal compositions and composing challenging for our field to understand. Lynda Walsh contends that

> Research on visual inscription practices in particular is finally building momentum after a long lag behind other communication-studies fields—perhaps because there was something initially about visual communication that seemed by definition to fall outside writing studies. But our field can now boast a substantial body of work on visual inscription, particularly in the arena of science, technology, engineering, and math (STEM) writing, where graphics dominate the page/screen. (4)

Scholars have studied adolescents constructing digital stories and videos (Hull and Nelson; Nelson, Hull, and Roche-Smith; Vasudevan, Schultz, and Batemen; Yang), graphic designer's processes (Graham & Whalen; Steiner), and interior design processes (Smagorinsky, Zoss, and Reed) as sites for multimodal compositions and composing. Others have even begun to discuss the variety of texts that can and should be under the purview of multimodal compositions including composite objects like ballet shoes with writing on them (Shipka) and clothing (Manthey). Writing studies has wrestled with the complexity of multimodal composing processes and visual communication through literate activities and practices, mediational means, design studies, and visual rhetoric theories. My own work attempts to follow suit with the work that Walsh highlights as well as extend the work and theories by providing data about multi-material multimodal composing processes from fashion design students that blend digital and tactile modes.

Further, multimodal composing processes of fashion design students are useful for our understanding of multimodality and digital writing because fashion design is not dominated by print, alphabetic texts and has a unique perspective of processes that have been multi-material and multimodal since their inception. This multi-materiality is evident not only in the final products these fashion design students create (garments, sketches, process books, and final portfolios) but also the wide variety of tools and materials incorporated in the creation of these products.

While multimodal composing processes in fashion design are not equivalent to composing processes and digital writing, fashion design processes have similar goals to digital writing processes. Fashion design students compose and convey messages and purposes through products and texts just like students writing in the composition classroom. Bridging the gap between fashion design and writing studies is further supported by Shipka's contention for a "communications approach" to writing studies that values and sees the relationship between writing and other modes of communication and representation. Further, as Takayoshi and Derek Van Ittersum contend, "writing is always and always will be a material process of making, crafting, composing" (84). Fashion design is, in many ways, the epitome of a material or rather a multi-material process that is driven by making and crafting material messages through clothing, sketches, mood boards, process books, and portfolios.

One goal of this larger study, and what I believe should be a goal of digital writing and composing processes research, was to capture the dynamic whole of composing. By capturing a wider view of composing, I believe that we can obtain a clearer understanding of the vast array of resources and habits that writers, composers, and designers incorporate into their processes. To capture the dynamic whole, I used multiple "multimodal methods"—i.e., methods that collect multiple streams of data simultaneously and allow researchers to attend to the multi-sensory experience of digital writing and multimodal composing processes as well as attend to the various participants within the network of composing (materials, tools, objects, environments, humans, and nonhuman actors).

By utilizing multimodal methods and collecting visual, sonic, oral, and tactile data, I was attempting to avoid what John Trimbur recognizes as how "the major images of writing from the process era neglect the materiality and visuality of writing" (191). Therefore, I employed multiple streams of data to provide a "less partial and more detailed understanding" of multimodal composing processes (Takayoshi 6). The multiple streams of data for the larger project included: classroom observations, interviews, multimodal process interviews, process sketches, reflections, project walk-throughs, and artifact collection. Takayoshi explicates that "this methodological variety provides a range of perspectives on literacy *as it is practiced*" and that "composition studies' research on individual writers in the moment of composing, provides a richer understanding of literacy [and composing] as a situated practice" (2). Thus, multilayered, multi-tiered, and multimodal data collection has allowed me to see more complexity in each case study's composing processes and further capture the dynamic whole of multimodal composing processes—and I believe of digital writing as well. Of this variety of methods, this chapter will focus primarily on the evolution of the multimodal process interviews and the methods that supported them.

Interviews

As part of my recruitment for the multimodal process interviews and as a means of obtaining more contextual information, I completed a series of initial interviews with students in the fashion design studio course. These interviews allowed me to better understand the ways that the students themselves interact and feel with their classroom, their context, and the program itself. They also served as an opportunity to ask them to participate in the multimodal process interviews and were essential for cultivating better relationships with potential participants. The primary goal of the initial interviews was to provide data about the participants' perceptions of their multimodal composing processes, with a specific focus on their tools, materials, environments, and habits that participate in their processes.

One issue I found with these interviews was approaching students to be interviewed in the first place. Had I planned more carefully I would have figured out a better method for recruiting during this phase other than awkwardly approaching students during classroom observations. Awkwardness aside, my status as a regular fixture in the classroom (I had been observing the class since early in the semester) afforded me the ability to approach the students in the first place. I also imagine being a white, cisgendered woman who often is mistaken for an undergraduate made me relatively nonthreatening. Further, my status in the classroom also altered my approach with students. I was in a grey area where the students saw me as simultaneously a peer but also as akin to an instructor because of how the relationships grew with my participants during observations but also how the instructor of the course positioned my presence (sharing with the class that I was a researcher and often including me in class discussion).

Because of my status in the classroom, these interviews were more of "active interactions between two (or more) people learning to negotiate contextually based results" (Fontana and Frey 646). I began with the guiding questions but also allowed the conversation to flow naturally and asked supplemental questions to further my understanding. I asked my participants about their typical composing habits, what tools they preferred to use, what practices they use for beginning their projects, how they research, and where they find their inspiration for their design work. As with all other aspects of my data collection, I aimed for these interviews to be "reciprocal, and often intimate, shaping of information . . . fundamentally influenced by the material realities and situated perspectives of multiple partners" (Selfe and Hawisher 37), which was aided by my participants' comfort with my presence and my own positionality within the classroom.

Using these interviews, I recruited three participants to participate in the multimodal process interviews based on convenience samplings. All three participants expressed interest in my project and agreed to participate. These participants were not necessarily representative of all fashion design students at this university but represent examples of some aspects of multimodal composing processes rather than a complete picture of one singular truth of multimodal composing.[2]

Multimodal Process Interviews

Throughout this larger project, the multimodal process interviews oversaw the most serendipitous changes. Originally, when collecting data of each case study participant's process, I intended to have my participants complete multimodal think-aloud protocols (Walsh), which would have them record traditional think-aloud protocols to coincide with the video and/or screen capture I was recording of their processes. Think-aloud protocols are typically used to record concurrent verbalizations of the cognitive processes associated with completing an action. Participants are asked to speak their thoughts out loud as a stream of consciousness. Peter Smagorinsky contends that think-aloud protocols are useful for the study of composing practices because they "can yield significant information about the structures of the processes" (465). He also argues, along with Elizabeth Daigle, O'Donnell-Allen, and Bynum, that think-aloud protocols are useful for tracing processes over multiple sessions of writing.

Walsh argues for think-aloud protocols as a "joint activity between" researcher and participant and that while the participant controlled the activity, she allowed dialogue between them, including requests for feedback from the participant or clarification questions from the researcher (9). Thus, my multimodal think-aloud protocols became a multimodal think-aloud instructional interview hybrid that

---

2. I will note that even though all three of my participants self-identified as female, it was not my intention to only study female students. I originally had a fourth self-identified male student who dropped out of the study. Conversely, my participants did represent a variety of perspectives in terms of race, religion, and socio-economic background. I believe that each of my participants' unique experiences and histories influence their composing processes.

I have deemed multimodal process interviews, which were comprised of audio recordings of verbal interactions between the researcher and participant, video and screen capture of actions within and beyond the screen and session field notes by the researcher. These multimodal process interviews resembled Cynthia Selfe and Gail Hawisher's feminist interviews in that they "were resistant... to the boundaries of single-session conversations" (39) and were more of an extension of our interactions from the time I observed them in class where my participants were conversational and instructional while working and describing their processes. Gloria Jacobs argues that "observing people ... provides deeper insights especially when observations are followed by interviews" (335), thus the hybrid nature of the multimodal process interviews, where interview, think-aloud protocol, and observations meld together, offers a layer of understanding that one of these methods alone could not provide.

This shift from a multimodal think-aloud protocol to a multimodal process interview was a natural evolution and primarily dictated by my participants—they asked the questions, they provided instructional explanations, they spoke in tangents, they engaged with me as they felt comfortable, which aligns with my beliefs of valuing the voice and positionalities of my participants. One even admitted that the traditional think-aloud protocol format was intimidating: "I was thinking about it because I'm like oh no I'm going to have to be thinking about what I'm doing. Normally, I just kind of do it, subconsciously I guess, and not really think about it." Because of this evolution, multimodal process interviews were made up of narrations of the participant's actions woven in with their interactions with other individuals within the space in natural conversation and questions they had for me, which made these observations feel more organic and similar to classroom and studio observations. Others had a more difficult time with narrating and discussing their work, so I had to prime them more often with questions to get them to talk. Some participants were more conversational and often had tangents discussing completely unrelated topics which required me to ask directly about the work being completed. Some even took an instructional approach where they were explicating their actions to ensure that I understood what task they were completing.[3]

The most fulfilling and interesting part of the evolution into multimodal process interviews was the transition between researcher and "interested other" in that my position became one of "asking participants for elaboration [and] encouraging them" (Selfe and Hawisher 42) because these sessions became more organic and better resembled the ways that my participants worked during class time or individual studio time. While this transition is evidence of the effect of my presence on my participants' processes, I believe that since there is no one singular truth nor one singular multimodal composing processes, any new actor (human

---

3. Many of these moments can be viewed as part of the videos that appear later in this chapter.

or non-human) being present would shift or shape their processes. Smagorinsky et al. note that, in their study, the think-aloud protocols they collected from Susan "included conversations between her and occasional visitors (her friend, her family members)" (377), so the interaction between the researcher and participant or the participant and other people within their spaces is not abnormal.

At the time, the evolution into multimodal process interviews felt almost like a mistake or a potential downfall of my study, but, in retrospect, it was ideal for the goals of my research. Not only did our observations feel more organic, but they were also very similar to the classroom observations I completed as part of the larger study. Moreover, the evolution as participant-driven aligns with my desire to honor and value my participant's perspectives and voices. Had I pushed the more rigid plan I intended for the think-aloud protocols, that participant who felt intimidated by the structure might have been entirely derailed from her "typical" processes. The evolution to the more interactive and instructional multimodal process interview serves as evidence of my participants being comfortable in my presence, as well as the presence of the camera, to interact normally with their peers. This level of comfort made the data collected during observations seem more authentic.

Collecting and Capturing: Video and Screen Capture

One of the biggest hurdles with multimodal process interviews is deciding which tools to use for capturing each session. I found myself questioning what camera should I use? Does camera selection even matter? I quickly learned that the answer is always yes. Some situations require different tools and technologies to capture as much as possible of the given situation. Thus, for my larger project, depending on what acts of composing each participant chose to do during each session, the session was either recorded solely on video or using both video and screen capture. Utilizing video, screen capture, and audio provided multiple layers of data for each composing session and allowed me to work towards capturing the dynamic whole. In her assessment of data collection methods for capturing composing processes, Takayoshi notes that screen captures are a more comprehensive, layered approach grounded in the moment of composing. She contends that these approaches allow us, as writing studies researchers, to gain a more complete understanding of the act of composing (6) as both video and screen capture provide videos that can be played back, spliced, reversed, and saved in chunks or as still images.

For video recording, I used two cameras—a Canon T3i and a GoPro. Looking back, I would not recommend using a Canon T39 for video recording because of issues I had while recording, which are further explicated in the Trials and Tribulations section of this chapter. On the other hand, the GoPro was a good choice for a secondary camera for two reasons: its portability and the video angle. The ease of moving the GoPro allowed me to follow the participant if/when they chose to move spaces or rooms. The wide-angle of the built-in lens allowed me to capture more environmental space than a standard camera lens.[4] Based on these experiences, I would recommend that researchers are far more careful in their camera selection than I was. However, I realize that many researchers, like myself, must make their camera choices based on access to technology. As a graduate student at the time of this study, I did not have the funding for a camera of my own, so I relied on borrowing my partner's Canon T3i and GoPro Hero 3 (both of which were dated at the start of this project). If I had the funding, I would have done more thorough research on video recording and selected other newer options.

As Landon Berry and Brandy Dieterle have noted, it is often necessary to use multiple cameras and multiple camera angles to capture the entire environment in which the participants are acting and to make all aspects of the composing process as visible as possible. For my study, each camera was placed at a different angle to the participant's workspace to best capture the space and the movement of the participant within the space. Figures 18.1 and 18.2 show an example of one camera set up I used during a multimodal process interview. The goal was to capture multiple sides of the dress form while the participant was working so that as she moved around the dress form, my focus when analyzing could follow her movements and avoid the issue of not being able to see her actions on the recording.

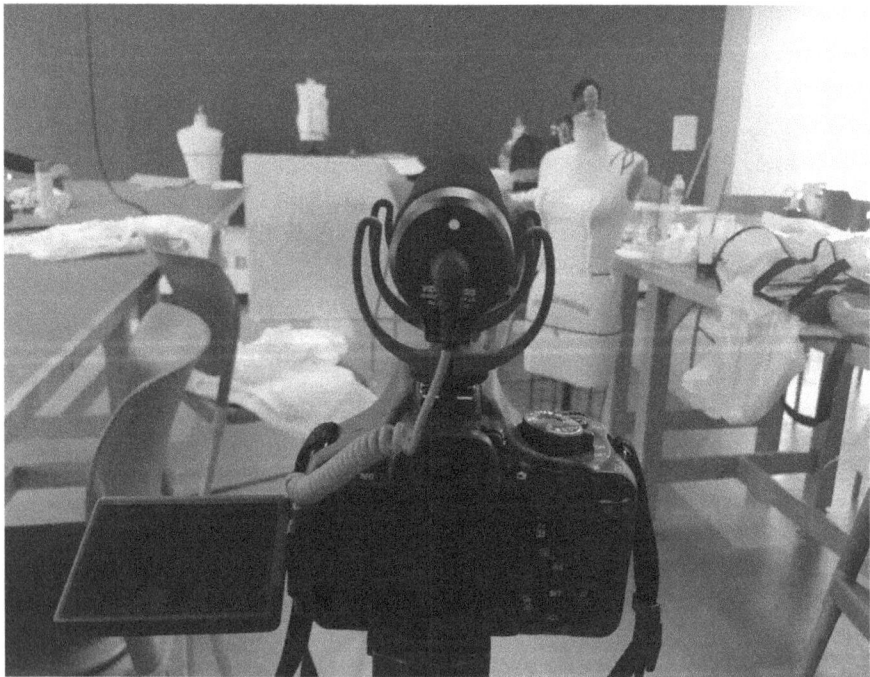

Figure 18.1. Sample Camera Set-Up

---

4. A wide-angle lens on a standard camera could also achieve this.

Figure 18.2. Sample Camera Set Up

Videos were used for situations when the participant's composing processes occurred beyond the computer screen. However, in situations including both digital and tactile forms of composing, I recorded the screen and videoed the actions outside of the screen.[5] By using both video and screen capture, I could correlate or connect actions performed in both the digital and physical environments. This dual recording permitted me to see other actions at play, such as the materials, objects, and tools the composer is employing as well as the nature of the environment around the composer. Capturing the environment using video is evocative of Rule's use of video to record her participants in their natural writing environments. Moreover, by both recording the screen and the environment around the screen, I worked to respond to the problem in digital writing research of ignoring the actions beyond the screen or the immediate actions of the composer. Observing and recording the environment in which the processes are cultivated and occur works to recognize the network of composing surrounding the processes.

---

5. Using a handheld digital recorder, I also audio recorded the multimodal process interviews to collect better quality audio than recorded by either camera or to serve as a backup for if audio failed on any of the other methods.

For screen capture, I used either QuickTime or OBS Studio to record their laptop screen. QuickTime was used because of convenience since most of the fashion design students owned a MacBook and QuickTime is a default program that supports screen capturing and audio recording simultaneously with limited difficulty or set up time. OBS Studio was used for screen capturing when the participant owned a PC and is an open-source software that can be used for screen capturing and audio recording as well. OBS Studio was particularly convenient for selecting only certain aspects of the screen that needed to be recorded as well as allowing for recording multiple screens in a dual monitor set up. Unlike QuickTime, OBS Studio requires time for downloading the software, initial program setup, and individual screen capture/audio recording set up. Both programs are extremely useful for screen captures as they have no limitations on the length of screen capture and are adaptable to many situations. As software primarily used by video gamers for recording their streams, OBS Studio offers a greater variety of screen capturing abilities including the ability to record multiple screens and/or sources. After this project, I would recommend OBS Studio over QuickTime because of these features despite the extra time for set up.

The primary benefit of video and screen capture is that they highlight the material, digital, and visual nature of writing that is often omitted when using solely voice, cognition, and cognitive data collection methods. They also provide data that more clearly represents and reproduces the multimodal, multi-sensory dynamic whole of composing process including an expanded view of the moment of composing and insight into how the designer/composer/writer employs ESSPs by altering, shaping, and shifting their environment and tools to better suit their composing needs.

Session Field Notes

Another layer to the multimodal process interviews beyond the video, screen capture, and audio recording was taking field notes during each session. Some might question the necessity of being in the space with the participant during the multimodal process interviews; however, there are two primary reasons for being present: 1) being in the room, observing, and taking field notes provided another layer of data to triangulate and supplement the video and screen capture data; and 2) I could provide tech support for the video, screen capture, and audio that was being collected. Also, as seen in my discussion of the multimodal process interviews, my presence is potentially what altered my data collection and encouraged my participants to resist the bounds of the traditional think-aloud protocol. However, I would still recommend being present when using video or screen capture.

My session field notes were inspired by Clay Spinuzzi's discussion of naturalistic observations where he took detailed field notes about the "work environment... interactions with others... interactions with texts... [and] movements from one space to another, along with any artifacts they took with them and artifacts they used in each space" (371). Since multimodal composing processes, and digital writing processes, do not solely happen within a computer screen or a video frame, screen capture, and video cannot record all that happens within a space. As part of the field notes, I also attempted to provide cues that would allow me to "sync" the field notes with the actions on the video or screen capture. After the observations were completed, I transcribed the field notes from my hand-written notes and jottings into full descriptions of each observation to use later in coding.

Streamlining

After collecting the data from the multimodal process interviews, I was faced with a hurdle that I should have anticipated—having multiple streams of data of a singular moment of composing and correlating which actions happen simultaneously. Thus, before analysis, I decided to streamline all the data to make analysis a more fluid process by editing the multiple video angles or video/screen capture combinations for each observation into single videos using iMovie software. This streamlining process did not include eliminating any data from any video or audio source, but it did allow me to transcribe and later codes to video the actions being performed from different angles or sources simultaneously rather than each data stream separately. Choosing to combine and streamline the multiple video angles and data sources was more for convenience rather than coming from any methodological standpoint or even guidance from other research projects. My primary goal was to make the transcription and coding process as straightforward and comparable as possible; however, I believe that editing the multiple angles and sources together allowed for a better understanding of the network of composing as more actions and environment were visible at once. Further, the ability to watch back moments on the screen with the actions outside the screen more closely resembles my own experience of observing the actions in real-time. Thus, streamlining the data streams into a single source became essential to my success.

From streamlining, there were multiple variations that I generated: video/screen capture combo, video cutaways, picture-in-picture, and side-by-side video. Each of these layouts had its own benefits and drawbacks. Figure 18.3 shows a screenshot of a video/screen capture combo.[6] By combining the screen and the video, I could see not only how the participant used their mouse, keyboard, and other tools outside of the screen as well as tools to work within the bounds of the screen as well. For example, in Figure 18.3, the video and screen capture combination allowed me to see how this participant was using the Wacom drawing tablet to control different sketching and painting tools in Illustrator or Photoshop on the computer while simultaneously using the keyboard and touchpad to change brushes, move windows, and select parts of the sketches (you can see this video at https://youtu.be/toaF__ps4Cw).

---

6. All media in this chapter has been reproduced with the consent of my participants.

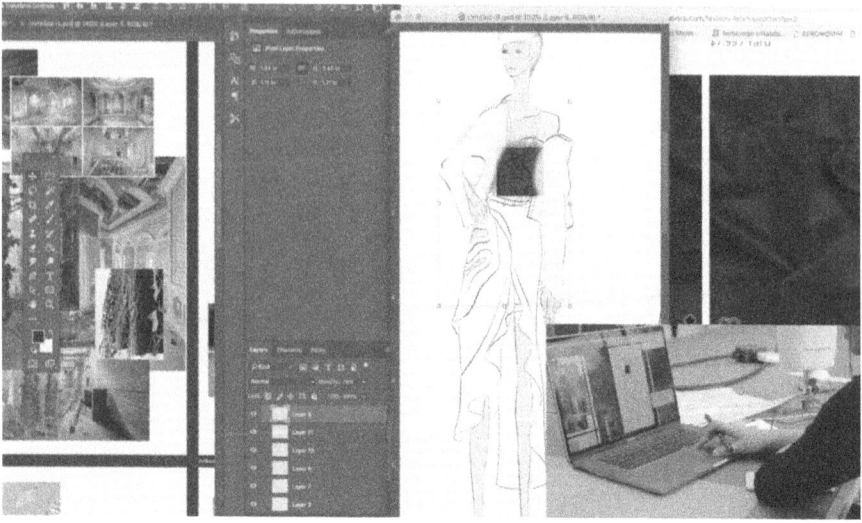

Figure 18.3. Video/Screen Capture Combination

As with the video/screen capture combo, the multiple video angles were also edited together. Depending upon the action happening within the frame, videos were either edited as cutaways with only one video visible, as a picture-in-picture video (see Figure 18.4) or as a side-by-side video (see Figure 18.5). The single video or cutaways were used in instances where only one angle of the video was usable. The picture-in-picture format was useful for instances where the entirety of each frame needed to be visible, though one frame is significantly smaller than the larger and slightly blocks part of the larger frame. For example, in Figure 18.4, we can see both an over the shoulder view of the participant's work in the bottom left corner but also a view of her work from across the table as the majority of the screen. When editing these videos together, I was cognizant of the placement of the smaller video to not block out any actions or environmental factors. Conversely, the side-by-side format was useful for instances where the positioning of the participant and the action within the frame allowed me to zoom and only show a portrait cropping of the side of the original frame by side.

In the video at https://youtu.be/QivAcUSEiX, which corresponds with Figure 18.4, I was able to see how this participant worked on her patterns from both aforementioned angles which allowed me to have a more complete view of her actions. In Figure 18.5, the dual video angles allow us to see the participant's movement around the dress form without the view being blocked with the left side showing the front and the right showing the back. Also, the multiple angles allow for a better view of which part of the project they're working on at different times. Her movement around the dress form and the benefit of the multi-angle view can be seen at https://youtu.be/EyWf6epIi6A.

Multimodal Methods 199

Figure 18.4. Picture-in-Picture Video

Figure 18.5. Side-by-Side Video

Trials & Tribulations of Recording and Streamlining

As with all research, especially research on multimodal composing and digital writing, these methods do not come without their trials and tribulations. One of the primary limitations or issues I had with these methods was selecting and using the camera. First, though I chose to use multiple cameras to collect data from different angles, I became aware that the eye of the camera is not without blind spots. There were moments where the participant left the camera frame or reached for something outside of either camera's view. Unfortunately, these blind spots are inevitable and cannot be entirely avoided.

Along with the limitations of camera frames, I also had issues with the recordings themselves. For instance, the Canon T3i proved to be a poor choice in camera because of problems with video recording as it wouldn't record for the full hour without stopping. To attempt to fix this issue, I had to restart the camera recording every 10 to 13 minutes to keep it from shutting off entirely without my knowledge. This led to momentary lapses in the data collection, but typically these lapses were less than a few seconds. Unlike the Canon, the GoPro could record for the entire time without stopping, if the battery was charged, and the memory card had enough space. However, in neither case did I end up having a single video file from either camera since the GoPro automatically broke the video into multiple files, which had to be combined during streamlining.

The primary issue with the multiple video clips for each session came when trying to streamline each multimodal process interview into a single video. I not only had to verify that the clips from the main camera (the Canon T3i) were in order, but I also had to sync those clips with the clips from the GoPro. I also chose to use the audio from the handheld recorder rather than the camera audio, so that file had to be synced with the video files as well. In retrospect, the process of combing and streamlining all these various data streams together was more tedious than I expected and required more time than I expected as well. However, the ability to view, code, and analyze all the streams of data from a single multimodal process interview simultaneously proved to be worth the tedium of streamlining.

Supplementing the Multimodal Process Interviews

Even though multimodal process interviews offer a wealth of data about multimodal composing processes, they cannot stand alone as a data collection method. To supplement the multimodal process interviews, and to capture as much as possible of the dynamic whole of multimodal composing processes, I continued my data collection after the multimodal process interviews. These methods include post-session reflections, final interviews, process sketches, final project walk-through, and artifact collection—each of which served to complement and provide more context to data from the multimodal process interview.

Post-Session Reflections

After each multimodal process interview, participants completed a reflection to gauge their emotions and perceptions about the work that just occurred. For my larger project, there were three reflections per participant. In this case, I asked the participants to reflect on questions like "how do you feel about the work you completed today?" "Did you feel productive? Or unproductive?" "Where does this work fit into your overall process?"[7] The purpose of these reflections was to gauge each participant's reaction to their work that day. Perceptions of productivity or lack thereof help with understanding how the participant felt about that day's work and if they felt the work done was typical or atypical of their "normal" workflow, which gave me insight into potential differences in processes across the multimodal process interview sessions.

Final Interview

After all multimodal process interviews and post-session reflections were completed for all participants, I interviewed each participant one final time. These final interviews were semi-structured and served as a roundup and final touchstone for understanding the multimodal process interviews and the participant's processes. Each participant reflected on the work they completed as part of this project and compared it to what they believe is their typical work and process. Also, they added a layer of triangulation between data points during the coding and analysis process and created a richer, more dynamic understanding of their processes.

Process Sketches

After completing the final interviews, my participants completed two final reflective activities; the first being a process sketch. Process sketches are drawings or diagrams completed by the participant that represent their processes. Prior and Shipka argue that asking participants to sketch out their process allows participants to negotiate what it means to be "in process" and what tools, environments, and activities are central to their process (185). For the process sketches, I was curious about what each participant integrated into their sketches but also how these process sketches might align or differ from their explication of processes provided in the interviews and observations of processes in the multimodal process interviews. The primary benefit of these sketches was seeing the thread of their processes come into view with each new layer of data.

In this case, I asked each participant to sketch their process and narrate their process while sketching. These sketches were audio-recorded, and screen captured and completed on an iPad Pro with an Apple Pencil using the Adobe Sketch application (see Figures 18.6 and 18.7). By having these process sketches completed digitally, I had a permanent copy of the sketches and the opportunity to screen capture the sketch being completed. Screen capturing and audio recording the participant's narration of the process sketch added a multi-dimensional, active layer to the already multimodal nature of the process sketches, as seen in a video at https://www.youtube.com/watch?v=7iL26o8ZbHc.

---

7. Many of these questions were inspired by Spinuzzi's observation-based questions.

Project Walk-Through

The final data collection method used was the walk-through of the finalized composition, which for all my participants was a process book and fashion portfolio. Depending on the final form of their process books and portfolios, these walk-throughs were either videoed or screen captured as well as audio recorded. This allowed me to align their narration and discussion of their projects with the physical location within the project itself. During the walk-through of their completed project, each participant reflected on the work they did and the decisions they made. My participants used this opportunity to discuss design inspiration, overall design choices, individual page content and design, and reflect on their overall process of creating the garments, process book, and final portfolio. Moreover, these walk-throughs allowed me to compare these reflections with their actual composing processes-in-action and my own analysis of those composing processes. As with the process sketches, the walk-throughs provided a reflective, multi-dimensional layer to the final multimodal compositions.

Artifact Collection

Along with the process sketches, reflections, and project walk-throughs, I also collected other artifacts related to each participant's multimodal composing processes. Spinuzzi contends that artifact collection is necessary to "keep track of what the participant touches, reads, writes, and uses. Especially look for artifacts that they use repeated, customize, . . . or hand off" (loc. 2137). Most of the artifact collection included photographs of tools, materials, and completed projects. For example, I took photos at the end of each multimodal process interview because seeing the progress between sessions is valuable for tracking progress across time, especially time not recorded (Figure 18.8). In retrospect, I wish I had taken more photos, including some at the beginning of each session because these photos served as references for where this session took place in the overall construction of the process books and portfolios as well as the overarching multimodal composing processes.

I also took photographs of each completed process book and portfolio to create a digital reconstruction (Figure 18.9). For one participant, their final book was entirely digital rather than tactile, so I was able to obtain a PDF copy of the final project rather than reconstructing it myself. Recreations or copies of the final projects not only demonstrated the evolution of different elements of the project observed during the multimodal process interviews. They also aided in understanding what the participant valued or liked enough from the process book to include in the final portfolio as well as any other versions of designs that were composed outside of the multimodal process interviews.

Figure 18.6. Sample Process Sketch

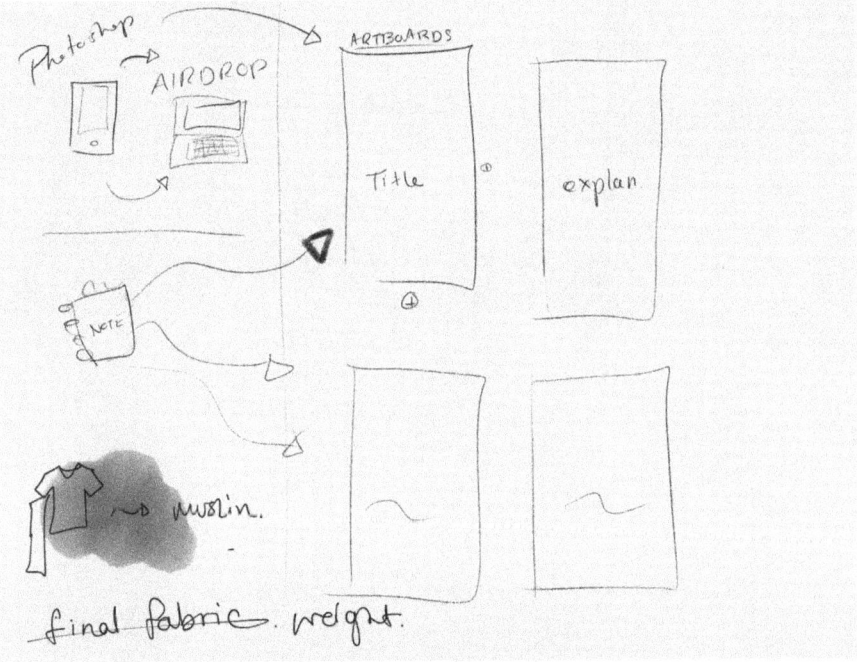

Figure 18.7. Sample Process Sketch

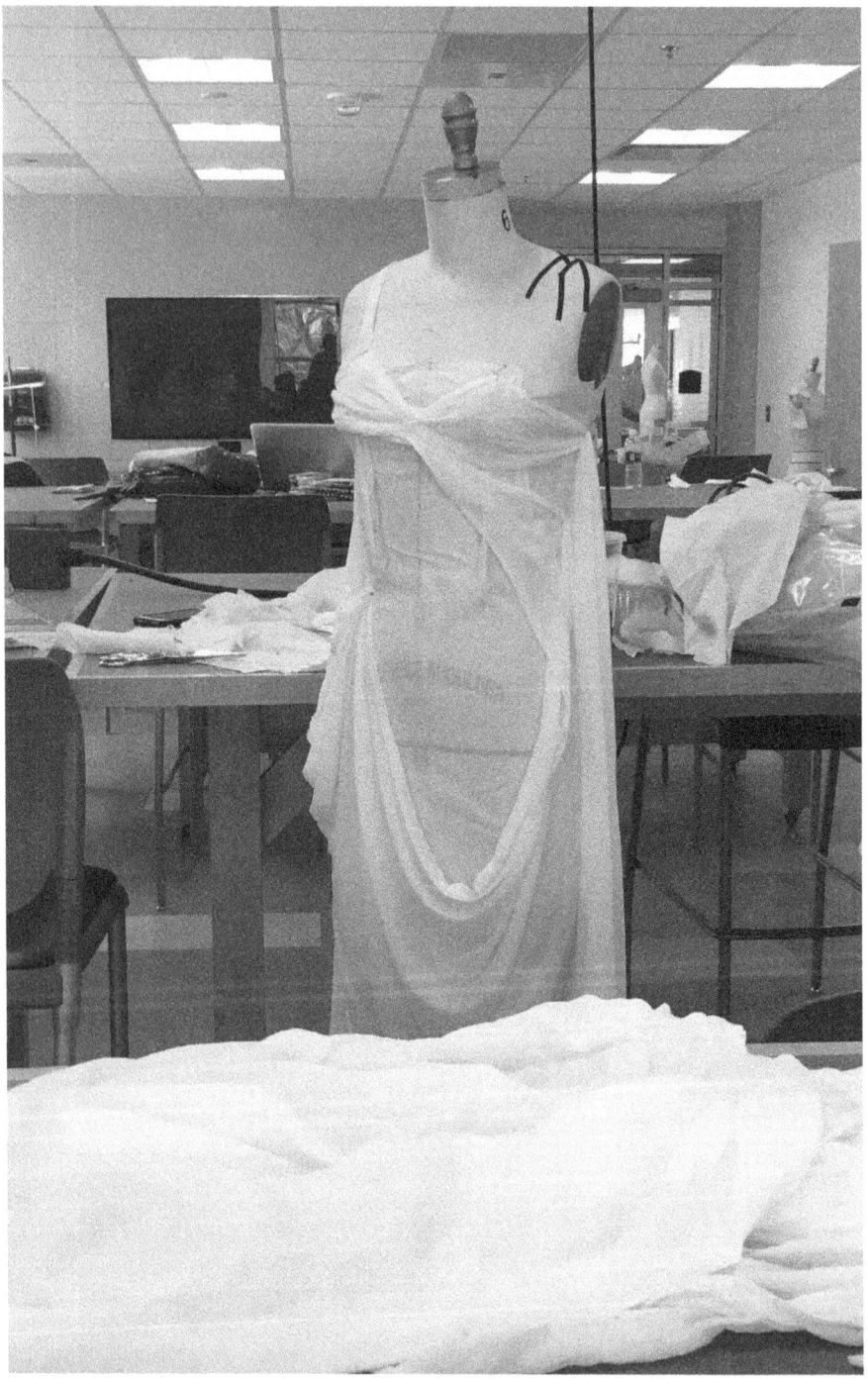

Figure 18.8. Artifact Photograph Example

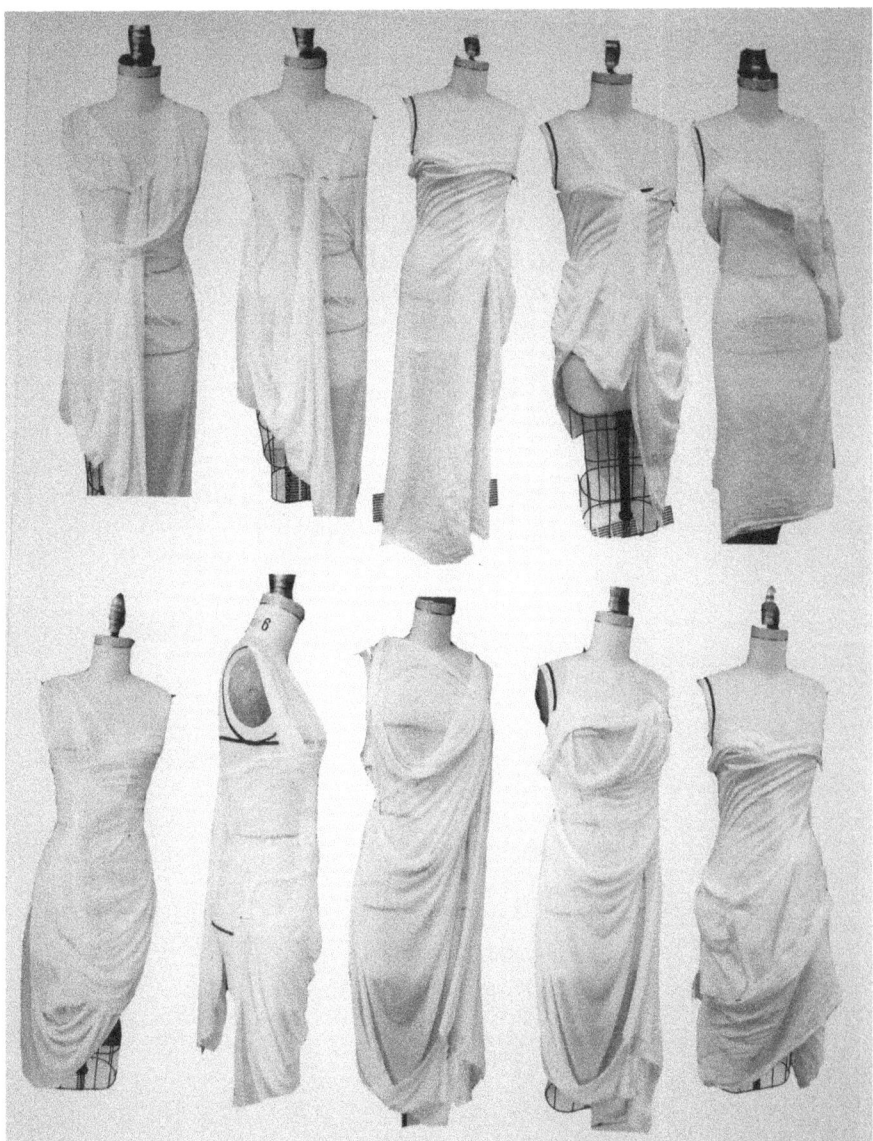

Figure 18.9. Process Book Page

Recommendations for Implementing Multimodal Process Interviews

This chapter has addressed how a multilayered, multi-tiered approach using multimodal methods can permit researchers to capture the dynamic whole of composing processes. Particularly, I focused on the use of multimodal process interviews as the primary data collection methods for researching multimodal composing and digital writing. The key takeaway I hope that other researchers of digital writing, multimodality, or composing processes find from this chapter is to be ready for the moment when methods seem to fail and must be modified to collect or capture a new situation or experience and to value those moments when your participants take the lead on sharing their processes. Had I not allowed the multimodal process interviews to naturally come into being by forcing my participants to strictly adhere to traditional think-aloud protocol standards, I may have missed out on many ESSPs or other composing habits of my participants. Multimodal process interviews are a highly appropriate and valuable method for examining multimodal composing processes and digital writing because of the dynamic, multi-faceted and multimodal nature of the data produced and truly work towards allowing writing studies to capture the dynamic whole of these processes. However, they are not without fault or flaw, so I call on other researchers to employ these methods in their own studies of digital writing and multimodal composing processes to validate the effectiveness and utility of these multimodal process interviews beyond the scope of my study.

Works Cited

Bennett, Jane. *Vibrant Matter: A Political Ecology of Things*. Duke UP, 2010.

Berry, Landon, and Brandy Dieterle. "Group Consultations: Developing Dedicated, Technological Spaces for Collaborative Writing and Learning." *Computers and Composition*, vol. 41, 2016, pp. 18–31.

Fontana, Andrea, and James H. Frey. "The Interview: From Structured Questions to Negotiated Text." *Handbook of Qualitative Research*, vol. 2, no. 6, 2000, pp. 645–72.

Graham, S. Scott, and Brandon Whalen. "Mode, Medium, and Genre: A Case Study of Decisions in New-Media Design." *Journal of Business and Technical Communication*, vol. 22, no. 1, 2008, pp. 65–91.

Gries, Laurie E. "Iconographic Tracking: A Digital Research Method for Visual Rhetoric and Circulation Studies." *Computers and Composition*, vol. 30, no. 4, 2013, pp. 332–48.

Hull, Glynda A., and Mark Evan Nelson. "Locating the Semiotic Power of Multimodality." *Written Communication*, vol. 22, no. 2, 2005, pp. 224–61.

Jacobs, Gloria E. "Troubling Research: A Field Journey through Methodological Decision Making." *Practicing Research in Writing Studies: Reflexive and Ethically Responsible Research*, edited by Katrina M. Powell and Pamela Takayoshi, Hampton Press, 2012, pp. 331–47.

Johnson, Lucy. "Contending with Multimodality as a (Material) Process." *Journal of Multimodal Rhetorics*, vol. 2, no. 1, 2018, pp. 13–27.

Manthey, Katie. "Wearing Multimodal Composition: The Case for Examining Dress Practices in the Writing Classroom." *Journal of Global Literacies, Technologies, and Emerging Pedagogies*, vol. 3, no. 1, 2015, pp. 335–43.

Nelson, Mark Evan, Glynda A. Hull, and Jeeva Roche-Smith. "Challenges of Multimedia Self-Presentation: Taking, and Mistaking, the Show on the Road." *Written Communication*, vol. 25, no. 4, 2008, pp. 415–40.

Palmeri, Jason. *Remixing Composition: A History of Multimodal Writing Pedagogy.* SIU Press, 2012.

Prior, Paul, and Jody Shipka. "Chronotopic Lamination: Tracing the Contours of Literate Activity." *Writing Selves, Writing Societies: Research from Activity Perspectives,* edited by Charles Bazerman and David R. Russell, The WAC Clearinghouse/Mind, Culture, and Activity, 2003, pp. 180–238, https://doi.org/10.37514/PER-B.2003.2317.2.06.

Prior, Paul. *Writing Disciplinarity: A Sociohistoric Account of Literate Activity in the Academy.* Lawrence Erlbaum, 1998.

Rivers, Nathaniel. "Tracing the Missing Masses: Vibrancy, Symmetry, and Public Rhetoric Pedagogy." *Enculturation: A Journal of Rhetoric, Writing, and Culture,* vol. 17, 2014.

Reid, Alex. "Composing Objects: Prospects for a Digital Rhetoric." *Enculturation: A Journal of Rhetoric, Writing, and Culture,* vol. 14, 2012.

Rule, Hannah J. "Writing's Rooms." *College Composition and Communication,* vol. 69, no. 3, 2018, pp. 402–32.

Selfe, Cynthia L., and Gail E. Hawisher. "Exceeding the Bounds of the Interview: Feminism, Mediation, Narrative, and Conversations About Digital Literacy." *Writing Studies Research in Practice: Methods and Methodologies,* edited by Gesa E. Kirsch, SIU Press, 2012, pp. 36–50.

Shipka, Jody. "Transmodality in/and Processes of Making: Changing Dispositions and Practice." *College English,* vol. 78, no. 3, 2016, pp. 250–57.

———. *Toward a Composition Made Whole.* U of Pittsburgh P, 2011.

Smagorinsky, Peter, Elizabeth Anne Daigle, Cindy O'Donnell-Allen, and Susan Bynum. "Bullshit in Academic Writing: A Protocol Analysis of a High School Senior's Process of Interpreting Much Ado About Nothing." *Research in the Teaching of English,* vol. 44, no. 4, 2010, pp. 368–405.

Smagorinsky, Peter. "The Reliability and Validity of Protocol Analysis." *Written Communication,* vol. 6, no. 4, 1989, pp. 463–79.

Smagorinsky, Peter, Michelle Zoss, and Patty M. Reed. "Residential Interior Design as Complex Composition: A Case Study of a High School Senior's Composing Process." *Written Communication,* vol. 23, no. 3, 2006, pp. 295–330.

Spinuzzi, Clay. *Topisight: A Guide to Studying, Diagnosing, and Fixing Information Flow in Organizations.* CreateSpace Independent Publishing Platform, 2013.

Steiner, Lindsay B. "Enacting Professional Literate Practice: A Snapshot of One Graphic Designer's Process." *Literacy in Practice: Writing in Private, Public, and Working Lives,* edited by Patrick Thomas and Pamela Takayoshi, Routledge, 2015, pp. 189–201.

Takayoshi, Pamela. "Methodological Challenges to Researching Composing Processes in a New Literacy Context." *Literacy in Composition Studies,* vol. 4, no. 1, 2016, pp. 1–23.

Takayoshi, Pamela, and Derek Van Ittersum. "The Material, Embodied Practices of Composing with Technologies." *The Routledge Handbook of Digital Writing and Rhetoric*, edited by Jonathan Alexander and Jacqueline Rhodes, Routledge, 2018, pp. 84–94.

Trimbur, John. "Delivering the Message: Typography and the Materiality of Writing." *Rhetoric and Composition as Intellectual Work*, edited by Gary A Olsen, Southern Illinois UP, 2002, pp. 188–202.

Vasudevan, Lalitha, Katherine Schultz, and Jennifer Bateman. "Rethinking Composing in a Digital Age: Authoring Literate Identities through Multimodal Storytelling." *Written Communication*, vol. 27, no. 4, 2010, pp. 442–68.

Walsh, Lynda. "Visual Invention and the Composition of Scientific Research Graphics: A Topological Approach." *Written Communication*, vol. 35, no. 1, 2018, pp. 3–31.

Yang, Yu-Feng Diana. "Multimodal Composing in Digital Storytelling." *Computers and Composition*, vol. 29, no. 3, 2012, pp. 221–38.

Contributors

Laura Aull is Associate Professor and director of the English Department Writing Program at the University of Michigan. She is the author of *First-Year University Writing* and *How Students Write: A Linguistic Analysis*, and her articles can be found in *Written Communication, Assessing Writing, Journal of Writing Analytics, Composition Forum,* and other journals.

Stuart Blythe is Associate Professor in the department of Writing, Rhetoric & American Cultures at Michigan State University. He teaches a range of courses in the undergraduate program in professional and public writing as well as the graduate program in rhetoric and writing.

Victor Del Hierro is Assistant Professor of Digital Rhetoric and Technical Communication in the English department at the University of Florida. His work focuses on the intersection between Hip-Hop, Technical Communication, and Community. Victor is an Associate Director of TRACE Innovation Initiative.

John R. Gallagher is Associate Professor at the University of Illinois, Urbana Champaign. He studies interfaces, digital rhetoric, participatory audiences, and technical communication. He has been published in *Computers and Composition, enculturation, Rhetoric Review, Transformations, Technical Communication Quarterly,* and *Written Communication.* His monograph, *Update Culture and the Afterlife of Digital Writing*, is available from Utah State University Press. He co-edited, with Dànielle Nicole DeVoss, *Explanation Points: Publishing in Rhetoric and Composition*, available from Utah State University Press.

Constance M. Haywood is an Assistant Professor in the English department at East Carolina University. Lying at the intersections of Black feminist literacies, digital writing, and research ethics, Constance's work aims to center Black women, their writing, and the ways in which they use their experiences and knowledge(s) to advocate for themselves and their communities. She maintains a deep-rooted interest and love for the ways that Black women navigate, create community within, and sustain digital spaces. Focusing in these areas not only allows her to engage the research that she does more critically and ethically, but it also supports her goals in making the systems and institutions that she is part of better and more equitable places.

Eric A. House is Assistant Professor of Critical Composition and Writing Studies at New Mexico State University where he teaches courses on cultural rhetorics and writing, and composition theory and pedagogy. His current research is focused on the composing practices of the Hip-Hop DJ as he argues that the DJ's emphasis on identity and technology offers visions of culturally situated digital writing practices that are critical of difference and power dynamics.

Whitney Lew James is Assistant Teaching Professor at the University of Notre Dame. She is currently working on a monograph titled *Algorithmic Identification:*

Predictive Technology, Agency, and Inequality, which develops a digital cultural rhetorics critique of predictive algorithms that reproduce and reinforce existing inequalities. Her work has been published in *Composition Forum* and is forthcoming in edited collections on artificial intelligence and non-traditional dissertations in the humanities. She earned her Ph.D. in Rhetoric and Composition from Texas Christian University, her M.A. from Emerson College, and her B.A. from the University of California, Santa Barbara.

Shannon Kelly is a doctoral candidate in the department of Writing, Rhetoric, and American Cultures at Michigan State University. She is interested in how institutions work and change, and her current research focuses on trauma-informed change management. As a former assistant Writing Program Director, she is also excited about curriculum design and the role of mentorship in how learners learn to teach.

Benjamin Lauren is Associate Professor at the University of Miami. His scholarly interests intersect technical communication, user experience, and institutional change. He has published broadly in technical communication, user experience, and organizational theory, including his book *Communicating Project Management: A Participatory Rhetoric for Development Teams*. His recent work includes supporting equity in accessing essential needs resources for college students and managing curricular and institutional change projects. In addition, during his time in higher education, he has collaborated with community partners on change projects in a variety of settings: Pre-K-12 schools, non-profit organizations, technology companies, and other professional organizations, such as the Society for Technical Communication.

Benjamin Miller is Assistant Professor of English/Composition at the University of Pittsburgh. He co-edited, with Amanda Licastro, the collection *Composition and Big Data* (University of Pittsburgh Press, 2021), and received a CCCC Emergent Research/er grant toward his data-analytical monograph, *Distant Readings of Disciplinarity: Knowing and Doing in Composition/Rhetoric Dissertations* (forthcoming from Utah State University Press); his scholarship has appeared in *College Composition and Communication* and *Kairos*. He is also a lead developer of the Writing Studies Tree (writingstudiestree.org), a crowdsourced, open-access academic genealogy for Composition, Rhetoric, and related fields, and part of the founding editorial collective of the *Journal of Interactive Technology and Pedagogy*.

Eric Manuel Rodriguez is Assistant Professor of Urban Humanities at Portland State University. His research and teaching weaves together cultural rhetorics, technical writing, and the rhetoric of health and medicine to understand how community-engaged writing practice encourages positive public health outcomes. He has worked on the Mellon-funded Building Healthcare Collectives, a project that seeks to build inter-disciplinary capacity between academics and medical practitioners to foster culturally specific communicative practices to better public health outcomes. His work has been published in *Kairos*, *Poroi*, and *Composition Studies*.

Christina Rowell earned her Ph.D. in 2020 at Kent State University, where she studied multimodal composing processes and was awarded the Stephen P. Witte Fellowship for her dissertation *Capturing the Dynamic Whole: Multimodal Composing Processes of Fashion Design Students*. During her time at Kent State University, she also coordinated the writing program and taught courses in technical writing and business writing. Since graduating, she has taught at Youngstown State University and Volunteer State Community College. Presently, she works as a content writer and designer, focusing on creating scientific journalism and marketing pieces for start-up companies.

Erika M. Sparby (they/them) is Assistant Professor of Digital Rhetorics and Technical Writing at Illinois State University. They research digital aggression, memes, and ethics, and their work has received national acclaim—including the 2016 Gloria Anzaldúa Rhetorician Award, the 2017 Hugh Burns Dissertation Award, and the 2019 Distinguished Book Award (with Jessica Reyman for the co-edited collection *Digital Ethics: Rhetoric and Responsibility in Online Aggression*)—and they co-founded the Digital Aggression Working Group in 2019. Sparby's work on digital aggression has also appeared in *Computers and Composition* and *enculturation*.

Crystal VanKooten is Associate Professor of Writing and Rhetoric at Oakland University in Rochester, Michigan, where she teaches courses in the Professional and Digital Writing major and in first-year writing and serves as co-managing editor of *The Journal for Undergraduate Multimedia Projects (the JUMP+)*. Her work focuses on digital media composition through an engagement with how technologies shape composition practices, pedagogy, and research. Her publications appear in journals that include *College English*, *Computers and Composition*, *enculturation*, and *Kairos*. Her digital book, *Transfer across Media: Using Digital Video in the Teaching of Writing*, was funded by a Conference on College Composition and Communication Emergent Research/er Award and is available online from Computers and Composition Digital Press.

www.ingramcontent.com/pod-product-compliance
Lightning Source LLC
Chambersburg PA
CBHW061207070526
44583CB00025B/3143